I0815734

FIRST LADIES AND THEIR ORCHIDS

— A Century of Namesake Cattleyas —

A. A. CHADWICK and ARTHUR E. CHADWICK

★ ★ ★ ★ ★ ★ ★

★ ★ ★ ★ ★ ★ ★

All photographs by A. A. Chadwick or Arthur E. Chadwick unless otherwise noted.

ISBN (hardback) 979-8-218-38586-6

Library of Congress Control Number: 2024905823

Published in 2024 by
Chadwick & Son Orchids, Inc.
1240 Dorset Road
Powhatan, VA 23139

For contact infomation regarding editorial and marketing in
the United States, see www.chadwickorchids.com.

Distributed by University Press of Florida.
For questions about sales or distribution, visit http://upress.ufl.edu

TABLE OF CONTENTS

★ ★ ★ ★ ★ ★ ★

Our 1939 Studebaker is a reminder of the glamour associated with the corsage era.

ARTHUR E. CHADWICK PHOTO

PREFACE

I first learned about the cattleya hybrids that are named after First Ladies of the United States by reading back issues of the American Orchid Society's magazine, *The Bulletin*.

My father, Arthur A. Chadwick, had all the old periodicals dating back to the turn-of-the-century in his library. I would leaf through them at night when I visited my parents and would stay up very late, riveted by the stories. If I thought something needed additional explanation, I would put a sticky note on the page and talk about it with dad at breakfast in the morning.

I remember reading about an orchid presentation that took place in 1962 at the Truman Presidential Library in Independence, Missouri that involved the former President, Harry Truman. The owner of Lines Orchids in Signal Mountain, Tennessee was in town that weekend for a big orchid show and had somehow managed to arrange for a personal meeting with Mr. Truman. There are no photographs but the touching story of how the flowers were originally intended for Harry who deferred to his wife *"who is more deserving"* reeled me in.

I asked my father about the Truman event and he explained that there have been a number of orchid presentations to First Ladies over the years and each has a compelling story. The flowers are almost always cattleyas which are the showiest and most glamorous of all orchids.

I then suggested to my father that maybe we should somehow be a part of the tradition of naming orchids after First Ladies. After all, we have greenhouses full of the best stock plants (many of which are historic) and can make new hybrids or remake old hybrids. We also have benches and benches of un-named crosses of all colors and styles just waiting to be registered.

My brilliant idea landed with a thud. *"Absolutely not! Never mix business with politics"* and he walked away.

For the life of me, I couldn't understand what he was talking about. Growers have been naming orchids after prominent women since the 1920s and if Lines, McLellan, Manda, Patterson, Rivermont, Hausermann, and others thought it was a good idea, there must be something to it.

His point was, if analyzed in a vacuum, that the lone act of naming a hybrid after a single First Lady could be construed as an endorsement of her husband and his policies, and, as such, might generate some opposition from the public. Obviously, the last thing we want to do is alienate any clients let alone an entire swath of them. However, if we take a broader view and look at the First Ladies as an American tradition - a legacy that is to be celebrated – then contributing even the smallest part is a noble gesture.

I respectfully disagreed with my father and promptly named an orchid after the First Lady at the time, Hillary Clinton or, should I say, Hillary Rodham Clinton as she was being referred to in the 1990s. The hybrid is a stunning semi-alba with a peachy orange throat and, a short while later, was awarded "Best in Show" at the Eastern Orchid Congress in Raleigh, North Carolina. The orchid world, at least, was abuzz with the new First Lady orchid.

Presenting the flowers to Mrs. Clinton, however, was a little more involved and took several years of political wrangling involving state and federal officials. I started out, rather innocently, writing a letter directly to the Office of the First Lady in Washington D.C. explaining my great deed and its significance to her and the horticulture world at large. A few weeks later, there in the mailbox was a letter from *The White House* addressed TO ME! Boy, this is easy I thought.

I carefully opened the letter, trying to preserve the official letterhead for future framing.

I would buy a very expensive frame – maybe gold embossed – and hang it in the living room. After all, this was a personal letter TO ME from the First Lady of the United States.

"Dear Mr. Chadwick", the letter began. *"I appreciate your thoughtfulness but my schedule does not allow for a personal meeting. Good luck with your future endeavors."* Her signature was stamped at the bottom.

I was devastated. Is an orchid presentation not the most important item on any First Lady's agenda? There must be a mistake.

I sheepishly told my father about this disastrous experience and, after rolling his eyes a few times and saying *"I told you so"*, he suggested that, if this is something that I really wanted to do, then I should contact one of my state politicians who is inherently skilled at communicating with the White House. Dads are usually right about important things like this.

I contacted my Virginia Senator, John Warner, who had previously purchased orchids from us at the Washington Flower Show and was a known horticulturalist. He was very excited about the idea of an orchid presentation and wrote a glowing letter to the White House, even offering to join us for the event.

A few weeks later, there in my mailbox was a letter from a *Senator of the United States* TO ME. This wasn't too hard I thought.

I carefully opened the letter and considered preserving the official letterhead for future framing. I might buy a mid-priced frame – maybe silver – and hang it in the living room. After all, this was a personal letter TO ME from a Senator of the United States.

"Dear Mr. Chadwick" the letter began. *"It appears that Mrs. Clinton's schedule does not allow for a personal meeting. Good luck with your future endeavors."* His actual signature was at the bottom.

Now, I was absolutely stumped. How could a powerful and worldly senior Senator like John Warner get a rejection from the White House? How did the other orchid growers of the past make their flower presentations? I must be missing something…

Again, I met with my father who proceeded to roll his eyes and say *"I told you so."* Then he mentioned the obvious. *"You have to go through the SAME political party"*.

By this time, I was skilled at writing cover letters to government officials and had a template ready to go. I contacted our Virginia Lieutenant Governor Don Beyer, Jr, a Democrat, who was just as excited about the orchid presentation as Senator Warner was. However, instead of writing a formal letter to the White House, he simply made a phone call.

I won't spoil the drama of the orchid presentation itself but, afterwards, the story appeared in dozens of newspapers and magazines around the world. It was particularly big news in the orchid community. Indeed, there was a little backlash but, generally speaking, the response was 99% positive.

Over the next 30 years or so, we named cattleya hybrids after the next four First Ladies - Laura Bush, Michelle Obama, Melania Trump, and Jill Biden and retroactively named Barbara Bush, Lady Bird Johnson, Eleanor Roosevelt, Grace Coolidge, Florence Harding, and Edith Bolling Wilson. The entire series now spans 19 consecutive administrations. Each hybrid is unique and has a compelling story.

I hope you enjoy reading about them.

Arthur Everett Chadwick
December 2023

ACKNOWLEDGEMENTS

This book has been 30 years in the making and is truly a test of stamina. Of course, my father is the overriding inspiration having written *The Classic Cattleyas* at age 76. With him, it was vitally important to get his historic information on paper since he was actually witness to the great corsage era.

First Ladies and Their Orchids, however, is an ongoing subject that doesn't really have an end. The term, *First Ladies*, will likely be changing to *First Spouses* in the near future but, other than that, the topic is open ended.

It is not possible to write a comprehensive work like this without the help of many wonderful people and organizations. First and foremost, the editor of *Orchids* magazine, Ron McHatton, who published every single First Lady article that I gave him over the past 15 years. This allowed me to get early feedback from readers and see how a true professional lays out a story.

The orchid registrar at the Royal Horticultural Society, Julian Shaw, who assisted with hundreds of emails that I sent him regarding the parentage of early hybrids and their breeders. Orchid nomenclature is, inherently, a quagmire and the first registrations weren't always well documented. He navigated me through with crisp answers that cleared up all doubt.

I am grateful to Justin Kondrat, Head Grower at the Smithsonian Gardens, for housing a duplicate collection of First Lady hybrids at their greenhouses and displaying them to thousands of visitors.

I am indebted to Laura Bush who sat in the front row of my Dallas lecture and gave me instantaneous feedback from a First Lady perspective.

My wife, Jane, didn't seem to mind my bringing very old and faded orchid reference books to bed every night.

My daughter and 24/7 cheerleader, Olivia, proofed each chapter TWICE and provided lots of supporting information.

My son, Arthur IV, and his cat, Tango, provided technical and emotional support.

Our company vice-president, Janis, allowed me to take an exorbitant amount of time off.

Richmond hobbyist and amateur orchid historian, Charlie Harkness, provided timely research.

Special thanks to my fellow cattleya addicts: Carson Barnes, Chris Loncke, David Toyoshima, Ken Reynolds, Keith Davis, Robert Thiessen, Jim Roberts, Ed Kidder, Harry Gallis, John Stanton, Stephen Kotarski, Brian Behm, Dave Off, Mark Peters, Bob Fuchs, Allen Black, Dennis Pavlock, Bob Scully, Erica Hannickel, Ed Merkle, Jason Fischer, and others who provided the stories and kept me focused.

Last but not least, my graphic designer, Scott Fields, who tied it all up in a pretty little package. ✯

Art Chadwick Sr. and his father, Arthur, building their first greenhouse in 1946.

A. A. Chadwick was active in numerous orchid societies over the years including Central Florida, Atlanta, and Dallas before settling in Delaware. He would take his young son, Arthur, to the shows.

ANNE CHADWICK PHOTO

A. A. Chadwick got started in orchids as a teenager in Elkins Park, Pennsylvania. His father had to build him a greenhouse to hold all the orchids that he brought home after school. OLIVE CHADWICK PHOTO

In 1989, A. A. Chadwick and his son, Arthur, opened a commercial location in Virginia. There was just one modest greenhouse open by appointment. ANNE CHADWICK PHOTO

DEDICATION

My father, Art Chadwick, Sr. did not live quite long enough to see this book get published. He did, however, contribute important historical sections to each of the nineteen First Lady chapters.

Since the age of 13, he had been collecting cattleyas and, until the very end, he couldn't wait to see what was in bloom each morning in his greenhouse. His lifelong interest began rather innocently, as a teenager walking home from school.

Growing up during the corsage era of the 1940s, young Arthur was exposed to orchid greenhouses at every turn. Commercial firms, estate growers, and hobbyists were all raising cattleyas because the demand for cut flowers far exceeded the supply. A single corsage was selling for as much as twenty dollars and women everywhere were wearing them.

Arthur's neighborhood of Elkins Park, Pennsylvania was particularly active in orchids and the second and third Presidents of the American Orchid Society lived there. Each day, Arthur would walk past the fancy estates and admire their greenhouses. Eventually, he befriended the growers who took him under their wing.

Over time, Arthur was given their extra orchids to experiment with. Initially, it was just a plant or two – perhaps the back pieces that occur when a specimen is divided. But it wasn't long before Arthur was carrying boxes full to his parents.

Arthur's father, a builder, soon realized that he had to construct a greenhouse for the expanding collection. The two Chadwicks bonded one summer and erected a redwood structure with top and side louvers and manual openers. This design would serve as a prototype for all of Arthur's greenhouses over the next 75 years.

The following summer, Arthur took a job at a commercial orchid nursery, Fetzer Greenhouses, in nearby Warminster, Pennsylvania. Their fertilizing technique was legendary and involved collecting sheep manure from the owner's front yard and soaking it for a week in burlap bags. The "tea" was then poured onto their cymbidiums which produced enormous heads of flowers. Arthur was glad that he wasn't responsible for collecting the manure.

When Arthur went away to college, his parents took care of his orchids but eventually the plants were sold. A single cattleya was spared - a 1930s wild collected species from Venezuela – and it survived on windowsills for many more years. Ultimately, Arthur named the variety after his father (who had the same name) and C lueddemanniana 'Arthur Chadwick' was launched into the history books – first getting an HCC/AOS in 1974 then upgrading to an AM/AOS in 2002. Even today, it remains one of the best pale lavenders.

Arthur graduated from Penn State in Agricultural Economics but, before accepting a major job offer and much to the dismay of his parents, he went into the cut flower cattleya business with a friend. Like any new venture, there was considerable risk and Arthur was more interested in the botanical nuances of each plant than the actual day to day production of blooms. Not surprisingly, Arthur sold out to his partner but not before selecting the very best Cattleya Bow Bells for himself.

In 1960, he entered the big white hybrid in the inaugural Central Florida Orchid Society show where it won Best Cattleya. Again, he gave his special orchid a family variety name – 'Anne Chadwick', after his new bride. The next day, she and the orchid were featured on the front page of the *Orlando Sentinel. "She, of course, was hooked on orchids from that day on,"* he often quipped.

After work and on weekends, Arthur began breeding cattleyas and took details notes of the process. He was fascinated in the genetics and photographed each flower, amassing an enormous library of Kodachrome slides. He was not deterred by the length of time it would take to raise the plants to maturity - typically seven years.

The tricky technique of planting seed or "flasking" was mastered on his kitchen table using a pressure cooker and glass beakers. Few hobbyists attempt this step given the absolutely sterile conditions required for germination but Arthur's mother was a nurse and had taught him the fundamentals of strict cleanliness. The newly planted flasks were promptly moved to a special incubation chamber in the basement.

Arthur made new hybrids, remade old hybrids, and did sibling crosses of his favorite species. His earliest recorded hybrid was in 1951 but he is widely known for his 1990 Laeliocattleya Powhatan (Princess Margaret x C dowiana) which produced some stunning white with purple lip varieties.

An avid reader, Arthur explored all the old orchid journals and was intrigued by the earliest primary hybrids dating back to the turn of the century. Unable to find examples in circulation, he simply remade long forgotten yellows - Lc Ophir (L xanthina x C dowiana) 1901, Lc Constance Wigan (L xanthina x C rex) 1902, Lc Gaston Doin (rex x tenebrosa) 1902, and C Triumphans (rex x dowiana) 1904, among many others.

He was particularly fond of the spring blooming species, Cattleya mossiae, which is the National Flower of Venezuela and can produce up to five flowers on a spray. He made sibling crosses of the best historic varieties - some of which were virused - but he would always "dry pod" the seed so that the offspring were clean. The resulting plants had superior genes and vigor and he bloomed them all, creating quite a show in his greenhouse each March.

In 1989, he lent his name and hard labor to a startup family business, Chadwick & Son

Gardening diva Martha Stewart had both Chadwicks on her TV show in 2006 where she reviewed their book, The Classic Cattleyas. *She was presented with her namesake orchid in front of a live studio and national audience. Art Sr. stole the show with his relaxed humor and silk orchid tie.* COURTESY OF MARTHA STEWART

Orchids Inc. The Virginia-based company began modestly with the construction of three of those old fashioned, hand built, redwood greenhouses with upper and lower louvers and manual cranks that his father had shown him fifty years earlier. The company just celebrated its 35th year and now has a dozen greenhouses and two retail stores.

Art Sr. and his wife, Anne, at a book signing for The Classic Cattleyas.

Arthur's love of orchids was apparent in the dozens of feature articles that he wrote for the American Orchid Society over half a century. He was a natural story teller and the editor, Jim Watson, suggested that he write a book. *The Classic Cattleyas* was published in 2006 and promptly landed him on *The Martha Stewart Show.* I was there to witness as he and Martha hammed it up in front of a national audience. The book consequently sold out and is now in its second printing.

Through it all, Arthur held on to his prized cattleya orchids – the corsage type, now numbering over 800. Hobbyists would send him plants all the time - just to keep, as though he was some kind of horticultural repository. In many ways, he was the keeper of historic cattleyas – a direct line to a time when corsages were king.

This is a responsibility that I now shoulder.

Arthur Everett Chadwick
December 2023

Bc Mount Hood 'Mary' AM/AOS (Deesse x C Claris) from 1962 is an example of a classic Brassocattleya or "Big Brasso." It has recently been reclassified as a Rhyncholaeliocattleya but, conversationally, and for purposes of this historic book, it remains a Brasso. PHOTO BY ARTHUR E. CHADWICK

A NOTE ABOUT NOMENCLATURE

It's been about twenty years since our first book, *The Classic Cattleyas*, was published, which is a relatively short time, given that the earliest cattleya discovered by westerners was in 1821. But in those two short decades, some well established orchid names have changed.

For example, Cattleya eldorado, named after the mythical gold in Brazil, is now C wallisii. Cattleya skinneri, the National Flower of Costa Rica, is now Guarianthe skinneri. Brassavola digbyana, the National Flower of Honduras, is now Rhyncholaelia digbyana.

To make matters worse, some names have changed twice. Laelia crispa first became a Sophronitis then a Cattleya.

And there are many other examples.

All of these changes leave the tens of thousands of orchid enthusiasts, who painstakingly memorized the fine details of their collections, to throw up their hands in frustration.

For over a century, the overly frilly lipped cattleyas were referred to as *"Big Brassos"* meaning that their genus included a Brassavola digbyana somewhere in the lineage. Now that familiar term no longer exists in the orchid lexicon. It would be like if maple syrup was now called something else or if Twitter was replaced with X. Paralysis.

While my father did make the case for moving the Brazilian Laelias to Cattleyas (L purpurata, etc), he didn't expect this change to happen in his lifetime.

First Ladies and their Orchids: A Century of Namesake Cattleyas is, by and large, a historical reference for it highlights the early growers, hybridizers, and explorers who made today's hybrids what they are.

So rather than add gasoline to the fire and in order to be consistent with our first book (and with much relief from our readers), we are using the nomenclature that is familiar to everyone – the old names.

Let's have a toast – to the old names: The cute little Slc's, the Big Brassos, and so much more. ✯

Cattleyas were in their heyday in the 1940's and were often carried by brides. This ad from Thomas Young Orchids shows a wedding bouquet with 10 semi-alba flowers of Lc Canhamiana.

COURTESY OF THOMAS YOUNG ORCHIDS

INTRODUCTION

For as long as orchid hybrids have been made, breeders have been naming them after prominent women of the day. European royalty were often honored and included queens, princesses, empresses, and baronesses. By the early 1900s, Queen Victoria, Queen Mary, Queen Elizabeth, and Queen Alexandra all had namesake cattleyas.

Naming orchids for royalty had a considerable benefit for the horticulture world. Cattleyas were associated with wealth and social status which increased people's interest in collecting them, exhibiting them, doing scientific research, and preserving their native habitats.

Royal titles are not part of the American culture so, in the United States, orchids are named for the wives of presidents. Woodrow Wilson's second wife, Edith clearly deserved a named cattleya because she coveted "canaries, bourbon, and orchids" and was given a fresh cattleya bloom every day by her husband. As did Doctor Jill Biden, who lives just minutes from the Chadwick home in Wilmington, Delaware, and spent half an hour with Art discussing orchids in the green room of the White House. All are part of a grand tradition; we now have nineteen consecutive First Ladies with namesake cattleyas. Each hybrid is as lovely and interesting as the women themselves.

The collection of first lady namesakes also presents a historical picture of the trends in cattleya breeding over a century – the Art Deco style of Mrs. Herbert Hoover and Eleanor Roosevelt, the classic corsage look of Mamie Eisenhower and Jacqueline Kennedy, the exhibition quality of Betty Ford and Nancy Reagan, the compact nature of Laura Bush and Michelle Obama… and so on.

In addition, the lineage of these hybrids provide an overview of the diverse family of cattleya species that exist in tropical cloud forests around the world – Colombia and Venezuela where they are the National Flower of their country, through Costa Rica, Brazil, Peru, and Ecuador. Many of the fine early varieties were painted and reproduced in the *Orchid Album* of the 1880s.

Then there are the renowned growers around the world who played a role in creating the hybrids – from the old English estates of Baron Schroder and Col. G. L. Holford to the large cut flower firms of the glamorous corsage era such as Patterson and Rivermont. Their stories are here, too.

The Chadwicks are responsible for much of this history. They acquired, bred, named, or presented the hybrids, got them awarded, corresponded with the First Lady (or her children or grandchildren) then donated the entire collection to the Smithsonian for safe keeping. It is, after all, a national treasure. ✯

The best of the Wilson seedlings are very dark including variety 'First Lady' whose flowers last six weeks and are particularly intensely colored.

ARTHUR E. CHADWICK PHOTO

President Woodrow Wilson showed off his new girlfriend, Edith Bolling Galt, at the 1915 World Series. She wore a quadruple cattleya corsage that day.

PHOTOGRAPH COURTESY OF ALAMY/THE EVERETT COLLECTION

EDITH BOLLING WILSON

"Usually the orchid wears the woman, but to the contrary with my dear Edith."

– Woodrow Wilson

There was controversy in Washington, D.C. in the spring of 1915. It was rumored that President Woodrow Wilson had a love interest. The nation was still in mourning from the unexpected death of First Lady Ellen Wilson just eight months earlier. The President was also in mourning – until he met the widowed Edith Bolling Galt by a chance encounter in a White House stairwell. In order to woo his new sweetheart, he gave her a fresh orchid every day.

Their whirlwind courtship included a highly publicized appearance at the World Series in which she wore a quadruple cattleya corsage. On December 28, 1915, the President married Edith and she became the new First Lady of the United States.

During her tenure in the White House, Edith Bolling Wilson stood by her husband's side, supporting his efforts for world peace, and eventually aiding in the nation's conservation efforts

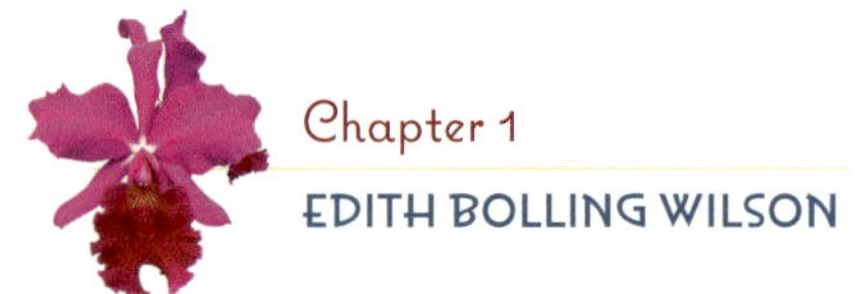

The primary hybrid, Lc Callistoglossa (L purpurata x C warscewiczii) from 1882, appears on both sides of the Wilson lineage. Shown is the heirloom variety 'Low' which honors the famed nursery man, Stuart Low of Crowborough, Sussex, England.

ARTHUR E. CHADWICK PHOTO

during the First World War. Like everyone else, the Wilsons were observing "Gasless Sundays", "Meatless Mondays", and "Wheatless Wednesdays."

Woodrow Wilson was a popular president and had three cattleyas named after him – 1916 C President Wilson (Fabia x *labiata*), 1917 Blc President Wilson (Bc Mrs. J, Leemann x Lc Lustre), and the rare yellow 1918 Lc President Wilson (Thyone x *C dowiana*). However, it was Edith who was the orchid lover in the family, and she had no namesakes. That all changed in 2016, when Chadwicks reached out to the Edith Bolling Wilson Birthplace Museum.

The Wilson non-profit organization which celebrates the life and legacy of the First Lady. The museum selected a fall blooming purple from our stock to honor Mrs. Wilson. The bloom season coincides with her October 15th birthday.

The new hybrid, Lc Edith Bolling Wilson (William Romanoff x *C dowiana*) was bred by A. A. Chadwick, who is known for his work with the large flowered cattleya species and early hybrids. The seedlings yielded a broad spectrum of purple shades and are reminiscent of an earlier Chadwick cross, Lc Powhatan (Princess Margaret x *C dowiana*) from 1990. Lc Powhatan produced mostly lavenders as well as some stunning semi-albas - and even a yellow. The Wilson cross produced some very dark seedlings and some possible award winners.

One parent, Lc William Romanoff (Cabazon x Morning Star), was originally bred in 1962, and named after the owner of Romanoff Greenhouses in Canterbury, Connecticut. William and his wife, Sally, operated the nursery from 1947 until 1988. Their business had humble

William Romanoff and his wife, Sally, operated Romanoff Greenhouses in Canterbury, Connecticut for over 40 years. His namesake was a parent to the Wilson hybrid.

PHOTO COURTESY OF SALLY ROMANOFF

We find the primary hybrid, C Hardyana from 1896, on both sides of the Romanoff lineage. Shown is A. A. Chadwick's fine variety.

ARTHUR E. CHADWICK PHOTO

beginnings, with the couple running a grocery store by day and dabbling in orchids at night. William "*read everything he could to discover how to grow and hybridize orchids.*" Their story is depicted in the book, *Canterbury – The First 300 Years*.

The hybrid was named by wealthy orchid hobbyist, Josephine Aronson. She and her husband, Charles, lived in Arcade, New York, on an estate called Hundred Acres and had a close association with the Romanoffs.

Lc William Romanoff comes from a long line of dark purple breeding. The lineage is complex, with 11 species being represented over six generations. Hybridizers chose dark varieties of Cattleya warscewiczii, labiata, and lueddemanniana. Most importantly, however, is an early cross that appears on both sides of the parentage – Lc Callistoglossa (L purpurata x C warscewiczii) that was registered in 1882.

Lc Callistoglossa, which translates into "*most beautiful tongue (lip)*", is one of the major building blocks of purple hybrids and was registered by James Veitch and Son of Exeter,

Laelia purpurata is found naturally in Brazil and comes in many flavors including this dark rubra form.

ARTHUR E. CHADWICK PHOTO

One parent of the Wilson hybrid is the naturally occurring yellow species, C dowiana, from Costa Rica and Colombia. C dowiana has been used extensively in breeding for over a century. Shown is A. A. Chadwick's stud plant, 'Meadowlark', which has proven to be rot resistant, long lasting, and quite fertile.

ARTHUR E. CHADWICK PHOTO

England. Veitch Nurseries were the leaders in orchid hybridizing during the late 1800's and are credited with making the very first cattleya hybrid. Their breeder, John Seden, produced a host of famous primary crosses starting with Lc Callistoglossa and followed by Lc Canhamiana (*L purpurata* x *C mossiae*) in 1885, C Empress Frederick (mossiae x dowiana) in 1888, C Fabia (labiata x dowiana) in 1894, and C Enid (*mossiae* x *warscewiczii*) in 1898.

Veitch describes Lc Callistoglossa, "*The gorgeous lip of this hybrid is scarcely equaled in colour by any of the species belonging to the grand race of orchids from which it is derived.*" Noted horticulturalist John Rolfe writes "*Undoubtedly the best of the hybrid Laelias, it was flowered in 1884 by Mr. Ballantine, gardener to Baron Sir J. H. W. Schroder…and was exhibited by him…where it deservedly awarded a first-class certificate. The flowers resemble those of Laelia purpurata; the sepals and petals are bright rose-colour, and the lip rich magenta-crimson shaded with mauve…*"

Lc Callistoglossa is a tall plant with pseudobulbs well over 24" high and leaves that are narrow, like its parents. A well grown plant can produce enormous heads of flowers. For example, the variety 'Low's', which dates back to 1910, makes as many as seven 9" wide blossoms.

Seden's breeding was not limited to cattleyas, or even orchids, as he produced a wide variety of plant material ranging from gloxinias and begonias to fruit trees. In recognition of his outstanding work in hybridizing, Seden was given the most prestigious award in British horticulture, the Victoria Medal of Honour.

The Wilson seedlings vary in shades of purple and generally bloom in the fall. The cross was made by A. A. Chadwick and several hundred plants were grown to maturity. Supporters of the Edith Bolling Wilson Birthplace Museum were each given a plant at the unveiling. ARTHUR E. CHADWICK PHOTO

C lueddemanniana is inherently a well shaped species that remains relatively compact. Shown is an un-named fine variety.

PHOTO BY ARTHUR E. CHADWICK

Orchid seed germination at the time of Lc Callistoglossa was a difficult proposition. Sterilized flasks and laboratory agar had not been invented yet. Growers were left to shake the seed pod over a pot of finely milled peat moss that had been boiled to kill any pathogens. The media was then covered with wet burlap and a glass jar and placed in a warm greenhouse. Growers were lucky to have any plants survive and most crosses saw only a dozen or so seedlings reach maturity.

Breeders were also not experienced in storing orchid pollen, so most early hybrids were between plants that flowered at the same time. Such is the case of Lc Callistoglossa, whose parents both bloom between late spring and early summer.

The other parent of Lc Edith Bolling Wilson is the familiar yellow species *Cattleya dowiana*, which has been used heavily in breeding for over a century. The flowers are relatively short-lived – just two to three weeks in August - though the blistering summer heat contributes to premature aging. Hybridizers use *C dowiana* for a variety of reasons – hoping to pass along the intense lip color (gold veining on a velvety purple throat), the sweet fragrance, or the blooming time, among other traits.

In the case of Mrs. Wilson's cattleya, Chadwick took advantage of a little known hybridizer's trick with *C dowiana*: When combined with a purple parent, the yellow color of its sepals and petals is known to darken the shade of purple in the offspring. Chadwick Sr. used his best

Edith Bolling Wilson outlived her husband by nearly 40 years. Here, she meets with former first ladies, Bess Truman and Eleanor Roosevelt. All three are outfitted with cattleya corsages. PHOTOGRAPH COURTESY OF ALAMY/THE EVERETT COLLECTION

This fine dowiana from The Orchid Album *illustrates the excellent qualities of the species. In particular, the intense yellow sepals and petals as well as the vivid veining in the lip.*

COURTESY OF THE ORCHID ALBUM.

C dowiana, variety 'Meadowlark', which had proven over many decades to be rot resistant and particularly fertile.

In September 1919, President Woodrow Wilson suffered a debilitating stroke that left him temporarily paralyzed. In the White House, the only two people with access to the President were his doctor and Edith. Scholars today debate the role of Edith Bolling Wilson in White House affairs during this period. In Edith's autobiography, *My Memoir*, she referred to this time as her "stewardship" of the presidency, and decided which matters of state were important enough to bring to the bedridden president.

Mr. Wilson never fully recovered from his stroke and died a few years after leaving office. Edith outlived her husband by nearly four decades and did not remarry. Until the end, Edith Bolling Wilson continued to promote her husband's legacy. She died on what would have been her husband's 105th birthday – the very day that she was scheduled to be the guest of honor at the dedication ceremony of the new Woodrow Wilson Bridge outside Washington, D.C.

Now, over a century after Edith Bolling Wilson first resided at 1600 Pennsylvania Avenue, she finally has a namesake orchid. The special hybrid was unveiled on October 15, 2017 at a fancy reception hosted by her birthplace museum in Wytheville, Virginia. All attendees received an "Edith orchid", growing instructions, and a copy of *Orchids* magazine which featured the Wilson hybrid.

PERSONAL LIFE

Edith Bolling was born in 1872 in Wytheville, Virginia. She struggled to obtain a solid education and spent her youth caring for her family, as she was one of eleven children. Her 12 year marriage to Norman Galt ended with his unexpected passing in 1908, and after suffering a difficult pregnancy resulting in the infant's death, she was unable to have any more children. Edith met recently widowed Woodrow Wilson in 1915, where Wilson took an instant liking to her and proposed that March. The pair was wed in December 1915.

Edith Bolling Wilson was First Lady of the United States from 1915 to 1921. During this time, World War I was being fought and she not only participated in rationing efforts but traveled to Europe twice to visit with the troops. Her presence among female royalty in Europe is thought to have helped secure the U.S. as a global power and improve the world view of First Lady in international politics.

Woodrow Wilson's sudden stroke in October 1919 caused Edith to take over many of the presidential duties, known to the American public as a "stewardship". She became the sole communicator between the bedridden President and his trusted cabinet, bearing most of the responsibility during the last 18 months of Wilson's presidency. Her legacy features a strong, capable, feminine leader who went above and beyond for her husband and the country. ✯

In anticipation of the orchid unveiling, Virginia Governor Terry McAuliffe's wife, Dorothy, hosted a gathering at the Governor's mansion. Attendees included the founders of her birthplace museum, Farron and Bill Smith, the museum's Executive Director, Shiloh Holley as well as Edith Wilson's great niece, Elizabeth Evans. Everyone wore oversized cattleya corsages as was Mrs. Wilson's style and posed for photographs besides a historical silver bowl full of blooming cattleya plants. ✯

In anticipation of the new Edith Bolling Wilson orchid unveiling, Virginia's first lady, Dorothy McAuliffe (white dress) hosted a gathering that included Edith's great niece, Elizabeth Evans (light blue), as well as birthplace museum executive director Shiloh Holley (dark blue), and founder, Farron Smith (white jacket). All wore oversized cattleya corsages as was Edith's style. JAY PAUL PHOTO

LC EDITH BOLLING WILSON

(2016 Chadwick)

There are 11 species in the lineage of Lc Edith Bolling Wilson – most notably C dowiana and C warscewiczii, both of which are summer bloomers. For the most part, this first lady hybrid produces flowers in the fall.

COMPOSITION

Species	%
C dowiana	55%
C warscewiczii	12%
C labiata	6%
L purpurata	5%
C lueddemanniana	5%
C schilleriana	3%
C trianaei	3%
C warneri	3%
C mendelii	3%
L pumila	2%
C mossiae	2%

LINEAGE

- *1962 Aronson/Pierson* **Lc William Romanoff**
  - *1941 Armacost* **Lc Cabazon**
  - *1943 Broughton* **Lc Morning Star**
- **C dowiana**

Former First Lady Florence Harding did not have a namesake orchid during her lifetime so we retroactively named one. The breeding is in keeping with the plants available during the 1920s.

ARTHUR E. CHADWICK PHOTO

Florence Harding was First Lady from 1921-1923.

PHOTO COURTESY OF LIBRARY OF CONGRESS/HARDING PRESIDENTIAL LIBRARY

FLORENCE HARDING

Cattleya Florence Harding honors the wife of the 29th President of the United States, Warren Harding, who served from 1921 until his death in 1923. Like her predecessor, Edith Bolling Wilson, Mrs. Harding did not have a namesake orchid during her lifetime while both their husbands were honored four times. Within a short two year window, we find Royal Horticultural Society registrations for Cattleya Warren G. Harding (1920), Odontoglossum President Harding (1921), Odontioda President Harding (1921), and Paphiopedilum President Harding (1920).

The former Florence Kling De Wolfe worked for many years with Warren Harding at his newspaper, the *Marion Star* in central Ohio and campaigned vigorously on his behalf for his many political offices. As First Lady, Mrs. Harding played an active role by helping to select cabinet members, write speeches, and regularly give personal tours of the White House. She also took an interest in social issues of the day and worked tirelessly to protect her husband's image. She displayed so many flowers throughout 1600 Pennsylvania Avenue that major renovations to the supporting greenhouses were required.

Octave Doin lived in the swanky Chateau de Semont in Dourdan, France and not far from his friend and commercial grower, Charles Maron. POSTCARD CIRCA 1900

Originally bred in 1899, C Octave Doin (dowiana x mendelii) yields intensely colored offspring with a sweet fragrance. It can be found in the lineage of hundreds of today's hybrids. PHOTO CREDIT - MICHEL BART

Cattleya Florence Harding is a recent effort but it took a team of skilled orchidists to bring it to fruition. The cross was originated by famed breeder, Andy Easton, of New Horizon Orchids in Salinas, California, who sold the flasks to cattleya aficionado, Ben Oliveros, of Orchids Eros. The seedlings were raised to near maturity on the Big Island of Hawaii then were sent to our nursery in Virginia to be finished off.

As the seedlings bloomed, we photographed them and set them aside for the First Lady project. It is unusual to find such simple lineage as most of today's hybrids are complex and up to a dozen generations long. We were specifically looking for flowers that could have actually appeared during the time period of the Harding administration.

We were delighted to see the flowers open as they were various shades of yellow, peach, and burgundy and exhibited some early breeding traits such as narrow petals and delicate substance. Nearly all the blooms have vibrantly colored lips and a sweet fragrance. Their blooming season is July to January.

The lineage contains only three species - *C dowiana*, *C mendelii,* and the newly discovered, as of 1906, C *jenmanii.*

C jenmanii was quite rare in the early 1900s with only a handful of closely guarded specimens to work with. The species was found in a remote part of Venezuela and was initially thought to be a variety of *C labiata* because the flowers were similar and can bloom at the same time.

Experts, in fact, still have a difficult time differentiating between the two species because *C jenmanii* is relatively nondescript with little uniqueness in the petals, sepals, or lip. There is no

Warren and Florence Harding in a rose garden.

PHOTO COURTESY OF LIBRARY OF CONGRESS/HARDING PRESIDENTIAL LIBRARY

The last discovered large flowered cattleya species was C jenmanii in 1906. Shown is variety, 'Dunsterville', which honors the Venezuelan explorer, G. C. K. Dunsterville. ARTHUR E. CHADWICK PHOTO

Most varieties of C mendelii are pale lavender. This species was widely used in the early days of breeding and included C Octave Doin (x dowiana) in 1899. ARTHUR E. CHADWICK PHOTO

distinctive fall-forward shape to the petals like *C mossiae* or cutesy curled sepals like *C schroederae*. There is no stripe down the lip like *C maxima* or a signature orange disk in the throat like *C eldorado*. It could be said that *C jenmanii* can be identified by its lack of individual traits.

The two species, *labiata* and *jenmanii*, come from neighboring countries – Brazil and Venezuela – and this geographic difference is sometimes used to differentiate between the two orchids. In addition, while their blooming times can overlap, *C labiata* was the fall blooming work horse of the 1930s cut flower era with varieties that opened in September, October, and November while the season of *C jenmanii* is more closely aligned with November.

C jenmanii was first discovered by westerners in 1906 and, thus, escaped, the mad rush of primary hybridizing that occurred in the late 1800s. Breeders rushed to make every combination they could as newly found species were pulled from the jungles. The classic dowiana primaries such as C Empress Frederick (x *mossiae*) 1888, C Fabia (x *labiata*) 1894, and C Hardyana (x *warscewiczii*) 1896 were all made before *C jenmanii* was known to exist. By the time pollen from *C jenmanii* was available, breeders had already moved on from the primaries and were focused on second, third, and even fourth generation plants.

In those days, it could take a decade between generations for the tiny orchid seeds to sprout, mature, bloom, and get re-pollinated given the rough and tumble growing conditions. Orchids were relatively new and horticulturalists were still trying to figure out how to effectively grow these exotic plants. The old timers could remember the ill conceived high heat stove houses used to propagate orchids, which, in most cases, caused their rapid demise. Seed sowing entailed ripe pods being shaken over damp beds of moss and the "success rate" was more accurately described as the "mortality rate". It wasn't until 1924 that reliable orchid seed sowing techniques were developed.

Cattleya Florence Harding was bred by a familiar name in the orchid world, Andy Easton, who was originally from New Zealand and made a name for himself in the U.S. with cattleyas and cymbidiums.

Mr. Easton began his long and illustrious career at age 13 with a win at the horse races which gave him the seed money to start an orchid business. He invested in stock plants and purchased a modest greenhouse from a retiring florist. After earning a botany degree, he moved to America for a Masters in Botany.

In no time, he was managing 60 greenhouses for a firm that specialized in roses with four acres set aside for cattleyas and cymbidiums. Along the way, he became an American Orchid Society judge.

The flowers of C Florence Harding vary from yellow to peach to burgundy. All have a sweet fragrance and bloom between July and January. ARTHUR E. CHADWICK PHOTO

Cattleya Ned Nash honors long time orchidist, Ned Nash (left), who credits Irene and Lou Holguin (center) and Ernest Hetherington (right) with his passion for orchids. PHOTO COURTESY OF NED NASH

After a short stint as General Manager of Dos Pueblos Orchids growing cymbidiums, he returned to New Zealand and founded Geyserland Orchids where the emphasis was on breeding heat tolerant cymbidiums and odontoglossoms. For most of the 2000s, he ran New Horizon Orchids in California and now resides in Colombia with his wife who is native to the country.

One of the parents used to make Cattleya Florence Harding is the primary hybrid, C Ned Nash (*jenmanii* x *dowiana*) from 2010, that was also bred by Andy Easton. Given the grand potential of the offspring, it's hard to believe that this hybrid wasn't made earlier. The resulting flowers are richly colored shades of lavender and quite fragrant.

Easton named it after his friend and fellow grower, Ned Nash, who has been a familiar name in the orchid world for nearly half a century starting with Dos Pueblos Orchid Company and Santa Barbara Orchid Estate in the mid 1970s. But it was his steady rise at Armacost & Royston, which later merged with Stewart Orchids, that put him on the map. He served as President of Stewart's from 1987 to 1995.

Here, he oversaw hundreds of cattleya crosses and clones that Stewart's sold all over the world. Their annual color catalog was eagerly anticipated and was filled with both new hybrids and remakes. The 75th Diamond Jubilee catalog of 1990 featured two pages of big purples headlined by Lc Susan Holguin, C Irene Holguin, and Blc Bryce Canyon plus a full page of big reds, whites, semi-albas, yellows, and greens. No other commercial grower offered the breadth that Stewart's did.

From here, Mr. Nash went to work for the American Orchid Society as Director of Education & Conservation following his career-long involvement with the organization as a judge, committee chair, and Trustee. His numerous books including "*A Pocket Guide to Orchids*", "*The World's Most Beautiful Orchids*", and "*Four Seasons of Orchids*" line the shelves of hobbyists everywhere. He credits his love of orchids to his mentors, Leo and Irene Holguin and Ernest Hetherington.

The other parent used to make Cattleya Florence Harding is C Octave Doin (*mendelii* x *dowiana*) from 1899. It was one of hundreds of registered hybrids created by the Charles Maron & Fils of Brunoy, France. This primary combines the spring blooming, generally pale lavender, *C mendelii* from Venezuela with the prized summer yellow, *C dowiana* from Costa Rica and Colombia.

Lavenders are known to intensify when bred with *dowiana* so many of the Octave Doin's and Ned Nash's are very dark purple. In addition, some degree of yellow veining and sweet fragrance also comes through.

Although C Octave Doin hasn't been in circulation for over a century, there have been some recent remakes. The primary hybrid honors fellow French grower and hobbyist, Octave Doin (1848-1919), who founded Editions Doin which specialized in books and periodicals about the sciences and nature. *Le Dictionnaire des Orchidees Hybride* and *Les Orchidees Manuel*

C Ned Nash is a recent primary hybrid made by Andy Easton that combines C dowiana and C jenmanii.
PHOTO COURTESY OF NED NASH

Amateur breeder Octave Doin made a number of important hybrids including his son's namesake, Lc Gaston Doin (L tenebrosa x C rex) in 1902. Shown is A. A. Chadwick's remake. ARTHUR E. CHADWICK PHOTO

de L'Amatuer were both edited by Doin in 1893. At one time, he was president of the Orchid Committee at the National Society of French Horticulture.

Mr. Doin lived the high life in Chateau de Semont – a sprawling three story estate with eight chimneys in suburban Dourdan, not far from Charles Maron et Fils in Brunoy. He kept an accomplished gardener, Sadarnac, and exhibited his best plants at flower shows.

The two men spent a lot of time together - trading plants and making crosses. About a dozen hybrids are registered to Doin including several primaries honoring family members, Lc Gaston Doin (*L tenebrosa* x *C rex*) in 1902 and C Madame Jeanne Doin (*quadricolor* x *dowiana*) in 1911. Maron thought so much of his friend that he honored him with a namesake in 1899

The species, Cattleya mendelii, is a direct grandparent of the Harding namesake and is native to Venezuela. Most varieties are similarly colored and loosely resemble this fine heirloom 'Jamesiana' whose watercolor painting by John Nugent Fitch is found in The Orchid Album. COURTESY OF THE ORCHID ALBUM

The famed C dowiana is a grandparent on both sides of the Harding namesake. Shown is the fine variety, 'Kathleen', which was given an Award of Merit from the American Orchid Society in 2007.
ARTHUR E. CHADWICK PHOTO

– C Octave Doin (*mendelii* x *dowiana*) which went on to directly parent over a hundred new hybrids and was ultimately in the lineage of thousands of future plants.

At the turn-of-the-century, a primary hybrid blooming for the first time was a reason to throw a party and C Octave Doin was no exception. The spring to summer-blooming seedlings varied from lavender to semi-alba and boasted various intensities of gold veining in the lips. The intense *dowiana* fragrance carried through and Octave was pleased with his namesake.

Octave also loved his stately Chateau de Semont and twice attempted to name an orchid after it. The first try was in 1902 when he combined C dowiana with C warscewiczii and submitted the name, C Semontiana. Record keeping and information sharing was rudimentary back then and, unfortunately for Octave, those two species had already been registered as C Hardyana six years earlier.

Another decade went by before he tried again. This time he combined C Hardyana with *C trianaei* and again submitted the name, C Semontiana. Sadly, prominent collector Norman C Cookson of Wylam, Northumberland, England had named that combination after himself in 1906. Following two setbacks, poor Octave never tried again to honor his chateau.

Charles Maron (1852 – 1926) was an exceptionally active breeder and one of the first orchid seed sowers in Europe. His crosses still reverberate in the horticulture world today. The primaries - C Leda (*percivaliana* x *dowiana*) 1900, Bc Empress of Russia (*B digbyana* x *C mendelii*) 1900, Mrs. J. Leemann (*B digbyana* x *C dowiana*) 1902, and C Triumphans (rex x dowiana) 1904 speak to the very core of the cattleyas and are still actively sought out by enthusiasts despite their high prices. Today, the going rate for a blooming size C Triumphans is $500+.

First and foremost, Maron named his crosses after wealthy clients including Captains, Duchesses, Empresses, Generals, Madams, Mademoiselles, Mistresses, Monseurs, Presidents, and Queens. Family members, friends, and neighbors were also represented and there are a few outliers such as local hero and romantic playwright, Victor Hugo. No doubt it was a challenge to think of hundreds of hybrid names.

What will be remembered about Florence Harding in the horticultural world is that she was a plant lover and was often photographed in the rose garden with her husband. While the President had four namesake orchids circa 1920, she had none until recently. We gave her a long overdue cattleya that is appropriate for the time period and simply combines two primary hybrids.

Special thanks to Robert Guichard – Secretary of the Societe Francais d'Orchidphile. ✯

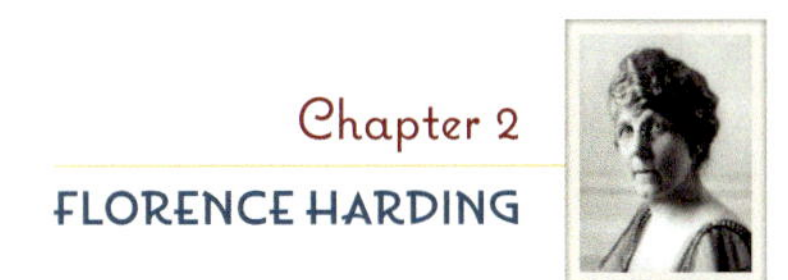

C FLORENCE HARDING

(2017 Chadwick/Easton)

COMPOSITION

- C dowiana................. 50%
- C mendelii 25%
- C jenmanii 25%

LINEAGE

2010 Easton
C Ned Nash

- **C jenmanii**
- **C dowiana**

1899 Maron
C Octave Doin

- **C dowiana**
- **C mendelii**

A dark variety of Bc Grace Coolidge (Cynthia x C Heathii).

JOHN STANTON PHOTO

A light variety of Bc Grace Coolidge.

JOHN STANTON PHOTO

First Lady Grace Coolidge along with Secretary of Agriculture, Henry Wallace, visit a greenhouse full of her namesake chrysanthemum.
PHOTO COURTESY OF ALAMY/ALPHA STOCK

GRACE COOLIDGE

Grace Anna Goodhue Coolidge was perfectly content as Second Lady of the United States where she could mingle in public relatively unnoticed and avoid all the hoopla associated with the highest office. But fate had other plans and when President Warren Harding passed away unexpectedly while on vacation in the summer of 1923, she was thrown into the lime light. In an instant, the Coolidges were moving to 1600 Pennsylvania Avenue.

As First Lady, Mrs. Coolidge steered clear of taking political stances and gave no interviews or public remarks. Instead, she hosted nearly weekly events with special interest groups and civic clubs. Her relaxed nature made her a popular figure and among her many visitors was famed aviator Charles Lindbergh.

She was a lifelong advocate of the Red Cross as well as the Clarke School for the Deaf, where she had previously been a teacher. Her famous photo with disability rights activist Helen

William Herbert St. Quintin was a British naturalist and amateur orchid hobbyist who registered 58 crosses between 1909 and 1919.

COURTESY OF SCAMPSTON HALL

The St. Quintin orchid collection at Scampston Hall was extensive and included this crop of nobile dendrobiums. Shown is their grower, Mr. Taylor, who worked under famed Head Gardener, Frederick C. Puddle.

COURTESY OF SCAMPSTON HALL

Keller helped raise $2M towards that cause. She was also a role model for young women pursing higher education with her four year degree from the University of Vermont.

Coolidge had a keen interest in plants and opened spring flower shows, planted trees, hosted garden parties, and oversaw the installation of a water lily pond on the White House property. She not only had a chrysanthemum named after her but personally visited, along with the Secretary of Agriculture, the greenhouse where it originated.

Now, she also has a namesake orchid.

Bc Grace Coolidge is a recent effort that combines two early primary hybrids that could very well have been in private collections in her day. Both parents as well as their offspring are perfect for windowsill growers because they stand less than a foot tall and bloom on short spikes.

The Coolidge namesake produces delightfully waxy and fragrant flowers in a wide range of lavender shades. The seedlings are vigorous and bloom for at least a month every autumn. Some even bloom twice a year. It was exciting to watch the variations unfold.

Bc Grace Coolidge (Cynthia x C Heathii) was bred by The Orchid Trail of Morrisville, North Carolina and is their fourth First Lady effort, having previously created C Lady Bird Johnson, Lc Eleanor Roosevelt and Jill Biden. Owner John Stanton ran a successful orchid business for two decades before retiring several years ago.

The Orchid Trail started in 2001 when it moved into the former greenhouses of the popular nursery, Bloomin' Orchids, which had introduced plant boarding into the Raleigh area in 1982. Stanton continued to offer boarding but modified it such that clients paid by the square foot of bench space rather than by the plant. He also required clients to repot their own collections.

Breeder John Stanton of The Orchid Trail in Morrisville, North Carolina, stands behind a bench full of his Laelia purpurata carnea siblings. He bred a number of first lady hybrids including Grace Coolidge.

PHOTO COURTESY OF SARA GALLIS.

British Naturalist and Amateur Hobbyist William Henry St. Quintin (1851 – 1933) owned a world class orchid collection at his Scampston Hall greenhouse that was overseen by his Head Gardener and future recipient of the Victoria Medal of Honor, Frederick C. Puddle.

PHOTO COURTESY OF SCAMPSTON HALL

St. Quintin resided at the sprawling country estate of Scampston Hall that had been in the family since the late 1600s when Sir William, 3rd Baronet and Member of Parliament acquired it.

PHOTO COURTESY OF SCAMPSTON HALL

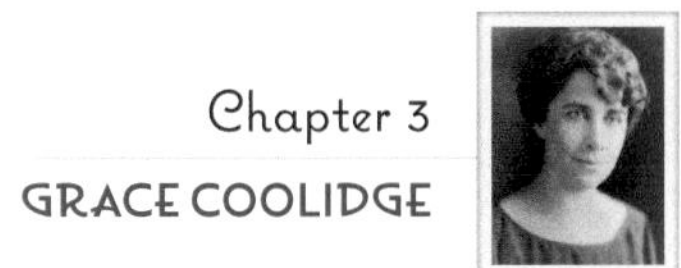

The boarding business paid the bills and allowed Stanton to follow his real passion of breeding cattleyas. He amassed an impressive collection of stud plants, many of which came from local nurseries, Breckinridge Orchids and Lenette Greenhouses as well as from area hobbyists, Courtney Hackney and Keith Davis. On his many buying trips to Florida, he would stop by Joe Grezaffi's greenhouse for additional breeder plants and when the legendary Stewart Orchids made their ill fated move to Mississippi, Stanton picked up their extras.

He bred cattleyas by the hundreds and the offspring filled an entire 30' x 96' greenhouse. As they bloomed, the seedlings were sold to walk-in clients but Stanton always kept the very best for himself. It was from this fine collection of cattleyas that Grace Coolidge's namesake was born.

The first parent of Bc Grace Coolidge is the primary hybrid, Bc Cynthia (B digbyana x C walkeriana), that was registered in 1917 by British naturalist and amateur hobbyist, William Herbert St. Quintin (1851-1933). He lived in a sprawling country estate in Yorkshire, England known as Scampston Hall that, today, is a tourist attraction. The 420 acre property had been in the family since the late 1600s when Sir William St. Quintin, Third Baronet and Member of Parliament, acquired it. William Herbert was a capable man and held many titles including Deputy Lieutenant, Justice of the Peace, and Fellow of the Zoological Society.

Every good estate needs a head gardener and, in 1900, Frederick Charles Puddle came on board, having trained under the legendary James Veitch & Sons of Chelsea. Puddle was assigned the task of building a world class orchid collection to fill the newly built greenhouse that served as the focal point of the gardens. A wide range of orchid genera was amassed with a preponderance for cattleyas, William Herbert's favorites.

The Scampston Hall greenhouse or "conservatory" was the long narrow type, stretching 120 feet with an octagonal atrium-style entrance in the middle. The structure was well built – with brick knee walls and painted wood A-frame construction. A long top ventilator and swiveling side louvers helped cool the plants through natural convection and external roll down slats tempered the summer sun.

A sizable boiler house was situated behind the greenhouse and piped in hot water when the night temperatures dipped below 60 degrees F. The orchids received the best possible growing conditions throughout the year and, by 1909, Puddle had acquired fine varieties of all known cattleya species, both unifoliates and bifoliates, and was registering new hybrids. He dappled with other genera as well including dendrobiums, oncidiums, and paphiopedilums.

This was tumultuous time for England and the threat of German bombings was ever-present. The city of Yorkshire received some direct hits and among Puddle's dozens of new hybrids were lady slippers that honored the end of the conflict – P Armistice, P Peace, and P General Petain (a war hero). It was Puddle's work with cattleyas, however, that left a lasting legacy as he would later receive the Victoria Medal of Honor for "*his work on the hybridization of orchids, rhododendrons, and other plants and for his cultural skill.*"

Puddle's cattleya crosses are considered to be first and second generation breeding and, in many cases, combine a species with a primary hybrid. One of his earliest efforts was in 1911 with a delightful art shade, Lc Scampstonensis, (La France x C dowiana), which paid tribute to the country estate, Scampston Hall.

Puddle was one of the few breeders who saw the hybridizing potential of C quadricolor whose flowers are notoriously scant and cupped. There can be a surprising amount of color inside

Grace Coolidge's namesake gets much of its charm from the species, C walkeriana which grows naturally in Brazil. This watercolor painting by John Nugent Fitch is found in The Orchid Album.

a quadricolor bloom once the half closed petals are artifically opened. He is credited with naming two *quadricolor* primaries - C Madonna (x *trianaei*) in 1913, and C Camilla (x *warneri*) in 1915.

He was also fond of another overlooked species - C walkeriana which has the unusual growth habit of blooming from a leafless growth as well as having diminutive foliage, and smallish flowers. His *walkeriana* primaries were not the big show stoppers that adorned the exhibition halls at flower shows but rather of a style that the public had rarely seen – compact and easily grown on a windowsill. They include C Hecate (x *labiata*) in 1915, C Edala (x *mendelii*) in 1916, and C Egerides (*x dowiana*) in 1917, as well as the future parent of Grace Coolidge's namesake, Bc Cynthia (x *B digbyana*) in 1917.

Stewart Orchids of Carpinteria, California offered clones of Bc Cynthia 'Lilac Gem' AM/AOS in the late 1980s. Noted breeder Fred Clarke of Sunset Valley Orchids obtained a plant and has grown it for 30 years. He writes that it "*blooms reliably in late April and what I remember*

The other parent of Bc Grace Coolidge is Bc Cynthia (B digbyana x C walkeriana) from 1917. Shown is 'Lilac Gem' AM/AOS, a late 1980s remake from Stewart Orchids that was grown for 30 years by noted hybridizer Fred Clarke. FRED CLARKE PHOTO

The intensely colored flowers of Grace Coolidge's namesake get much of their color from the species, C harrisoniana.

ARTHUR E. CHADWICK PHOTO

C walkeriana is ideal for breeding compact hybrids because the foliage is less than a foot tall. In addition, the flowers have a short stem which keeps them close to the leaves.

ARTHUR E. CHADWICK PHOTO

most about it is the perfume-like fragrance."

The other parent of Bc Grace Coolidge is the primary hybrid, C Heathii (harrisoniana x walkeriana), that was bred in 1907 by William Heath (1810 - 1892) & Son of Cheltenham, located about 100 miles west of London. The company was part of Veitch's massive Royal Exotic Nurseries conglomerate which was comprised of an astonishing eleven plant divisions – orchid, fern, new plant, decorative, tropical, soft-wooded, hard-wooded, vine, propagating, seed, and glass – making it the largest of its kind in Europe.

Heath's full time grower, Mr. Treseder, was in charge of a wide range of orchids and had a fascination with breeding. In one reported case, in 1897, he bloomed 300 zygopetalum seedlings just to see the variation and presented his findings at a monthly meeting of the Royal Horticultural Society.

Treseder registered his very first orchid hybrid in 1888 from the cattleya alliance with the novelty cross, L crispa x C loddigesii, and named it after himself, Lc Tresederiana. There are no known plants in existence today but the flowers must have been unusual as L crispa is rarely used in breeding due to its small twisted petals and sepals. He was drawn to the idea of preserving his own legacy through namesakes and next delved into the oncidium alliance with O Tresederianum (nobile x specatissimum) in 1893 followed by Odo Treseder (Zygo mackayi x Onc nobile) in 1897.

Just for fun, he remade a natural hybrid in the phalaenopsis family that Veitch had flowered twenty years earlier but never registered, respectfully naming it Veitchiana (equestris x schilleriana). The horticultural magazine of the day, *The Gardener's Chronicle*, noted his work, "*The parentage was proved by Mesers. Heath and Son in 1896.*" He soon launched into a slew of primary hybrids using newly discovered lady slipper species and, after a brief stint with Masdevallias in which Treseder honored his boss with Masd Heathii (ignea x veitchiana) in 1899, it was back to cattleyas, his true love.

His final foray in orchid breeding came in 1907 with two more primary hybrids – both compact cattleyas and a continuation of Heath namesakes - Sc Heathii (S coccinea x C schroederae) and C Heathii (harrisoniana x walkeriana). He exhibited the latter at an RHS meeting in 1907 where *The Gardener's Chronicle* wrote that C Heathii was "*...a home-raised hybrid...and resembling C O'Brieniana*" (dolosa x loddigesii). There weren't many compact cattleya hybrids at the time and the judges weren't sure what to make of the results.

Over the next century, however, C Heathii has been used many times by breeders looking to make new and exciting compact hybrids. Nurseries such as Cal-Orchids, Hawaii Hybrids, Dogashima, and Gold Country have all registered Heathii crosses in recent years. Hobbyists love these little plants because they don't take up much space and can be grown on a windowsill. The Coolidge orchid is solidly in this category.

What will be remembered about Grace Coolidge in the horticultural world is that she was truly a flower enthusiast and personally visited the nursery that bred her namesake chrysanthemum. She was photographed in the greenhouse along with the Secretary of Agriculture and thousands of blooms. She never had her own orchid, however, until recently. Her hybrid combines two century old primary hybrids and could have been in circulation while her husband was in office. ✯

Chapter 3

GRACE COOLIDGE

One of the parents of Bc Grace Coolidge is C Heathii (harrisoniana x walkeriana) from 1907. Shown is a modern remake by The Orchid Zone.
TONY WELLS PHOTO

While much of the frills and color of B digbyana is lost when paired with C walkeriana, it remains an important grandparent of Bc Grace Coolidge by increasing the size and fragrance of the flowers. ARTHUR E. CHADWICK PHOTO

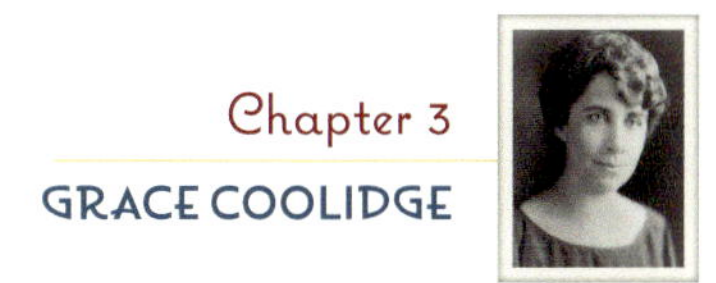

BC GRACE COOLIDGE

(2021 Chadwick/Orchid Trail)

COMPOSITION

- C walkeriana 50%
- B digbyana 25%
- C harrisoniana.......... 25%

LINEAGE

1917 St. Quintin
Bc Cynthia

- **B digbyana**
- **C walkeriana**

1907 Heath
C Heathii

- **C harrisoniana**
- **C walkeriana**

Blc Mrs Herbert Hoover (Pervenusta x Bc British Queen) was bred in 1929 by Joseph Manda and Sons of Bridgeport, New Jersey. The hybrid is noteworthy for many reasons not the least of which is the fantastic shape of the flowers.

ARTHUR E. CHADWICK PHOTO

Mrs. Hoover was a flower enthusiast but it is unclear if she ever saw her namesake orchid.

HOOVER PRESIDENTIAL LIBRARY PHOTO

LOU HENRY HOOVER

Several months before the stock market crash of 1929, a new cattleya hybrid was introduced that honored the wife of the President of the United States. Never before had an orchid been named after an American First Lady. It had always been their husbands who received the distinction. This hybrid would make history as it started a tradition of First Lady namesakes that continues today.

Lou Henry was born in 1874 in Waterloo, Iowa. She met her husband, Herbert Hoover, while attending Stanford University. The couple was proficient in Chinese as his first job was overseas near Shanghai, China. They returned to the U.S. where he served as head of the Food Administration under Woodrow Wilson during World War I. He would later be Secretary of Commerce under Presidents Harding and Coolidge.

As First Lady, Lou Hoover gave regular radio broadcasts to the American people about the importance of volunteering. She also promoted the Girl Scouts, having previously served as national president. Mrs. Hoover oversaw the development of a presidential retreat located at Rapidan Camp in Madison County, Virginia in what was the precursor to Camp David.

Lou Hoover's namesake orchid is noteworthy not just because it was the first to be named for the wife of an American president, nor because it started a tradition that has lasted over a century. The flowers, themselves are most unusual and are nothing like anyone has ever seen before. Not surprisingly, we put the hybrid on the cover of this book.

It's rare to have photographs of orchids from the turn of the century. This picture shows a pale C mendelii with two single flowers in a clay pot as grown at Scampston Hall in England.

COURTESY OF SCAMPSTON HALL

One parent of the Hoover namesake, Bc British Queen, was bred by wealthy English hobbyist, Samuel Gratrix, of Whalley Range, Manchester in 1922. He was horticulturally inclined and first started outdoors with peaches and nectarines.

PHOTO COURTESY OF THE ORCHID WORLD

Hobbyist Samuel Gratrix lived on a splendid estate called West Point in northwest England. His gardener, Mr. J Brown, was in charge of an extensive orchid collection as well as seventeen acres of cultivated grounds.

PHOTO COURTESY OF THE ORCHID WORLD

A large commercial grower from New Jersey was responsible for developing and distributing the Hoover orchid. Joseph Manda and Sons was a sizable cut flower operation in Bridgeport with over one acre of cattleyas under glass. Their market was primarily the wholesale trade in the Northeast but they also had a potted plant division that targeted the collector.

In breeding this orchid, Manda did not use any of the large round cattleya species that were so popular and entrenched as corsage flowers. There is no C trianaei, C mossiae, or C labiata. Instead, the lineage drew upon such starry species as L tenebrosa, C dowiana, and C warscewiczii as well as B digbyana on both sides of the parentage.

One parent of the Hoover namesake is the novelty hybrid, Blc Pervenusta (B digbyana x Lc Bletchleyensis) from 1914. The breeder, Charlesworth, catered entirely to the English hobbyist who was always looking for something a little different. These flowers have extremely narrow petals and an exaggerated hairy lip like the species grandparent, B digbyana, which happens to be the National Flower of Honduras.

The Pervenusta petals remain narrow due to the other grandparent, Lc Bletchleyensis (L tenebrosa x C warscewiczii), from 1899. This primary hybrid was named after Bletchley Park, England by the owner of the estate, Sir Herbert Leon. These flowers are dramatic and remakes of this cross can be found in circulation today.

The other parent of the Hoover namesake honors the wife of King Edward V, Mary of Tech, who was on the throne at the time. Bc British Queen (Empress of Russia x C Lord Rothschild) was bred in 1922 by wealthy English hobbyist, Samuel Gratrix who lived for decades on a splendid estate called West Point in Whalley Range, Manchester. Gratrix was horticulturally inclined and first started outdoors with peaches and nectarines before being forced inside by the poor air quality of nearby factories.

It is not known what color form of C gaskelliana was used by Sander in 1893 to make C Lord Rothschild, but they are all very similar, as shown in this grouping.

ARTHUR E. CHADWICK PHOTO

Lou Hoover was an active First Lady and participated in numerous events and ceremonies. Here, she plants a tree while her husband looks on. PHOTO COURTESY OF ALAMY/ALPHASTOCK

Lou Hoover delighted in wearing cattleya corsages to all the important events of the day including the World Series of 1929. Note the other ladies and their corsages. PHOTO COURTESY OF ALAMY/EVERETT COLLECTION

The primary hybrid, Lc Bletchleyensis (L tenebrosa x C warscewiczii), was originally made in 1899 by Sir Herbert Leon of Bletchley Park, England. There are remakes of this cross in circulation today.

ARTHUR E. CHADWICK PHOTO

The Hoover namesake gets much of its pizzazz from the 1899 primary hybrid, Bc Empress of Russia (B digbyana x C mendelii). Many RHS awards were given to this cross which, back then, was known as Bc Digbyano-Mendelii.

ARTHUR E. CHADWICK PHOTO

Gratrix excelled in greenhouse plants and was best known for his work with cypripediums (now paphiopedilums) culminating in a new species being named for him, *P gratrixianum*. His collection was "*healthy and very vigorous*" with the slippers having as many as "*five growths*" according to an early RHS newsletter account. The head gardener, Mr. J. Brown, was in charge of not only the extensive orchids but also seventeen acres of cultivated grounds.

Gratrix had modern greenhouses which included lath roller blinds and rarely seen humidity control which he had invented. His best plants were exhibited at the Manchester Orchid Society where watercolor artists painted all the award winners. He had individual houses for the lady slippers, dendrobiums, odontoglossums, and, most importantly, cattleyas.

The RHS reporter noted that the pedigree cattleya collection included the "*...much prized Brassavola hybrids – Bc Digbyano-Mossiae, the elegant Bc Mrs. J. Leemann, and Bc Mrs. M. Gratrix.*" Also blooming were "*rare albinos such as C percivaliana alba...along with fine varieties of Slc Marathon...C Iris, C Fabia, and Lc Canhamiana. Suspended in baskets from the roof were several masses of the recently imported Laelia gouldiana.*"

With this kind of fire power, it's no surprise that Gratrix bred a hybrid fit for the Queen of England. The flowers were a pleasing concolor, pale to medium lavender with fullish petals and an oversized ruffley lip. The RHS gave three flower quality awards to Bc British Queen – AM/RHS in 1923, 'Splendens' FCC/RHS in 1924, and 'Stonehurst' FCC/RHS in 1932 as well as numerous culture awards. Not only were the flowers well-shaped and plentiful but the foliage was vigorous. Manda would later use a select variety to make the Hoover namesake.

It takes seven years to bloom a cattleya from seed and, sure enough, Blc Mrs. Herbert Hoover (Pervenusta x Bc British Queen) was registered in 1929 – exactly seven years after the

Brassavola digbyana imparts its wonderful shape onto the Hoover namesake like no other species could. Shown is John Nugent Fitch's artistic rendition from The Orchid Album.

COURTESY OF THE ORCHID ALBUM

parent, British Queen. Manda sold his new first lady hybrid briefly but, within six months, America fell into the Great Depression and there were few buyers. President Hoover took much of the blame for the Depression and his wife's namesake fell out of favor rather quickly. Even my father, who is a lifelong orchid history buff, did not have this plant in his collection.

One day in the 1990s, however, lightening struck when we attended a monthly Delaware Orchid Society meeting. There on the show table with all the other blooming orchids that had been brought in by members to discuss was something very unusual. The tag was hand written, faded, and barely readable. Blc Mrs. Herbert Hoover!

We immediately sought out the owner who was more than glad to give us a piece. Over the years, she had divided the mother plant many times and traded divisions with other society members. Clearly, it pays to attend orchid meetings.

The Hoover namesake is noteworthy for a number of reasons. Aside from its fantastic shape and radiant color, the hybrid is known to bloom twice a year, usually with two large flowers. The foliage is modest and takes after the digbyana so the effect is that of a smallish plant with big blooms. Lastly, Manda chose the more formal approach to naming after married females in which the prefix Mrs. appears before the husband's name.

Orchid historians will note that Mrs. Hoover had a second cattleya named after her in 1949, five years after her death. This hybrid corrected the naming issue of the first one (the use of Mrs.) and was simply called C Lou Henry Hoover.

What will be remembered about Lou Hoover in the horticultural world is that her 1929 namesake cattleya survived not only the stock market crash but nearly a century more and can still be found in collections today. In addition, the flowers are so interesting that they made the cover of this book. ✯

PERSONAL LIFE

Lou Henry grew up participating in a variety of outdoor activities, including equestrianism, camping, taxidermy, and mining. Her tomboy nature continued through her youth as she moved to California. She graduated from high school and pursued a Bachelor's degree in geology from Stanford, where she met her future husband Herbert Hoover. Upon their graduations, Herbert cabled her a wedding proposal, which she immediately accepted by return wire. The pair was wed in 1899 and had two sons together, Herbert and Allan – both of whom also graduated from Stanford. Today, the Lou Henry and Herbert Hoover House is the official residence of the President of Stanford. ✯

HOOVER PRESIDENTIAL LIBRARY PHOTO

We don't know what color form of L tenebrosa was used by Leon in 1899 to make his famous Lc Bletchleyensis. Shown is an un-named bronze variety showing the narrow petals and dark lip.

ARTHUR E. CHADWICK PHOTO

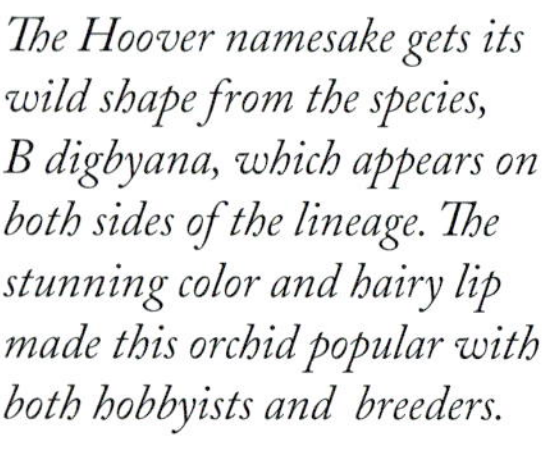

The Hoover namesake gets its wild shape from the species, B digbyana, which appears on both sides of the lineage. The stunning color and hairy lip made this orchid popular with both hobbyists and breeders.

ARTHUR E. CHADWICK PHOTO

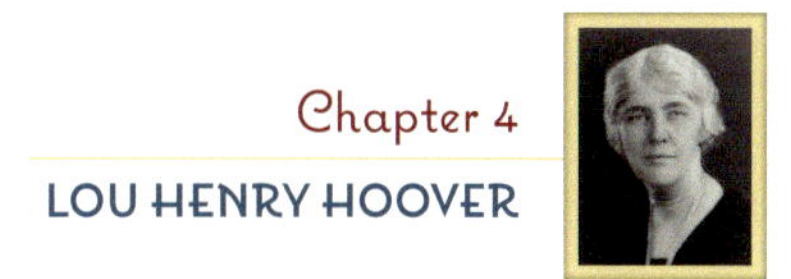

BLC MRS HERBERT HOOVER

(1929 Manda)

COMPOSITION

Species	Percentage
B digbyana	37.5%
C mendelii	12.5%
C warscewiczii	12.5%
L tenebrosa	12.5%
C gaskelliana	12.5%
C dowiana	12.5%

LINEAGE

1922 Gratrix
Bc British Queen

1904 Charlesworth
Blc Pervenusta

1900 Maron
Bc Empress of Russia

1893 Sanders
Lord Rothschild

B digbyana

1899 Leon
Lc Bletchleyensis

Although she's not wearing cattleyas, this lovely hand colored picture shows her love of orchids and a rare odontoglossum corsage.

COURTESY OF ALAMY/THE EVERETT COLLECTION

ELEANOR ROOSEVELT

★ ★ ★ ★ ★ ★ ★

The 1930s was a challenging time for the United States. Gone were the days of bathtub gin and the extravagances of the roaring twenties. The Great Depression left banks insolvent, businesses bankrupt, and millions of Americans without a job. Politicians could only hope that some new government program might ease the suffering and put people back to work. It was of utmost importance that elected officials appear modest and frugal.

Eleanor Roosevelt was First Lady during this tumultuous period and into the Second World War. Her husband, Franklin Delano Roosevelt, was the 32nd President and had been wheelchair bound since 1921. Together, they formed a strong political partnership. Due to his limited physical ability, she regularly made appearances and gave lectures on his behalf.

Mrs. Roosevelt was groundbreaking in every respect - she was the first president's wife to testify before a Congressional committee, the first to hold press conferences, and the first to speak before a national party convention. Her life was of such interest to the public that, for 26 years, she wrote a syndicated newspaper column, "My Day", that was read by millions. She was a strong advocate for social justice and equality and, although controversial, she is remembered as one of the notable figures of the twentieth century.

Like many First Ladies, Mrs. Roosevelt's namesake cattleya was not hybridized while her husband was in office (1933 – 1945). Some historians believe that she did not wish to display wealth and glamour at a time when the nation was in distress. Instead, her orchid is a relatively recent development using authentic lineage from that era.

One parent of the Roosevelt orchid is Lc C.G. Roebling (L purpurata x C gaskelliana) which was named by the legendary English firm, Frederick Sanders & Co, in 1895. The hybrid honors an American businessman, Charles G. Roebling, who was president of the company that built the Brooklyn Bridge. Roebling also had one of the finest orchid collections in the United States in the late 1800s.

It is common practice for commercial growers to bestow their best clients with gifts, even going so far as to name new hybrids or recently discovered species after them. Sander had recently opened a U.S. location in Summit, New Jersey which was a short train ride south to Roebling's greenhouses in Trenton, New Jersey. The two developed a close relationship as Roebling was regularly adding to his stock of fine cattleyas and Sander had some of the best varieties in existence. It was just a matter of time before Sander honored Roebling with a namesake orchid – in this case, one of the most spectacular primary hybrids the world had ever known.

Lc C. G. Roebling 'Beechview' AM/AOS (L purpurata x C gaskelliana) was first made in 1895 and named by Roebling's supplier and mentor, Frederick Sander. It was later remade as a coerulea and can still be found in collections today. ARTHUR E. CHADWICK PHOTO

Charles Roebling (left) was an accomplished businessman and engineer with nearly a dozen steel mills in New Jersey. Here he works on the Brooklyn Bridge with his assistant engineer, Wilhelm Hildenbrand.
COURTESY OF ROEBLING SUSPENSION BRIDGE HISTORY & HERITAGE

Charles Roebling and his brother, Washington, are credited with building the Brooklyn Bridge that their father, John, designed. It was opened to great fanfare in 1883. COURTESY OF ALAMY/WORLD HISTORY ARCHIVE

One secret to Roebling's high level of success as an orchid hobbyist was his grower, Henry Clinkaberry, who did everything from making new crosses to exhibiting at flower shows. Shown is his namesake C trianaei 'Clinkaberryana' which is a perennial favorite of A. A. Chadwick.

ARTHUR E. CHADWICK PHOTO

With its tall pseudobulbs and starry flowers, Laelia purpurata imparts the strongest influence of the four species in the Roosevelt hybrid. ARTHUR E. CHADWICK PHOTO

Roebling's greenhouses were immense and he scored innumerable awards at horticultural societies in Massachusetts and New York. Like his mentor, Sander, Roebling sent expeditions into the jungles of South America in search of rare species. All told, the massive hobby collection was estimated to have cost several hundred thousand dollars.

Britain's *Orchid Review* magazine featured Roebling's extensive operation in their November 1894 issue. (This rare original RHS publication, Volume 2, resides in A. A. Chadwick's personal orchid library.)

"These are Mr. Roebling's pets: and neither money nor pains have been spared to make this a leading collection", wrote the reporter, referring to the cattleyas. This greenhouse, alone, was sixty feet long and used *"canvas shades above the glass"* to keep it cool in the summer. There were a total of five greenhouses on the property, arranged by temperature requirements and genus.

A sampling of the plants shows Roebling's true love of white cattleya species as well as his excellent growing conditions. There was a *"...gaskelliana alba with 4 leads ...mossiae alba with 4 leads,... schroederae alba with 5 leads... C labiata was at its best, many dozen blooms being fully expanded."*

Like many hobbyists, Roebling named his best varieties after family members. *The Gardener's Chronicle* of February 1895 wrote *"C trianaei 'Miss Emily M. Roebling' ...which bears the name of the eldest daughter of the house, is a charming flower with white sepals and petals"*...while her sister's namesake, 'Miss Ellen Roebling' has similar coloring *"on which appears the most delicate pearly blush."* There was even one Roebling namesake awarded in England - a splash petal, C trianaei 'Roebling' AM/RHS as shown by Charlesworth in 1916.

Aside from Roebling's immense wealth which allowed him to acquire the best orchids and growing facilities, the key to his success was his gardener, Mr. H. (Henry) T. Clinkaberry who was passionate about the collection and did everything from making new crosses to exhibiting at shows. On one occasion, he sent a box of cut cattleya flowers to England (by ship) to be evaluated by the judges. The Gardener's Chronicle continues *"...not withstanding the long journey, have come to hand in a remarkably fresh condition. Taken throughout, they represent, by far, the best series of fine forms of C trianaei which we have seen this season."*

Clinkaberry's namesake trianaei, known as variety 'Clinkaberryana', is a perennial favorite of A. A. Chadwick, who keeps several plants of the century old species for display as well as for breeding. The flowers are a glistening light lavender with very wide petals and, like all trianaeis, seem to last forever. The name, itself, is endearing.

When Charles Roebling wasn't tending to his pedigree orchids, he was actively philanthropic at the highest level and built an entire town just to house the workers of his many steel and wire mills. The steel was used in the Brooklyn Bridge, the Golden Gate Bridge, and many others, while the wire went into the elevator cables for the Empire State Building and the Chicago Board of Trade. Charles ran the businesses with his older brother, Washington, who was somewhat of a Civil War hero having seen action in numerous battles including Gettysburg.

In 1912, tragedy struck as Charles's only son and heir to the family business, Washington, Jr., went down with the Titanic. Several years later, the main Roebling steel wire plant in Trenton, New Jersey, burned to the ground in what historians believe was arson. Disheartened, Charles became a recluse and died in 1918 at the age of 69.

Roebling had been a widower since 1903 and his two surviving daughters were not in-

In 1912, tragedy struck as Charles's only son and heir to the family business, Washington, Jr., went down with the Titanic. COURTESY OF WIKIMEDIA COMMONS/FRANCIS GODOLPHIN OSBOURNE STUART (PHOTOGRAPHER)

Tragedy struck again in January of 1915 when the main Roebling steel wire plant in Trenton, New Jersey burned to the ground. Historians believe the fire was caused by arson. Wire spools are visible in the foreground.
COURTESY OF THE LIBRARY OF CONGRESS

terested in maintaining the prized orchid collection. It was sold shortly thereafter to another well-known collector, Mrs. Frederick Dixon of Elkins Park, Pennsylvania for $28,000. (Coincidentally, Dixon was a neighbor of A. A. Chadwick who, over the years, had befriended the estate grower. Chadwick's earliest plants came from Dixon and included some of Roebling's).

Laeliocattleya C. G. Roebling has been remade numerous times over the years as breeders sought to recreate the fine qualities of the hybrid which included four to five well-spaced large blooms on a stem. In 1969, a blue version was introduced by Carson Whitlock and Fred Stewart as Stewart's launched a new line of coerulea cattleyas. Blues are always in fashion and nearly a dozen varieties have received awards from the American Orchid Society. Even today, many hobbyists have clones of 'Beechview' AM/AOS, 'Sentinel' or 'Blue Indigo' in their collection.

The other parent of the Roosevelt orchid is not without its own drama. Cattleya Undine (intermedia x mossiae) was registered in 1906 by Sir George Holford of the famed Westonbirt House and Arboretum. This cross was pure white and two varieties received First Class Certificates from the Royal Horticultural Society - one of which graced the cover of *The Orchid Review* in December of 1910. The only problem was the hybrid wasn't named Undine. It was named Dusseldorfii.

Historic prints best capture the old varieties available to the early breeders. Shown is L purpurata 'Russelliana' plate 195 by John Nugent Fitch which is a variety that Sander could have bred with to make Lc C. G. Roebling in 1895. COURTESY OF THE ORCHID ALBUM

C Undine (intermedia x mossiae) was originally made in 1906 as an alba. It was later remade as a coerulea and as this splash petal. Shown is 'Buena Suerta' HCC/AOS from 1997.

ARTHUR E. CHADWICK PHOTO

Cattleya Undine alba (intermedia x mossiae) was featured on the cover of the December 1910 Orchid Review. The only problem is, it wasn't labeled Undine.

ARTHUR E. CHADWICK PHOTO

The French firm, Charles Maron & Fils, had made the cross, C intermedia x mossiae, in 1904 – two years before Holford – and gave it the German name, Dusseldorfii. The judges wrote of Dusseldorfii 'Undine' FCC/RHS (which was coincidentally exhibited by Holford), *"It is a charming pure white variety, with a primrose yellow disk in the lip…a very free-growing and floriferous hybrid..."* Since Dusseldorfii (1904) was named earlier than Undine (1906), it should be the true and final name.

Unfortunately for Maron and the name, Dusseldorfii, the orchid registrar at the time was Frederick Sander who had a strong bias against everything German, having fled the country as a teenage refugee during Kaiser Wilhelm II's reign. As a result, the name, Dusseldorfii, was largely ignored and Sander gave preference to Holford and the name, Undine.

To complicate matters, a third name was introduced by authors Rolfe and Hurst in *The Orchid Stud – Book* of 1909. Here, the hybrid is listed as having been made in 1903 – three years before Undine and one year before Dusseldorfii by Right Hon. Joseph Chamberlain of Highbury in Moor Green. Cattleya Mackayi, as it was referred to, honors the Highbury grower, John Mackay who presumably made it. However, orchid registrars generally only recognize published dates of naming and it appears that Mackayi wasn't actually named until the stud book came out in 1909. Consequently, Undine survived another challenge.

Of course, there is much more to Cattleya Undine than nomenclature drama. The word, Undine, is a mythical water spirit as many early hybrids were named after classical characters – real or fictional.

Intuitively, combining two floriferous, spring blooming species such as intermedia and mossiae is bound to make a winning hybrid. Indeed, Undine was a major stud plant for medium sized hybrids with 28 registered crosses through 1945. There is even one AOS awarded variety – a splash petal, 'Buena Suerte' HCC/AOS – from 1997.

Like Lc C.G. Roebling, C Undine was remade as a coerulea many years after its introduction. Dr. Edgar McPeak of Kensington Orchids in Kensington, Maryland led this effort and his best seedlings would likewise become part of Stewart's legendary blue breeding program on the west coast.

The Roosevelt hybrid is a little unusual in that it was made using an alba parent and a coerulea parent – the outcome of which can only be lavender. Breeder John Stanton of The Orchid Trail in Morrisville, North Carolina made the cross in 2004 and was aiming for interesting shaped flowers on tall foliage rather than an exotic color. Technically speaking, his cross was Lc C. G. Roebling 'Beechview' AM/AOS x C Undine alba.

We named Eleanor Roosevelt soon after seeing a batch in bloom in The Orchid Trail greenhouses as the results were impressive enough for a First Lady. The blossoms are large and open-shaped, typical of the 1930s and the best varieties are worthy of consideration by the American Orchid Society judges. There does not appear to be a specific flowering season.

It has been exciting to watch the several hundred seedlings grow to maturity and bloom – each similar to one another but different enough to receive unique tag numbers. As they outgrew their pots, they were divided and, over the years, we've probably made 500 plants. The strongest influence of the four species that make up this hybrid is, undoubtedly, Laelia purpurata, which is found in the treetops of coastal Brazil and produces very tall pseudobulbs.

In later years, Eleanor Roosevelt continued to wear orchid corsages. Here, she sits with Frank Sinatra.

COURTESY OF ALAMY/GEM COLLECTION

When three first ladies get together, it's a grand affair and worthy of orchid corsages for all. Shown are Bess Truman, Eleanor Roosevelt, and Edith Bolling Wilson.

COURTESY OF ALAMY/EVERETT COLLECTION

After leaving The White House, Eleanor Roosevelt traveled the world with the United Nations and regularly wore cattleya corsages. Here, she visits Richmond, Virginia.

PHOTO COURTESY OF THE RICHMOND TIMES-DISPATCH

Mrs. Roosevelt wore a cattleya to dinner with the Allen family in Adrian, Michigan in 1959. She had just spoken to the local university on United Nations Day.

PHOTO COURTESY DAVID ALLEN

As the United States recovered from the war, Cattleya orchids hit their heyday of corsage fashion. Mrs. Roosevelt was courted by politicians to consider running for public office, but she chose to focus her later years on various duties within the United Nations. She traveled the world giving countless lectures and was regularly seen wearing Cattleya corsages.

We would like to thank her granddaughter, Anne Roosevelt, for assistance with this project. She resides in Maine and is President of the Goodwill Industries of Northern New England. At her request, the Roosevelt seedlings were sent to family members around the country as well as to her favorite horticultural venues – the Coastal Maine Botanical Garden as well as the New York Botanical Garden – where they are on public display. ✯

Eleanor Roosevelt doesn't have any surviving children but she does have a number of grandchildren including Anne Roosevelt (above) who resides in Maine and is the President of the Goodwill Industries of Northern New England. Here, she opens a box of cut Roosevelt flowers from Chadwick's. COURTESY OF ANNE ROOSEVELT

This grouping of Roosevelt seedling shows the lovely variations of the cross. ARTHUR E. CHADWICK PHOTO

While all the Roosevelt seedlings are various shades of lavender, there is one outlier – a dramatic two tone magenta variety, #15.

ARTHUR E. CHADWICK PHOTO

One of the best of the Roosevelt seedlings is this richly colored dark variety, 'First Lady' AM/AOS, with five flowers.

ARTHUR E. CHADWICK PHOTO

Another very fine Roosevelt is variety #25, with five flowers.

ARTHUR E. CHADWICK PHOTO

LC ELEANOR ROOSEVELT

(2012 Chadwick/Orchid Trail)

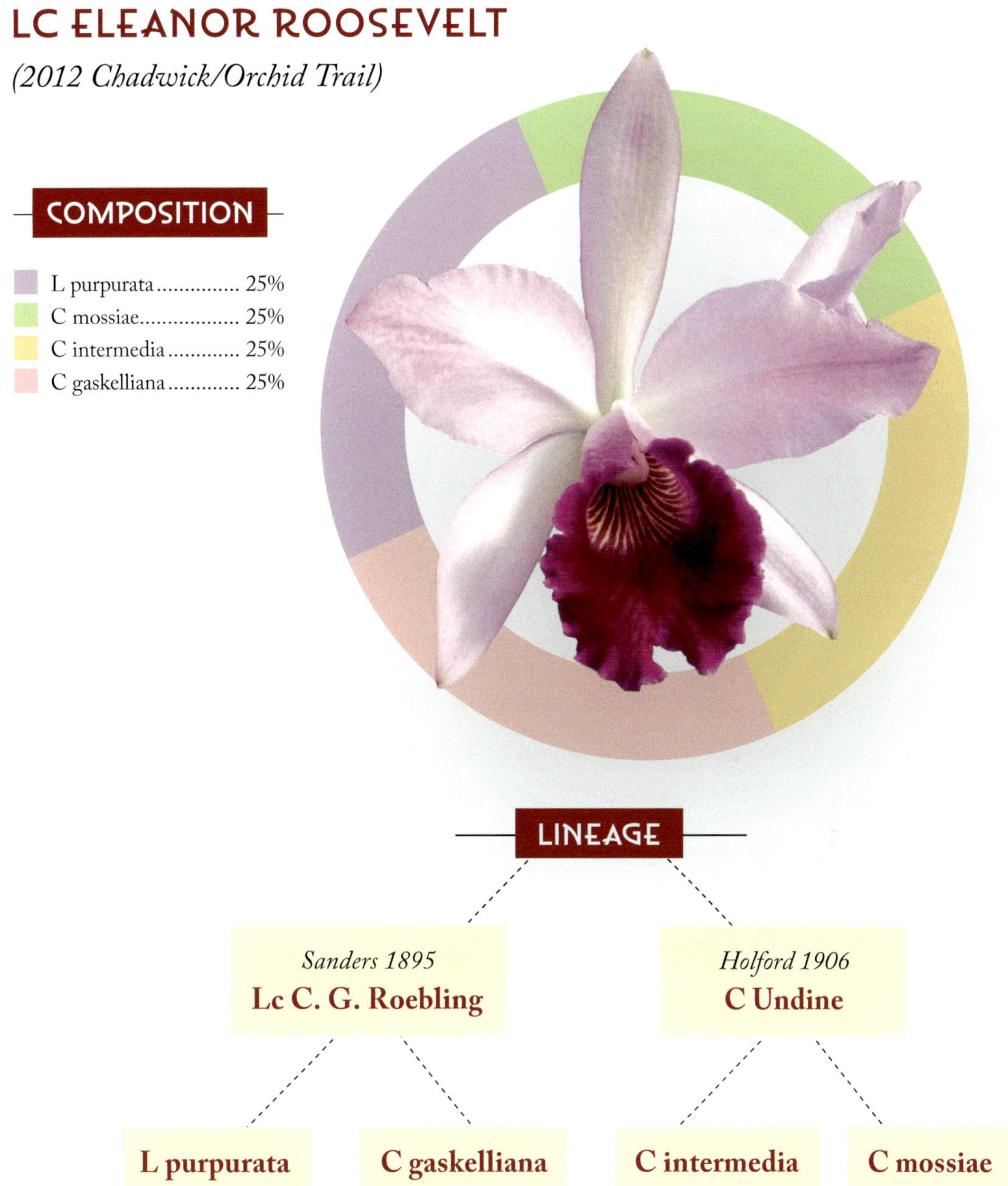

COMPOSITION

- L purpurata 25%
- C mossiae 25%
- C intermedia 25%
- C gaskelliana 25%

LINEAGE

Sanders 1895
Lc C. G. Roebling

- **L purpurata**
- **C gaskelliana**

Holford 1906
C Undine

- **C intermedia**
- **C mossiae**

Cattleya Bess Truman is a classic semi-alba from the breeding efforts of John Lines. He registered the hybrid in 1962 and personally presented the flowers to Harry Truman. Shown is a specimen plant of "Surprise Package" AM/AOS which is thought to have been the variety used as "the surprise" for Truman.

ARTHUR E. CHADWICK PHOTO

BESS TRUMAN

★ ★ ★ ★ ★ ★ ★

The world of cattleya corsages was elevated to new heights in 1945 when Bess Truman became First Lady of the United States. Not only were the glamorous flowers a regular part of her ensemble, but she often wore two or three at a time. She even featured her orchids while on "whistle stop" campaign tours with her husband.

Mrs. Truman had a tremendous love of plants and, while First Lady, was honorary chair of the Woman's National Farm & Garden Association. She reinstated the formal White House social season, which had been interrupted by the war, and took great interest in the planning of all events from state receptions to casual teas. It would be another decade after Mrs. Truman left Washington, however, before she would get her very own namesake orchid hybrid.

The 4th Mid-America Orchid Congress in the spring of 1962 must have been quite a show. Aside from the spectacular orchid displays, the weekend included a slate of big-name speakers as well as a trip to the Truman Presidential Library, where the former President was expected to make a personal appearance.

The star-studded event was held at the historic Muehlebach hotel in downtown Kansas City. Built in 1915, the twelve story structure was frequented by celebrity guests including sitting President Harry Truman who, not surprisingly, would stay in the "Presidential Suite". The posh room was subsequently named after him.

The Muehlebach hotel hosted the 4th Mid-America Orchid Congress of 1962. Noteworthy speakers included second generation orchid grower John Lines who had a special treat in store for Mr. Truman.
COURTESY OF THE MUEHLEBACH HOTEL

Legendary grower Oliver Lines worked for several years under Clint McDade of Rivermont Orchids in Chattanooga, Tennessee where he learned the finer points of the cut flower business. Lines would soon join his son, John, and form the powerhouse, Lines Orchids. COURTESY OF RIVERMONT ORCHIDS

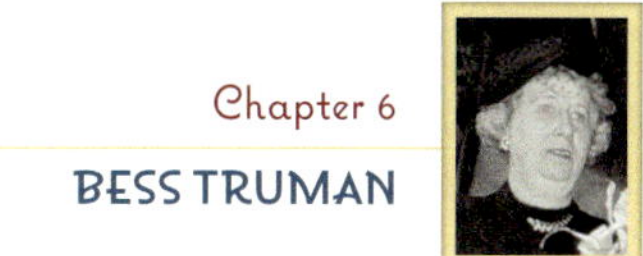

Speakers included Mr. and Mrs. Lewis Vaughn, who would later donate their West Palm Beach estate to the American Orchid Society for use as the new headquarters. Another prominent orator was Dr. Robert Gillespie, curator of the Missouri Botanical Garden, which had recently hosted the 1st Annual World Orchid Congress. The lecture of the day, however, was given by John Lines - a second generation orchid grower from Signal Mountain, Tennessee, who had a special treat in store for Mr. Truman.

John Lines' father, Oliver, was legendary in the orchid world. As co-founder of Lines Orchids in 1947, his resume included overseas stints with the orchid greenhouses of the British colonial secretary, Right Honorable Joseph Chamberlain, the Westonbirt estate of Sir George Holford, and the commercial firm, Charlesworth. Oliver then moved to the United States, where he was head grower of the famed Arthur Cooley collection in Pittsfield, Massachusetts – a position he held for a decade. After the Cooley collection was acquired by Fitz Eugene Dixon of Elkins Park, Pennsylvania in 1925, he would become their head grower for the next 20 years.

By the time the Mid-America Orchid Congress was held, Lines Orchids was a thriving cut flower cattleya operation. John Lines had spent three years working with Clint McDade at

John Lines credits much of his breeding success to the semi-alba stud, C trianaei 'Trenton' which originated in the collection of Charles Roebling.

ARTHUR E. CHADWICK PHOTO

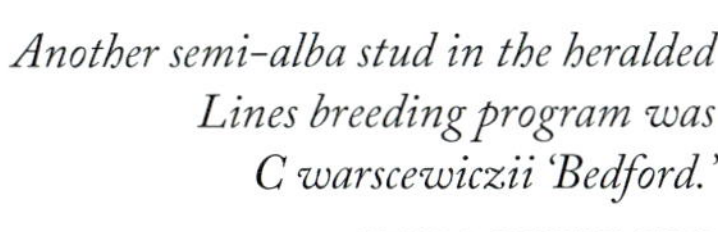

Another semi-alba stud in the heralded Lines breeding program was C warscewiczii 'Bedford.'

ARTHUR A. CHADWICK PHOTO

John Lines was a prolific cattleya breeder and was especially proud of his semi-albas. He detailed his love for this color form in a six page article for the American Orchid Society's magazine, The Bulletin. Note the two varieties of C Bess Truman as well as its parent, C Clotho. COURTESY OF THE AMERICAN ORCHID SOCIETY

Lines Orchids of Signal Mountain, Tennessee, had become a 4th generation family business when the author visited in 2013. Shown is the daughter of John Lines, Joan, in a greenhouse full of blooming purple cattleyas. ARTHUR E. CHADWICK PHOTO

Rivermont Orchids in Chattanooga, Tennessee, learning the finer points of the orchid business and had accumulated an impressive stock of breeder plants for his new venture.

He especially loved the semi-albas and explained this fascination in a six page spread for the American Orchid Society magazine, The Bulletin, detailing the intricacies of each hybrid. The lineage was traced back not just to the species, but to the actual varieties used in the original crosses – C trianaei 'Trenton', C mossiae reineckiana 'Youngs', L purpurata 'Orchid Knoll', C warscewiczii 'FMB' and 'Bedford', and C labiata 'Charlesworthii'.

One hybrid that John Lines was particularly proud of making was C Clotho x C Ardmore

Bess Truman's namesake cattleya gets much of its mossiae shape from the 1938 stud, C Ardmore (Enid x mossiae). Shown is the lavender variety, 'Kensington'. ARTHUR E. CHADWICK PHOTO

Oliver Lines was head grower for Fitz Eugene Dixon of Elkins Park, Pennsylvania for two decades. Numerous orchids were named after Dixon during this time including the lovely Bc F. E. Dixon (Digbyano-Schroederae x C dowiana) in 1925. ARTHUR E. CHADWICK PHOTO

C Bess Truman's parent, C Ardmore, was bred by the Sherman Adams Company of Wellesley, Massachusetts in 1938. The firm catered to the hobbyist and exhibited at all the major flower shows.

COURTESY OF THE SHERMAN ADAMS COMPANY

PARTIAL VIEW OF OUR GERMINATING-HOUSE

Seeds require six to nine months before the tiny plants can be removed to community pots.

The Sherman Adams Company did all their own flasking and specialized in cattleyas and paphiopedilums.

COURTESY OF THE SHERMAN ADAMS COMPANY

as he would later name this for Mrs. Truman. He describes his stud, C Clotho 'Lines', as follows - *"We raised 200 plants of this cross and this is the only variety we kept. It has proven to be a fine parent and we predict it will have a great influence of future late-winter and spring flowering semi-albas."* When combined with the heavily C mossiae influenced C Ardmore, the results *"show the progress made through very selective breeding."*

John Lines took his striking white with colored lip hybrid, C Clotho x C Ardmore, to the Congress that weekend. He boarded the tour bus for a 30 minute ride from Kansas City to Independence and the Truman Presidential Library. Upon arrival, John and the other orchid show attendees entered the building and were each personally greeted by the former President – a gesture that reminded everyone just how genuine the Trumans really were.

It was at this time that John Lines informed Mr. Truman that he wanted to name this special hybrid in his honor. Mr. Truman replied, *"So many things have already been named after me. Would you name it after Bess?"* Thus, Cattleya Bess Truman was born.

The Adams stud, C Ardmore, went on to breed many fine hybrids including the semi-alba cut flower, C Eileen Patterson (x Catherine Patterson) in 1964. ARTHUR A. CHADWICK PHOTO

The Sherman Adams catalogs were chock full of fantastic cattleya hybrids including remakes of "Big Brassos" from the turn of the century such as Bc Madame Charles Maron (B digbyana x C warscewiczii). Shown is variety 'Lines'. ARTHUR E. CHADWICK PHOTO

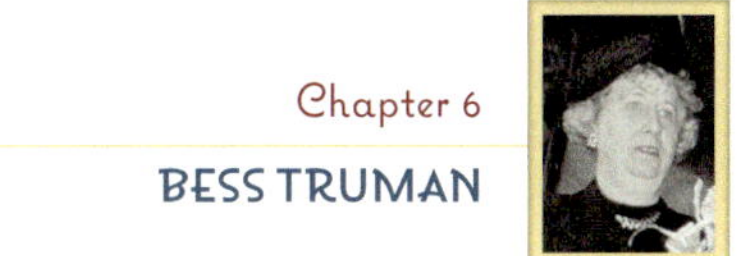

Of course, none of this excitement would have been possible without the parent, C Ardmore (Enid x mossiae), which was bred by the L Sherman Adams Company of Wellesley, Massachusetts in 1938. *"Orchids are ideal for city dwellers"* says the opening page of their catalog. Their nursery was different than most in that they catered to hobbyists *"who have a small greenhouse or lean-to"* at a time when nearly everyone else was focused on the corsage industry. An astonishing number of genera were represented – over fifty - from aerides to zygopetalum and everything in between.

The Adams greenhouses were only open to the public on weekends, as most of their business was mail order. Each year from 1937 to 1952, an extensive catalog was sent to subscribers around the country. Their slogan - *"Hybridists, Importers and Growers."*

Their pitch was simple – make orchids seem easy and inexpensive. These exotic plants *"take less room, and produce more flowers with greater lasting qualities"*...and at *"prices to fit any purse."* There were plenty of cattleya offerings and the "Brassos" alone would make modern day enthusiasts jealous – Bc British Queen, Cliftonii, Empress of Russia, Madame Charles Maron, Mrs. J Leemann, Queen of the Belgians, and many more. Imagine what these plants would sell for today.

Other exciting Sherman Adams offerings included the famed, Bc Mrs. J. Leemann (B digbyana x C dowiana), which can be found in the lineage of many yellow hybrids today. ARTHUR E. CHADWICK PHOTO

Bess Truman's namesake orchid is only three generations from the species. This painting from the late 1800s is an example of the fine varieties available to the early breeders. Shown is the semi-alba C warscewiczii 'Franconvillensis', formerly known as C gigas. COURTESY OF THE ORCHID ALBUM.

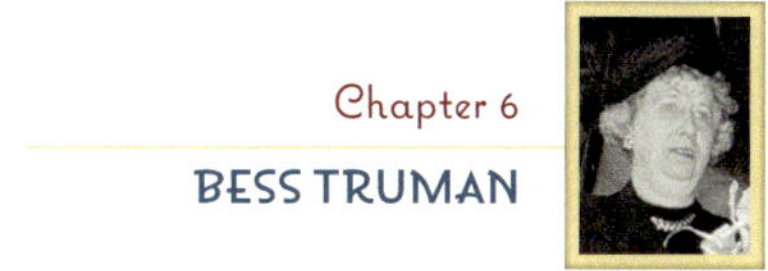

The adventurous collector could peruse the pages of unflowered, un-named cattleya crosses or jump into entire sections *"of interesting and beautiful species."* The catalog also offered basic growing instructions because *"practically all the literature upon the culture of orchids comes from English sources."* Hobbyists, who are new to the sport, might not realize that the orchid craze was started across the ocean by westerners who imported the species, made the first hybrids, and wrote a great deal on the subject.

Interestingly, C Ardmore is not found in any of the early Sherman Adams catalogs. From 1937 to 1939, it was listed in the "un-named crosses" section as "C Enid x C mossiae" and readers could purchase a flowering size seedling in a 4" or 5" pot for $10 - $15. This was a straight semi-alba cross and there would be no surprises.

Finally, in their 1951 Spring Offering, under the "Whites – Colored Lip" heading was C Ardmore (cross #2848) (Enid alba x mossiae wagneri 'La Belle'). By popular demand, they had remade their own cross and now were offering very small seedlings in 1 ¾" pots for $3.00 each.

The very best C Ardmore seedlings were given variety names and elevated to stud duties or used in trades with other commercial firms in the area, such as Patterson and McDade. Ardmore is a classically floppy cattleya – perfect for corsages but maybe not awards.

Sherman Adams registered nearly a hundred cattleya crosses over its brief fifteen years in the business but the company's main emphasis was always lady slippers. They also had a sizable representation in cymbidiums and dancing ladies.

What is most striking about the nearly four hundred total Sherman Adams orchid registrations is, generally speaking, their use of nonsensical hybrid names. While many breeders name their crosses after friends, relatives, or other important people, places, or things, Adams used a technique that combined fragments of each parent's name into one made-up word. Here are three examples:

- C Ariel x Lc Luminosa = Lc Arielosa
- Lc Carmencita x C Hardyana = Lc Carmyana
- Lc Britannia x Lc Schroederae = Lc Roedannia

All of this makes for strange record keeping for the hobbyist as the names are not obvious or easy to remember and adds to the already confusing lingo that is orchids.

Fortunately, C Ardmore is the rare Adams hybrid name that makes perfect sense, as it is a town outside Philadelphia about 300 miles down the coast from their greenhouses in Wellesley. It is speculated that perhaps Adams honored a wealthy client in the Ardmore area by naming the cattleya hybrid after the town.

C Ardmore is, in fact, one of the most significant crosses that Sherman Adams ever made, as it went onto to parent several dozen additional hybrids including the likes of C Chickamauga (x Thetis), C Eileen Patterson (x Catherine Patterson), C Olive Chadwick (x Lily Pons), and another first lady's namesake, C Jacqueline Kennedy (x Enid). Their most acclaimed cattleya cross, interestingly, is a yellow - Blc Xanthette (Midenette x Xanthedo), which was a widely used stud for mid century art shades, including the famed Blc Fortune.

In a strange coincidence, the other parent of Bess Truman was also listed in the Adams catalog. Seedlings of their 1910 C Clotho remake, in lavender, were offered for $12 to $18 depending on size. The description was enticing: *"Blush to delicate lavender, with orange and purple on the lip. Winter Blooming."*

While the L. Sherman Adams Company was named after Mr. Sherman Adams, his wife, Helen, was very active in the business and, in some ways, eclipsed her husband. She was a frequent speaker on the orchid circuit, drawing big crowds at such places as the Horticultural Society of New York. She left a lasting legacy by helping to create the American Orchid Society judging system in 1949, along with commercial growers Robert Gore and Norman & Jean Merkel, as well as hobbyists Norman Lind, and Gordon Dillon.

While much is known about C Ardmore, the information about the other C Bess Truman parent, C Clotho, is scant. Lines had remade it as a semi-alba but it was originally made in England by Charlesworth in 1910 as a lavender using the great stud, C trianaei 'Grand Monarch' FCC/RHS (1909). There is one award of C Clotho, in 1918, for variety 'General Pershing' FCC/RHS, a perfectly round flower as exhibited by the breeder.

Bess Truman's namesake cattleya can still be found in collections today, as it was publicized following the presentation in Independence. We are fortunate to own several varieties including

First Lady Bess Truman wore corsages every chance she could. Here, actress Ingrid Bergman pins a corsage on her for an event. COURTESY OF THE NATIONAL ARCHIVES

The Trumans were genuinely interested in flowers and orchids specifically. Here, President Truman takes time out of his busy schedule to attend a National Capital Orchid Society show in 1950.
COURTESY OF THE NATIONAL CAPITAL ORCHID SOCIETY

the lone flower quality award winner, 'Surprise Package' AM/AOS. This plant is thought to have been given the variety name by Lines after his "surprise" to Truman.

In 1995, a specimen C Bess Truman was displayed at the Michigan Orchid Society Show with an astounding 44 flowers, where it stole the show and earned a Certificate of Cultural Merit from the American Orchid Society. (The exhibitor, Darlene Cation, dedicated the plant to her late father with the variety name, 'Memoria Paul Cation's Elation' CCM/AOS.)

Mrs. Truman connected with the everyday American and made it a point to personally respond to each of the thousands of letters that she received at the White House. Although her namesake orchid came into existence a decade after her husband left office, it was widely regarded by hobbyists and remains one of the showiest of all the first lady hybrids. Following her years in Washington, DC (1945-1953), she and her husband returned to the place they loved – Independence. ✯

PERSONAL LIFE

Elizabeth 'Bess' Virginia Wallace was born in 1885 in Independence, Missouri. She and her husband, Harry S. Truman, met in primary school and were inseparable, marrying in 1919 and having one daughter, Margaret.

During her time at the White House, Bess served as Honorary President of the Girl Scouts, along with leading the Washington Animal Rescue League and the Women's National Democratic Club. She was the longest living First Lady in U.S. history - 97 years of age. ✯

First Lady Bess Truman was a fantastic advertisement for cattleyas during her husband's eight years in office. She even wore them on their high profile "Whistle Stop" campaign tours.

COURTESY OF ALAMY/ASSOCIATED PRESS

C BESS TRUMAN

(1962 Lines)

COMPOSITION

- C mossiae.................. 50%
- C trianaei.................. 25%
- C warscewiczi 25%

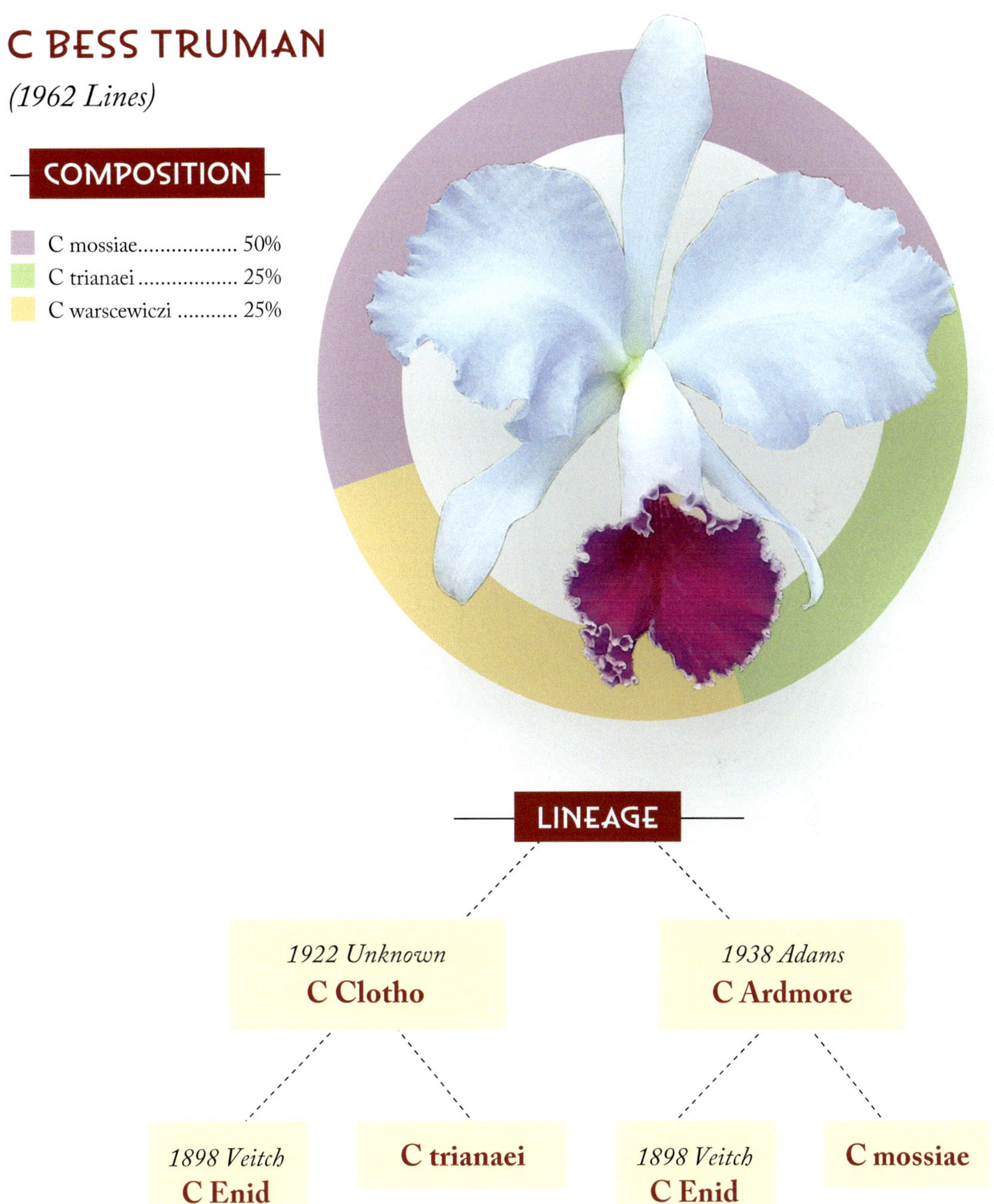

LINEAGE

1922 Unknown
C Clotho

1938 Adams
C Ardmore

1898 Veitch
C Enid

C trianaei

1898 Veitch
C Enid

C mossiae

Lc Mamie Eisenhower (Chevalier x Britannia) is a splashy purple from 1953 and honors the wife of President Dwight Eisenhower.

ARTHUR E. CHADWICK PHOTO

On inauguration day, 1953, the new First Lady pinned a cattleya corsage on her lapel and, in so doing, became the best spokesperson cattleyas could ask for.

MARK KAUFMAN PHOTO

MAMIE EISENHOWER

★ ★ ★ ★ ★ ★ ★

Having won the greatest war of the 20th century, President Dwight Eisenhower in 1953 ushered in eight years of calm and stability not seen in the United States for fifty years. In so doing, he also opened the golden age of cattleya orchids. First Lady Mamie Eisenhower was the symbol of prosperity and elegance. She loved cattleyas and was rarely seen in public without a corsage of two or three flowers during her husband's entire two terms.

Her love for cattleyas was so obvious that the orchid giant, Rod McLellan Company of South San Francisco, named a hybrid after her. At the time, she was only the second U.S. First Lady to be so honored (Lou Hoover was first in 1929). Suddenly, the practice of naming an orchid after a First Lady looked like it might even become a tradition.

In the 1950s, cattleya corsages were worn to nearly every social event, from dinners and luncheons to afternoon teas, the theater, opera, and high school dances. Growers had trouble keeping up with the demand for flowers and many fortunes were made in the industry. Springtime was especially busy with floral holidays - Easter and Mother's Day, as well as proms and June weddings. In selecting a cattleya for Mrs. Eisenhower, McLellan chose a floriferous spring bloomer with a pedigreed parentage.

The very first World Orchid Conference was held in 1954 in St Louis and Mr. Rod McLellan, himself, was a speaker. He declared that corsages are always in fashion – *"as a wristlet, or on a handbag, on the shoulder or at the waist, and sometimes in the hair."* The quintessential promoter, he further encouraged cut orchids *"for every room of the house"*.

Mamie's namesake cattleya was actually bred the previous decade by Rod's father's company, E.W. McLellan, for use as cut flower stock. In the early 1950s, Edgar divided his company between his two sons and gave the orchid division to Roderick, who immediately began selling off the corsage plants.

Nicknamed "Acres of Orchids", the newly formed Rod McLellan Co. was a tremendous operation with one greenhouse alone containing 200,000 cattleya seedlings. The flasking house was filled with countless sterilized glass bottles and had its own Superintendent, Geneticist, and Laboratory Technicians. The extensive mail order catalog featured over a hundred new cattleya hybrids, a line of custom potting materials including Supersoil and Wonderbark, and every imaginable accessory for the hobbyist.

1955 saw the first Rod McLellan public offering of Lc Mamie Eisenhower (Britannia x Chevalier) as full page advertisements appeared in both the American Orchid Society Bulletin and the Orchid Digest magazine. The plant was glamorously portrayed as a painting by local artist, Naomi Sandl. The wording of the ad was flattering: *"This outstanding lavender hybrid with a rich purple lip is so charming we named it in honor of our gracious First Lady (with Mrs. Eisenhower's permission)."*

Mr. Rod McLellan was a quintessential promoter of cut cattleyas and declared that corsages are always in fashion.
COURTESY OF THE ROD MCLELLAN CO.

The Eisenhower namesake was bred by the Rod McLellan Company of South San Francisco and was a tremendous operation with one greenhouse alone containing 200,000 seedlings.

COURTESY OF THE ROD MCLELLAN CO.

The McLellan flasking room contained countless sterilized glass bottles and had its own superintendent, geneticist, and technicians.

COURTESY OF THE ROD MCLELLAN CO.

First Lady Mamie Eisenhower was rarely seen in public without her corsage of two or three flowers during her husband's entire two terms.

COURTESY OF THE RICHMOND TIMES DISPATCH

1955 saw the first public offering of Lc Mamie Eisenhower as full page advertisements in orchid magazines with select varieties selling for as much as $75.

COURTESY OF THE AMERICAN ORCHID SOCIETY ARCHIVES

First Lady Mamie Eisenhower flaunts her double waist corsage of Brasso-cattleyas while her friends show off their "sash" corsages.

COURTESY OF ALAMY/EVERETT COLLECTION

McLellan did, in fact, get permission to name the hybrid via their local congressman, U.S. House of Representative J. Arthur Younger – an act which is commendable given the considerable logistics that an orchid presentation entails. Cattleya flowers are only fresh for a few weeks and the grower has to get them to the recipient as fast as possible.

Contact with the White House usually takes place after the hybrid is named and getting help from a local politician is the best way of connecting with a First Lady. The average person can't just call for an appointment due to the sheer number of inquiries they receive as well as the potential security threat.

We have further discovered that it is almost essential to work with a politician who is of the same party as the First Lady. For example, our proposed presentation to Mrs. Clinton in 1993 was met with polite rejections for several years when our very kind Republican U.S. Senator

While there are no known plants of Lc Mamie Eisenhower's 1903 parent, Lc Britannia (Canhamiana x C warscewiczii) in existence, the hybrid could be remade. Shown is a fine semi-alba variety of the grandparent, Lc Canhamiana (L purpurata x C mossiae). ARTHUR E. CHADWICK PHOTO

contacted her office but instantly accepted when our Democratic Lieutenant Governor made the same pitch.

The First Lady's physical acceptance of the orchid is her implied consent to the naming and, realistically, who would say, "No, I don't want an orchid named after me"? Every White House press secretary would agree that a namesake flower makes for a fantastic feel good story and is a win for everyone.

The McLellan ad went on to say *"Nine out of ten Mamie Eisenhower plants have been of exhibition quality, with superior size, substance, and texture."* This all sounds wonderful but what do these fancy descriptive words mean in relation to orchids?

"Exhibition quality" means that the blooms on a plant present themselves well. The flowers are large, of reasonable shape and not crowded. Of course, this description applies to all cut flower cattleya species and since Mrs. Eisenhower's namesake is made up almost entirely of these species, this is not exactly news.

The term, *"substance"*, is what a flower feels like and refers to the thickness of the sepals and petals. The description was used extensively during the corsage era when growers needed blooms that would resist bruising. Today, its value is debated because orchids are used as potted plants and not worn.

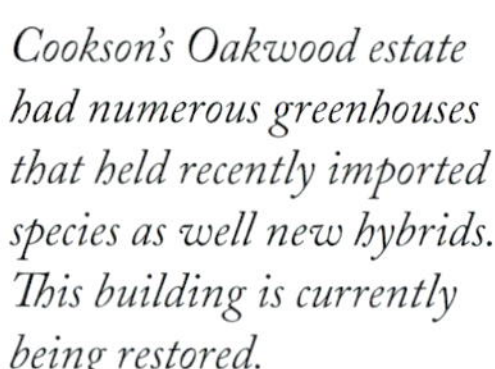

Cookson's Oakwood estate had numerous greenhouses that held recently imported species as well new hybrids. This building is currently being restored.

ANDREW CURTIS PHOTO

The rare hybrid, Lc Britannia, honors British patriotism and is often represented by a female warrior holding a trident and shield. Many English coins carry this symbol.

COURTESY OF WINTER COINS

Thick substance is often misinterpreted to mean long lasting flowers but there is no correlation between these terms. The blooms of C trianaei have the best longevity of all the cattleya species - six weeks or more - yet its substance is paper thin. A. A. Chadwick used to drill this point into every hobbyist who would listen.

"Texture" describes what the surface of a bloom looks like. Orchid judges, nowadays, use specific words like matte, waxy or crystalline and the McLellan ad's *"Superior texture"* doesn't really have a meaning.

Lc Mamie Eisenhower is an outstanding display plant as well as a prolific stud. McLellan thought very highly of its First Lady hybrid and, in 1955, charged as much as $75 for select varieties – a hefty sum at a time when gasoline was 29 cents a gallon. The catchy ads were effective and the company sold all its Eisenhower plants.

Springtime was the greatest market for cut flowers and the Eisenhower hybrid combines only April, May, June, and July blooming species. There is no C labiata, C percivaliana, or C trianaei. Mamie is all springtime.

The pedigree lineage all began innocently in 1893 with the primary hybrid, Cattleya Harold (gaskelliana x warscewiczii). Industrialist Norman Cookson registered the cross and named it after his third of four sons. The other boys had primaries as well but Harold's became well known.

C Harold was one of the very first large flowered cattleya hybrids ever made and combines two tall growing summer blooming species – neither of which is known for its good shape as both are somewhat starry. However, well grown plants can be tremendously showy with four or five blooms on a stem and C Harold managed to earn two flower quality awards from the Royal Horticultural Society.

The first RHS award was given the same year that the plant was introduced and it must have been quite a conversation piece at the judging table. There is no official variety name but it

The primary hybrid, C Harold, was registered by Industrialist Norman Cookson who lived at the swanky Oakwood estate in Wylam, England. The property is currently being restored. ANDREW CURTIS PHOTO

CATTLEYA MOSSIÆ DECORA.

The species, Cattleya mossiae, can be found on both sides of the Eisenhower lineage. This lavender variety, 'Decora', is representative of the fine varieties available at the turn of the century. COURTESY OF THE ORCHID ALBUM

was a richly colored lavender and was exhibited by Norman Cookson himself where it received an Award of Merit.

Twenty years later, a second C Harold was awarded – also an Award of Merit – this time for a lovely semi-alba variety, 'Fowler', as exhibited by hobbyist and RHS Orchid Committee Chairman, Gurney J Fowler.

Norman Cookson had an impressive orchid collection in the north of England that required 20-30 gardeners to maintain. He made his fortune in the mining industry and had interests in Mexican silver and New York metal works. He was also head of a local coal company and lead smelter but always found time for his beloved orchids.

Cookson was a well respected businessman and *"a gentleman of rare culture and scientific attainment"* as well as *"a recognized authority of vegetable biology and the hybridization of plants, particularly orchids."* His estate in Wylam, "Oakwood" was once described as *"the Mecca of orchid growers."* Many of his variety names pay homage to this estate including C labiata 'Oakwoodiensis' CCC/RHS from 1904.

Cookson used to send his very best specimens six hours by train to the RHS London shows, packed in large pine chests with carrying handles at each end and cushioned with sphag-

The species, Cattleya gaskelliana, is one parent of the famed C Harold and grows wild in Venezuela.

ARTHUR E. CHADWICK PHOTO

Among the many fine varieties that Cookson had in his collection was this 1895 awarded C labiata 'Cooksoniae' FCC/RHS. An original division of this plant made its way to Arthur A Chadwick's collection.

ARTHUR E. CHADWICK PHOTO

Cattleya Harold (gaskelliana x warscewiczii) from 1893 is one of the very first large flowered cattleya hybrids and imparts much of its showiness to the Eisenhower namesake.

ARTHUR A. CHADWICK PHOTO

num moss. It was at these events that he received many of his flower quality awards including the famed C labiata 'Cooksoniae' FCC/RHS [1895] (of which Chadwick's has original divisions of).

When Cookson died in 1909 at the age of 67, he left a year's wages to each servant who had been with him for ten years. His funeral was attended by all the area notables including the Duke of Northumberland. Today, the Oakwood estate still exists and is being restored along with some of the original greenhouses.

Sadly, Cookson didn't live quite long enough to see his head gardener, Henry James Chapman, receive the Royal Horticultural Society's Veitch Memorial Medal in 1910. In many respects, Chapman eclipsed his boss in the orchid world. He got his start at the famous Veitch Nursery in Chelsea and was soon hired as the head gardener for R. H. Measures of Camberwell who, like Cookson, was a successful industrialist.

Chapman was an educated man with an eye for detail and edited the third edition of William Watson's widely circulated book, *Orchids, their Culture and Management*, published in 1902. This was the standard work on orchid cultivation of its day and Chapman provided all the pictures. The preface describes Chapman as *one of the most able orchid growers and hybridists in the country.* In addition to the Veitch medal, Chapman served on the RHS Orchid Committee for 30 years.

In many respects, Cookson's head gardener, Henry James Chapman, eclipsed his boss in the orchid world. In 1910, he received the RHS's Veitch Memorial Medal.

COURTESY OF ANDREW CURTIS

The other parent of Lc Mamie Eisenhower is Lc Britannia (Canhamiana x C warscewiczii) of 1903 which must have been quite a masterpiece. Five flower quality awards from the Royal Horticultural Society were given to the hybrid, encompassing all three color forms - purple, semi-alba, and white. Of particular relevance to Mamie's namesake is the first award as exhibited by Sir George Holford in May of 1913 for the very round purple, 'Westonbirt' FCC/RHS.

Sander's choice of the hybrid name, Britannia, is timely because this terminology was in vogue at the turn of the century. The word generally symbolizes British patriotism and is often represented by a female warrior holding a trident and shield. This symbol appeared on English coins - half penny and penny - for 150 years, and well into the mid 20th century.

The name, Britannia, was also used with a number of English boats including King George V's famed racing yacht, HMY Britannia. Even today, most Brits know, at least, the chorus to the 1700's patriotic song, "Rule, Britannia!" Lc Britannia is not known to exist today but its parent, Lc Canhamiana (L purpurata x C mossiae), is still in circulation so Britannia could be remade.

Unlike many U.S. Presidents, Dwight Eisenhower was not a career politician, but rather a five-star general and hero during World War II. The Eisenhowers had been married 37 years prior to moving into the White House and were very close. Dwight called his wife *"my invaluable, my indispensable,...my lifelong partner."*

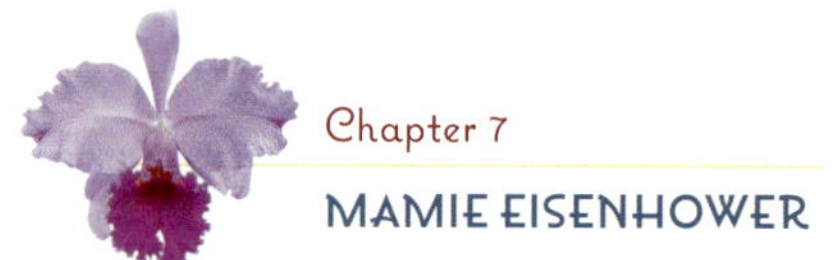

Mamie loved to entertain and was a popular hostess. Her specialty was holiday parties, for which she had the White House decorated in the appropriate theme. Just as the Trumans before them, the Eisenhowers campaigned by train across the country. Mamie's own popularity helped to bolster her husband to win two terms as president. On inauguration day in 1953, the new First Lady proudly pinned a cattleya corsage on her lapel and, in doing so, became the best spokesperson cattleyas could ask for.

What will be remembered about Mamie Eisenhower within the orchid community is her true love for cattleya flowers. She glamorized corsages like no First Lady before or since. Her namesake orchid, Lc Mamie Eisenhower, was a prominent hybrid for its time and, although rare today, remains a historical treasure. ✯

Cattleya warscewiczii used to be called C gigas because the flowers are often gigantic. It appears on both sides of the Eisenhower lineage. ARTHUR E. CHADWICK PHOTO

The presidential couple ushered in eight years of calm and stability not seen in the United States in fifty years. COURTESY OF ALAMY/ASSOCIATED PRESS

PERSONAL LIFE

Mary Geneva Doud was born in 1896 in Boone, Iowa. She grew up in Iowa, Colorado, and Texas, and finished her education at the Wolcott School for Girls. She met Dwight Eisenhower in 1915 and the two immediately hit it off. The pair was married a year later and had two children.

Mamie became known for her beautiful clothes, gracious hosting, and confidence. Her fondness for a particular shade of light pink popularized the color among households and dresses. She excelled in fulfilling the traditional role of a First Lady: prioritizing the home, her family, and entertaining. ✯

LC MAMIE EISENHOWER

(1953 Rod McLellan)

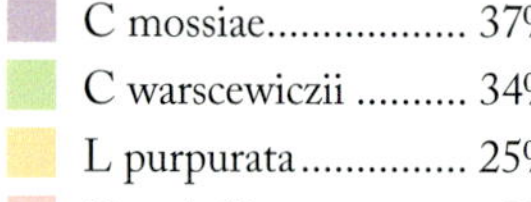

- C mossiae.................. 37%
- C warscewiczii 34%
- L purpurata............... 25%
- C gaskelliana.............. 3%

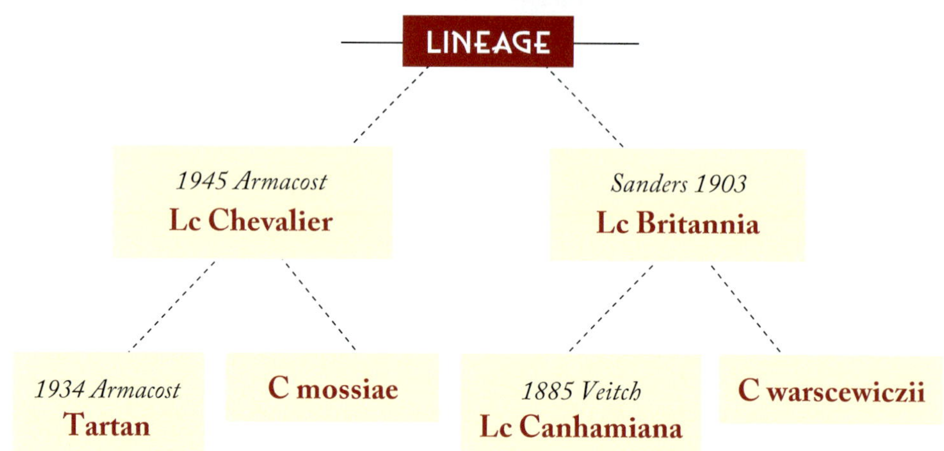

Mamie Eisenhower was the greatest advertisement for cattleya corsages that anyone could hope for. Her enthusiasm spoke volumes about her love of orchids.

COURTESY OF ASSOCIATED PRESS

It was a pleasure to meet Mamie Eisenhower's granddaughter, Mary Jean, at The Harry S. Truman Little White House in Key West, Florida. She explained the significance of orchid corsages to the First Lady. "They were protocol." GRACE HOUSHOLDER PHOTO

Patterson Orchids named the second of two Kennedy hybrids in 1961 with C Jacqueline Kennedy (Enid x Ardmore).

ARTHUR E. CHADWICK PHOTO

JACQUELINE KENNEDY

★ ★ ★ ★ ★ ★ ★

John F. Kennedy was only 43 years old when he became President of the United States in 1960, and he introduced a feeling of youth and excitement into the White House. His two young children were always underfoot and his young wife, Jacqueline, aged 31, was a fashion statement not only in the United States, but overseas as well. Kennedy's administration became known as Camelot – the mythical realm of King Arthur's famous "Round Table" and both Republicans and Democrats embraced his policies. He gave America a new aura of greatness when he announced that he would send astronauts to the moon.

Everything Jacqueline Kennedy touched seemed to acquire a feeling of glamour, whether it was her long pearl necklaces, stylish pillbox hats, or elegant dresses. Simplicity ruled her wardrobe and orchid corsages were unnecessary to enhance the effect. The youthful Mrs. Kennedy wasn't about to *wear* cattleyas as this reminded her of her elders. She was, however, willing to *carry* cattleyas.

On her wedding day in 1953 in Newport, Rhode Island, Jacqueline Lee Bouvier carried a fabulous bouquet of mostly pink and white cattleyas. Many in the bridal party wore cattleya corsages includes the groom's sister, Eunice Kennedy Shriver. More than 800 guests attended.

After she became First Lady, Mrs. Kennedy continued to carry cattleyas…as pocketbook corsages when she went out. The look was simple – her favorite handbag adorned with a single frilly orchid and she could put the ensemble down at any time. It wasn't long before the public caught on to this fashion statement and started to emulate it.

The White House was always full of colorful flower arrangements, many of which had cut orchid sprays of early white phalaenopsis hybrids and standard cymbidiums. The flowers were

ABOVE PHOTO COURTESY JOHN F. KENNEDY LIBRARY

Mrs. Kennedy became First Lady at the tender age of 31 and wasn't about to wear the corsages of her elders.

PHOTO COURTESY JOHN F. KENNEDY LIBRARY

The new First Lady created a fashion statement when she started carrying cattleya corsages attached to her pocketbooks.

COURTESY OF ALAMY/INTERPHOTO

The Kennedy family attended John and Jacqueline Bouvier's wedding in 1953 including the groom's sister, Eunice, who prominently wore a cattleya corsage. COURTESY OF ALAMY/TONI FRISSELL

seasonal and grown in local greenhouses. The containers were often antique urns and bowls, long forgotten from previous administrations.

Her major floral legacy was the establishment of an office dedicated to solely flowers. The Office of the White House Florist was created in 1961 and included a Chief Floral Designer responsible for all the floral decorations of the first family, their private entertaining and official state functions. There was even consideration given to the First Lady's attire and the customs of visiting dignitaries.

Mrs. Kennedy's designer was Elmer "Rusty" Young who was instructed to create natural bouquets with an airy, informal look. Designers stay on for years or even decades. We know the current designer, Hedieh "Roshan" Ghaffarian, who was selected by Michelle Obama in 2015.

Mrs. Kennedy's immediate predecessor, Mamie Eisenhower, left a lasting impression of the importance of cattleyas to a First Lady's image. The Rod McLellan Co. had capitalized on this popularity with their highly publicized hybrid honoring Mrs. Eisenhower in 1953. So it was no surprise that, in 1960 and 1961, two of the largest nurseries on the East Coast, Rivermont Orchids and H. Patterson & Sons, each submitted applications to register a cattleya for the new First Lady, Jacqueline Kennedy.

The names of orchid hybrids are currently governed by the Royal Horticultural Society. However, at the 1960 World Orchid Conference in London, the organization had just taken on this responsibility. Prior to this and dating back to the very first hybrid in the mid 1800s,

Rivermont Orchids named the first of two Kennedy hybrids in 1960 with Lc Jacqueline Kennedy (Elissa x Derryname). It was primarily a purple cross but there were a few semi-albas including this 'Jilltara' variety.

ROBERTA WILSON-WOOD PHOTO

Firmin Lambeau built two state of the art orchid ranges in the early 1900s to hold his collection of 10,000 plants.

COURTESY OF THE ORCHID WORLD

Firmin Lambeau was a wealthy Belgian hobbyist who had an extensive orchid collection in the early 1900s.

COURTESY OF THE ORCHID WORLD

Rivermont Orchids was a massive two acre operation near Chattanooga, Tennessee. They bred the first Kennedy hybrid in 1960.

COURTESY OF AOS ARCHIVES

English commercial grower Sanders of St. Albans had the duty. (By the 1960s, new orchid registrations were numbering in the thousands and Sander's could no longer keep up with the paperwork so the RHS took over.)

According to strict orchid registration rules, the first application received for a given genera gets to use the proposed name. As luck would have it, both Rivermont and Patterson got approved due to subtle differences in orchid nomenclature. (One is a Laeliocattleya meaning a laelia is in the lineage while the other is simply a cattleya. Today, the names would be the same but back then and in this historical book, they are different.) When the two are blooming, however, there is no confusing them since one is purple and one is semi-alba. This was the first time in history that a U.S. First Lady had two namesake orchids.

The 1960 hybrid, from Rivermont Orchids in Signal Mountain, Tennessee, was a stunning purple named Laeliocattleya Jacqueline Kennedy (Elissa x Derrynane). Rivermont's cross was a display of the best purple stud plants of the day, from Lc Princess Margaret to Lc Ishtar. They were dark, round, and beautiful.

Tracing the lineage a little farther, Lc Lustre (Callistoglossa x C lueddemanniana) appears on both sides of the parentage which contributes to the well shaped floriferousness of the Kennedy hybrid.

One unsung hero in the lineage occurred in 1906 with the primary hybrid, Cattleya Dupreana (warneri x warscewiczii). It was bred by the wealthy Belgian hobbyist, Firmin Lambeau, whose name is still mentioned in orchid circles today. He is responsible for bringing the very first alba C warscewiczii into circulation with his 'Firmin Lambeau' FCC/RHS of 1912.

Monsieur Lambeau's estate was located in Villa Vogelsand, near Brussels, and boasted two greenhouse ranges with over 10,000 plants. The structures were state of the art and included a

Hobbyist Firmin Lambeau was immortalized by his introduction of the first alba C warscewiczii, 'Firmin Lambeau' FCC/RHS (1912), and he remains a household name today among growers.

ARTHUR E. CHADWICK PHOTO

propagating house for seedlings as well as a central head house for repotting. Redundant heaters with wrought iron pipes kept everything warm and his custom shading system was ahead of its time. *"The method of rolling the lath blinds up and down by means of gearing is ingenious"* wrote *The Orchid World* in 1913.

Lambeau was known to donate expensive prizes to local orchid shows. At the Royal International Exhibition of 1912, he offered an engraved gold medal, valued at 700 francs, for *"the exhibitor whose collection contains the most interesting hybrid orchids."* At the 1913 Ghent Show, he gave a *"valuable work of art for the best trade exhibit."*

Nearly all orchid types were represented in his collection but Lambeau's favorites were white cattleyas. It was not uncommon for him to exhibit ten of the same alba species at one time – as he did with C labiata 'Harefield Hall', 'Purity' and others at one show.

As much as Lambeau loved white cattleyas, he wasn't able to make an alba C Dupreana because one of the alba parents (C warscewiczii) hadn't been discovered yet. Thus, we find two awards for purple varieties of Dupreana – Charlesworth's AM/RHS in 1911 and 'The Dell' FCC/RHS in 1912 – and a purple Dupreana would become a great grandparent of Jacqueline Kennedy's namesake.

The 1960 Kennedy hybrid is surprisingly complex for its time with ten species involved going back seven generations. Such unlikely species as C schilleriana and L tenebrosa are used

Rivermont's most famous hybrid is C Bob Betts (Bow Bells x mossiae) from 1950. It remains the most awarded white of all time. Shown is 'White Lightning'. ARTHUR E. CHADWICK PHOTO

Patterson Orchids of Bergenfield, New Jersey was a multi generation business with all the children and grandchildren involved. At the time of their Kennedy hybrid, they had 100,000 square feet of growing space.

COURTESY OF AOS ARCHIVES

while the heavy hitters are the cut flower studs - C warscewiczii, C dowiana, C labiata, and C trianaei.

Rivermont's nursery was a massive two acre operation with 15 greenhouses located near Chattanooga. The owner, Clint McDade, was well known in the orchid world for creating outstanding white hybrids using the famed C. Bow Bells. His C. Bob Betts (Bow Bells x mossiae), registered in 1950, was the first Bow Bells cross to bloom in the United States and it remains the most awarded white cattleya in the history of the American Orchid Society – at last count 68 awards.

Throughout the 1950s, Rivermont ran full page back cover advertisements in the AOS magazine. These ads featured some very unusual marketing campaigns, including one in 1955 in which the company promoted irradiated orchid seed from a nearby nuclear power plant. Other ads showed a close-up of a sprouting pseudo-bulb, an x-ray image of a cattleya flower, and a glamorous model covered in cut phalaenopsis. Many aspiring commercial growers, including John Lines, went to work for McDade, only to start their own orchid businesses later.

Like Mrs. Kennedy herself, Rivermont's purple hybrid was not without a little mystery and intrigue. Bred from a long line of rich purple ancestors, the cross produced a few unlikely semi-albas, including 'Jilltara' which appeared in Beall's 1975 catalog and was later sold at Lenette Greenhouses. In addition, Lines Orchids was selling their semi-alba variety of Lc Jacqueline Kennedy as late as 1994. Today, there are few known plants of either the purple or the semi-alba in existence.

One of the great studs of all time is C warscewiczii 'Frau Melanie Beyrodt' FCC/RHS (1904) which is found in the background of many semi-alba hybrids. The variety name is often abbreviated, F. M. B. ARTHUR E. CHADWICK PHOTO

Although Rivermont's Laeliocattleya Jacqueline Kennedy was named first, it was Patterson's Cattleya Jacqueline Kennedy that took over the orchid world. Patterson's plant was a beautiful semi-alba with glistening white sepals and petals and a fantastic magenta lip. The company made thousands of them before the hybrid was even named. Harold Patterson, who did the breeding for H. Patterson & Sons, made and remade the cross a whopping 18 times between the years of 1957 and 1960.

Patterson was aiming for large quantities of near-perfect mid-May blooms for their cut flower trade. They were also selling seedlings in 2 ¼" pots for $3.00 to orchid hobbyists. Remarkably, all 18 of these identical crosses were created before any had bloomed and while John Kennedy was still Senator of Massachusetts.

In stark contrast to Rivermont's complex purple, Patterson's semi-alba is exceedingly simple. There are only two species involved and it could be remade right now if someone was so inclined. The hybrid combines C. Enid with C Ardmore (Enid x mossiae).

The secret to the success of this cross is the *variety* of the two species. While C warscewiczii and C mossiae are common in modern collections, the stud varieties are very rare today. Let's take a closer look at C warscewiczii 'F.M.B.' FCC/RHS and C mossiae reineckiana 'Young's'.

The original Cattleya Enid (warscewiczii x mossiae) was made by James Veitch in 1898 and it was purple. He described it as *"having a light rose-purple sepals and petals and a finely crisped lip of deep crimson-purple with a rich yellow throat."* Breeders soon remade Enid with semi-alba parents.

C warscewiczii 'F.M.B.' or 'Frau Melanie Beyrodt' is a fantastic semi-alba and it was given a rare First Class Certificate by the Royal Horticultural Society judges in July of 1904 when exhibited by her husband, Otto Beyrodt. (The lengthy variety name, Frau Melanie Beyrodt, is difficult to pronounce so growers abbreviate it to just the initials, F.M.B.). The valuable pollen was traded to other breeders and nearly all fine Enid's produced during this period had F.M.B. as a parent.

C mossiae reineckiana 'Young's' was originally an imported jungle plant from Venezuela in the late 1920s. It proved to be an excellent stud plant and was kept under lock and key for many years by Thomas Young Orchids of Bound Brook, New Jersey. One division escaped and, through a comedy of errors, eventually ended up in the Patterson collection.

The term, reineckiana, harkens back to 1856 when Reichenbach described a form of C mossiae as *"having pure white sepals and petals and an Amethyst-purple labellum."* He named it Reineckiana in honor of Reinecke, who was the *"gardener to Herr Decker, in whose collection the plant first flowered."* To this day, the "old growers" use the term, reineckiana, to mean semi-alba.

C mossiae reineckiana 'Young's' did not become available to breeders until the late 1940s and Patterson promptly went to work making hybrids with the new stud plant. It wasn't long before his Enids garnered awards from the American Orchid Society including a rare First Class Certificate.

Harold Patterson kept detailed breeding notes and employed a cytologist to count the number of chromosomes of his stud plants. He declared that *"The future in Cattleya breeding will be decided through the thorough knowledge and application of Polyploidy....with regard to growth habits: namely season, strength of growth, color, stem length, texture, and size of flower."* Some of Patterson's Enids and Ardmores were, in fact, tetraploids (double the normal chromosomes), which gave them superior flower quality and vigor. When making Mrs. Kennedy's namesake flower 18

The very first semi-alba C mossiae discovered by westerners was in 1856 and was given the name, 'Reineckiana'. It honors Reinecke, who was the gardener to Herr Decker, in whose collection the plant first flowered.

COURTESY OF THE ORCHID ALBUM

times, he tried many combinations of each parent in his pursuit of perfection.

Stewart's legendary breeder Ernest Hetherington described Patterson's Kennedy hybrid as *"truly outstanding, and of excellent vigor, with flowers often up to 8-9 inches across."* We also found the hybrid to have superb "carriage", meaning that the buds fully clear the sheath and open unencumbered. Without a doubt, C Jacqueline Kennedy is suitable for both cut flowers or as a display plant.

The Patterson nursery, nicknamed "Orchidhaven", was a multi-generation business with all the children and grandchildren involved. The first greenhouse was built in the early 1930s and by their peak in the 1960s, there was 100,000 square feet of growing space. Harold Patterson is credited with making such classic hybrids as Lc De Loris Ziegfeld, C Barbara Billingsley, and C Catherine Patterson. Their Cattleya Jacqueline Kennedy became widely circulated and can still be found in collections today.

What will be remembered most about Jacqueline Kennedy and her two namesake cattleyas is that she entered the White House at the tender age of 31 sporting a fashion style that was much different than her predecessors. Orchids were not to be worn but rather carried and enjoyed in flower arrangements. ✯

The primary hybrid, C Enid (warscewiczii x mossiae), was first made as a purple by James Veitch in 1898. It was remade as a semi-alba and both colors rose to fame as studs.

ARTHUR E. CHADWICK PHOTO

C mossiae reineckiana 'Young's' was originally a jungle plant from the 1920's that became a prominent stud at Thomas Young Orchids before making its way to Patterson's breeding program. The "old growers" use the term, reineckiana, to mean semi-alba.

ARTHUR E. CHADWICK PHOTO

PERSONAL LIFE

Jacqueline Lee Bouvier was born in 1929 in Southampton, New York. She spent her childhood in Manhattan practicing ballet, learning various languages, and horseback riding. She met U.S. House Representative John F. Kennedy in 1952 and the pair was wed the following year. They had four children.

Mrs. Kennedy was First Lady of the United States from 1961 to 1963. She was involved in various preservation projects of American History and the Arts but her main focus was restoration of the White House. She sought to upgrade the Executive Mansion with authentic, historical, and distinguished furnishings. Jackie also hosted numerous social events.

She led the country through a period of mourning after her husband's assassination in November 1963 and, for the remainder of her life, she was dedicated to preserving his memory through the John F. Kennedy Presidential Library. ✯

Jacqueline Kennedy carried a bouquet of mostly pink and white cattleyas on her wedding day in 1953. COURTESY OF ALAMY/TONI FRISSELL/JOHN F. KENNEDY PRESIDENTIAL LIBRARY

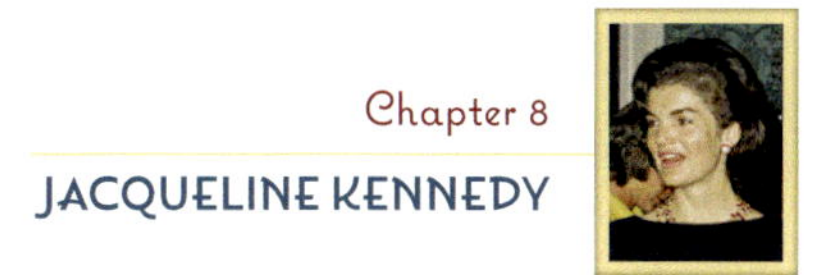

LC JACQUELINE KENNEDY (1960)

(Rivermont)

COMPOSITION

Species	%
C warscewiczii	26%
C dowiana	18%
C labiata	16%
C trianaei	12%
C warneri	7%
C lueddemanniana	6%
C schilleriana	6%
C mossiae	5%
L purpurata	3%
L tenebrosa	1%

LINEAGE

1943 Broughton
Lc Derryname

1934 Alexander
Lc Elissa

1934 Alexander
Lc Balkis

1930 McBeans
Lc Princess Margaret

1925 Holford
Lc Istar

1919 McBeans
C Dinah

C JACQUELINE KENNEDY (1961)

(Patterson)

COMPOSITION

- C mossiae................62.5%
- C warscewiczii 37.5%

LINEAGE

- *1898 Veitch* **C Enid**
  - **C mossiae**
  - **C warscewiczii**
- *1938 Adams* **C Ardmore**
  - *1898 Veitch* **Enid**
  - **C mossiae**

A well grown C Jacqueline Kennedy can produce four or five blooms on a stem and can be used for cut flowers or as a specimen plant. ARTHUR E. CHADWICK PHOTO

Two of Cattleya Lady Bird Johnson seedlings shows the variations in the flowers.

ARTHUR E. CHADWICK PHOTO

LADY BIRD JOHNSON

★ ★ ★ ★ ★ ★ ★

"Where flowers bloom, so does hope."

On the centennial anniversary of Lady Bird Johnson's birth, a special namesake orchid was presented to her oldest daughter, Lynda Bird Johnson Robb. The timing was perfect – Mother's Day – a fitting tribute to one of the most horticulture-minded of our First Ladies.

Lady Bird Johnson became First Lady just two hours after the death of John F. Kennedy on November 22, 1963 when her husband, Lyndon B. Johnson, became the 36th President of the United States. She was no stranger to politics, as her husband was elected to Congress just three years into their marriage nearly three decades earlier.

While First Lady, Johnson actively campaigned for the Highway Beautification Act of 1965 that called for control of outdoor advertising and encouraged scenic improvement along the nation's roadways. She was a lifelong advocate of flowers and at age 70, she co-founded the National Wildflower Research Center (later renamed the Lady Bird Johnson Wildflower Center, www.wildflower.org) – a nonprofit organization devoted to preserving and reintroducing native plants. Johnson was fond of saying *"Where flowers bloom, so does hope."* Today, every state grows wildflowers along its highways and there is no doubt that this effort has preserved more than a few of our native orchids.

America's landscapes are beautiful. The roadsides in the spring are awash with blossoms of

ABOVE PHOTO COURTESY OF ALAMY/EVERETT COLLECTION

Corsage pinning often took a team of experts and spare flowers just in case there were issues. Note the white gloves and pearls. COURTESY OF ALAMY/L.B.J. PRESIDENTIAL LIBRARY

Lady Bird Johnson sports a double corsage on her lapel while chatting with Muriel Humphries, the Vice President's wife. COURTESY OF ALAMY/EVERETT COLLECTION

Cattleya Lady Bird Johnson (David Hill x mossiae) produced many fine varieties including this 'Select'.

ARTHUR E. CHADWICK PHOTO

all shapes, sizes, and colors. Drivers can often tell what part of the country they are in simply by looking at the flowers along the highway. Lady Bird Johnson grew up in Texas where seemingly endless stretches of barren interstates now greet travelers with fields of bluebonnets and more.

Cattleyas are wildflowers in Central and South America, where they grow on trees. In many cases, they are the National Flowers of their respective countries. The pedigree lineage of this First Lady orchid relies heavily on Cattleya mossiae, the National Flower of Venezuela, which blooms in the spring.

One of the great stud plants for much of the 20th century is C mossiae reineckiana 'Young's' which was originally a jungle plant from Venezuela.

ARTHUR E. CHADWICK PHOTO

In order to fully appreciate Cattleya Lady Bird Johnson, one has to trace the history back to the early days of breeding. The background of this hybrid includes one of the great cattleya species of all time, a semi-alba variety called C mossiae reineckiana 'Young's.' (The term, reineckiana, harks back to 1871 with the very first FCC/RHS award of a semi-alba mossiae. The grower gave it the variety name, 'reineckiana', and over time, the word came to refer, unofficially, to all semi-alba mossiaes. This is a great example of "cattleya slang.") C mossiae reineckiana 'Young's' was originally a jungle plant sent by a friend in Venezuela during the 1920s to cut flower mogul, Thomas Young, of Thomas Young Orchids, in Bound Brook, New Jersey.

Mr. Young was very protective of his C mossiae and gave away only one division - and that was to his good friend Fitz Eugene Dixon, who was the second President of the American Orchid Society. Dixon later sold his collection to his neighbor Wharton Sinkler, who was the third President of the American Orchid Society. The plant was so valuable that Sinkler's personal orchid grower would trade just the tiny flower pollen in exchange for the latest cattleya hybrids.

Ultimately, Sinkler was forced to sell his entire collection and Thomas Young's arch rival, H. Patterson & Sons of Bergenfield, New Jersey, acquired it. The two cut flower nurseries were only 45 miles apart and each wanted to have the best stud plants. This would be the fourth time that the prized C mossiae had changed hands since being imported into the United States.

Patterson was intent on using C mossiae reineckiana 'Young's' extensively in its breeding program. The firm started out by remaking the 1898 primary hybrid, C Enid, (mossiae x warscewiczii) using superior varieties of both species. Their combination with C warscewiczii 'F.M.B.' FCC/RHS (1904) was remade over a dozen times and resulted in improved semi-alba offspring for years to come.

One of the parents of this First Lady hybrid is C David Hill (Catherine Patterson x Trimos) which was made by Joe Grezaffi in 1983. ARTHUR E. CHADWICK PHOTO

C Hardyana alba (dowiana x warscewiczii), which was first made by Norman Cookson in 1896, imparts much of its lip color to C Lady Bird Johnson. ARTHUR E. CHADWICK PHOTO

One such offspring was in 1952 with C Catherine Patterson (Enid x Mrs. Frederick Knollys). The flowers had a clear, crisp white color to the sepals and petals and a rich marbled purple throat. The blossoms were enormous and opened in early May, which was ideal for the Mother's Day corsage trade.

Enthusiasts occasionally hear mention of the other Catherine Patterson parent, C Mrs. Frederick Knollys (Hardyana x mossiae), but this early hybrid hasn't been seen in decades. It was made by wealthy English hobbyist, Frances Wellesley, in 1906, at his "Westfield" estate in Woking, Surrey. A writer for the Royal Horticultural Society visited the estate and wrote nothing but glowing comments for the June 1905 *Orchid Review* - *"Orchids are now so numerous and varied...his four houses are filled with a choice selection in thriving condition".*

Wellesley also kept plants of the Knollys parent, C Hardyana, which was then only known as a natural hybrid from Colombia between dowiana and warscewiczii. *"Two very diverse plants of C Hardyana were pointed out, one much like C dowiana in appearance and imported with it while the other was imported with C warscewiczii which it much resembles."* It must have been fascinating back then to bring in species from abroad and occasionally find a natural hybrid mixed in.

This side view of the primary hybrid, C Enid alba (mossiae x warscewiczii) from 1898, shows how large flowers can be on a modest plant. Note the endearing curly sepals. ARTHUR E. CHADWICK PHOTO

Like all good estate owners, Wellesley hired fine watercolor painters of the day to capture his best flowers. Cattleyas are only in bloom for a month or so and an artist's depiction of a fine variety could be used as bragging rights during the other eleven months. We find portraits of C labiata 'Mrs. Frances Wellesley' AM/RHS (1904) as well as several awarded primary hybrids featured in the article.

Aside from having a sizable collection, Wellesley was also an amateur orchid breeder but most of his potential offspring never made it to fruition. The RHS writer cited one example while visiting that day, *"120 attempts to intercross them have been made and the net result, at present, is one small seedling."* Back then, the seed germination technology was in its infancy and mortality was, unfortunately, the norm.

The idea that an orchid hybrid could be called "Mrs. So and So" clearly defines this time period in England. Married women were often seen as extensions of their husbands and there are several hundred RHS orchid registrations using the format of Mrs. before a surname or full name. It was, essentially, the who's who of the British orchid world at the turn of the century.

Wellesley himself registered over 50 cattleya hybrids over his relatively short career of orchid breeding from 1903 to 1913. Many of these began with the title "Mrs." including one for his own wife, Bc Mrs. Frances Wellesley (digbyana x lueddemanniana) from 1906. He is largely

One of the grandparents of this First Lady hybrid is the cut flower semi-alba, C Catherine Patterson (Enid x Mrs. Frederick Knollys), which was made by Patterson Orchids in 1952.

ARTHUR E. CHADWICK PHOTO

Commercial grower Joe Grezaffi exchanged heartfelt correspondence with fellow cattleya aficionados including A. A. Chadwick and wrote in fabulous cursive letters.

ARTHUR E. CHADWICK PHOTO

Joe Grezaffi was an orchid hobbyist turned commercial grower. He registered over 450 crosses during his nearly 50 year career.

DAVID OFF PHOTO

forgotten today with the notable exception of his association with the Knollys namesake.

As we approach the direct parents of C Lady Bird Johnson, we encounter C David Hill (Catherine Patterson x Trimos) from 1983. It was bred by hobbyist turned professional Joe Grezaffi of Melbourne, Florida. Anyone who had the pleasure of knowing Mr. Grezaffi was probably rewarded with their own namesake orchid.

For nearly five decades, starting in 1971, Grezaffi registered an astonishing number of new orchid hybrids as well as remade an untold number of existing crosses. Many of the largest nurseries in the country never came close to this level of productivity. Most surprising was his choice of hybrid names which reflected his humble beginnings as a hobbyist.

Of his 450 Royal Horticultural Society registrations, over 80 were named after family members – living and not. There is Frank, Jill, Mary, Joe II, Florence, Paula, Joey, Sara, Shawn, Sam, Polly, Tom, Carrie, Roger, Lena, Cayla, Davis, Peggy, Amanda, Buddy, Aimee, Tammy, Karen, Jacob, Jet, Mark, Benny, Johnny, Luke, Sadie, Mandela, Bobbie, Roberta, Tina, Michelle, and Elizabeth. The remaining hybrids were mostly named after friends and acquaintances, including an area dentist, David Hill. It was this plant that would sire Lady Bird Johnson's namesake.

While many cattleya breeders focus on species, standards or the latest trends, Grezaffi seemed to combine anything that struck his fancy at the moment. We find standards, minis, novelties, unifoliates, bifoliates, whites, purples, semi-albas and art shades in his history. He also made time for breeding other genera such as dendrobiums, vandas, and even phalaenopsis.

His focus was not on winning American Orchid Society awards though he did garnish three dozen over the years. His best success was with C Allen Condo (Summerland Girl x Mrs. Mahler) which earned two very rare First Class Certificates. In most cases, Joe knew more than the judges.

Like many commercial growers, Grezaffi started out strictly as an amateur. He was a popular social studies teacher at Palm Bay High School for many years before retiring at the age of 53. His home was on a two acre parcel and he leased an additional four acres which gave him room for seven greenhouses. He sold everything from flasks and seedlings to blooming size and specimens.

Grezaffi was a true "cattleya man" and could talk for hours on the genus. He and my father would regularly discuss the old hybrids and trade back bulbs of this or that. He had fabulous handwriting and, in written correspondence, would sign his name in flowing cursive letters.

In later years, conversation with Joe would invariably digress to "the neighbors" who apparently called the police regularly on his business. The greenhouses were located in a residential area of Melbourne and customers would regularly park along the street and for hours at a time. Through it all, he remained a bright star in the orchid world and sadly passed in 2020 at age 86.

Over the past decade or so, we have thoroughly enjoyed blooming the Lady Bird Johnson seedlings which are all lovely semi-albas with distinctive two tone magenta/orangey-yellow lips. The foliage stays fairly modest which makes for nice pot plants. With one notable exception, we have kept all the namesakes.

On Mother's Day of 2012, we had the opportunity to present Mrs. Johnson's daughter,

Lynda Bird Johnson Robb accepts her mother's namesake orchid from Art Chadwick on Mother's Day, 2012 at her home in McLean, Virginia.

COURTESY OF LYNDA ROBB

C warscewiczii 'Bedford' AM/AOS is a fine semi-alba that was recently awarded after being exhibited by Linden Burzell.

PHOTO BY ARTHUR E. CHADWICK

Lynda Bird Johnson Robb, with her mother's orchids. The Robbs live in northern Virginia and are a short drive from our nursery in Powhatan. We had previously donated a blooming LBJ plant to the United States Botanical Garden (USBG) in Washington, D.C. and had to borrow this plant back for the presentation as none of ours were in bloom at that moment. Ah, the drama of orchid presentations.

The USBG gladly accommodated our request and Lynda was truly excited to see the flowers. The plant was nestled in a gold decorative pot and had two enormous blooms in perfect condition. Lynda lamented that there wasn't an entire camera crew to witness the event.

As the daughter of a President, she was used to the bright lights but became a worldwide sensation in 1967 when she got married at the White House as millions watched at home on TV. By contrast, our down to earth orchid presentation was photographed by her personal assistant in several rooms. The best shot was taken in front of a framed portrait of the First Lady and we aptly gave the special orchid the variety name, 'Mother's Day'.

The Lady Bird Johnson cattleyas bloom each spring and are a constant reminder of the wonderful work that Mrs. Johnson did in beautifying the highways on which we drive every day. ✯

PERSONAL LIFE

Claudia Alta "Lady Bird" Taylor was born in 1912 in Karnack, Texas. As a young child, her nursemaid would commonly say she was "as pretty as a ladybird" and the name stuck throughout her life. She spent a great deal of her youth outside in nature and was known to be shy and quiet. Lady Bird was introduced to Lyndon Johnson, then a Congressional aide, and reportedly described the experience as "a moth drawn to a flame". The pair was wed in November 1934 and bore two daughters.

Lady Bird and Lyndon Johnson had two teenage girls when they moved into The White House.
NORMAN DIETEL PHOTO VIA UNIVERSITY OF NORTH TEXAS LIBRARY

Lady Bird Johnson was First Lady of the United States from 1963-1969. During her time at the White House, she worked to reinvent the role of First Lady. She was the first woman in the position to have a press secretary and staff, communicate directly with Congress, write a novel and campaign alone for her husband.

Mrs. Johnson received many awards and honors, including the Presidential Medal of Freedom in 1977 and the Congressional Gold Medal in 1988. Lady Bird's continued popularity ensures she will forever hold a place in America's heart. ✯

This late 1800's painting by John Nugget Fitch of C mossiae 'Mondii' from The Orchid Album is an example of the fine varieties available to breeders at the time. COURTESY OF THE ORCHID ALBUM

C LADY BIRD JOHNSON

(2011 Chadwick/Orchid Trail)

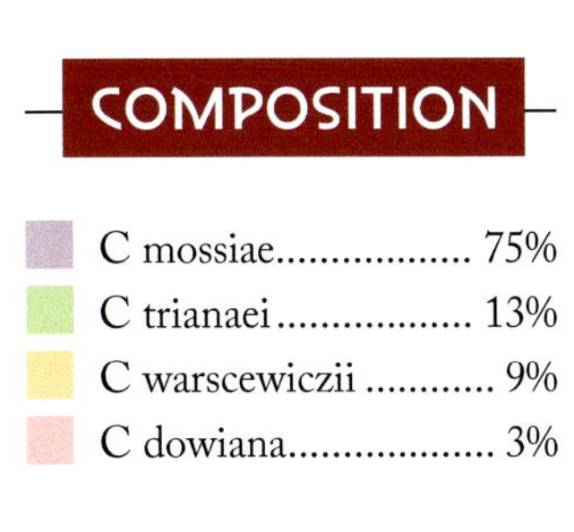

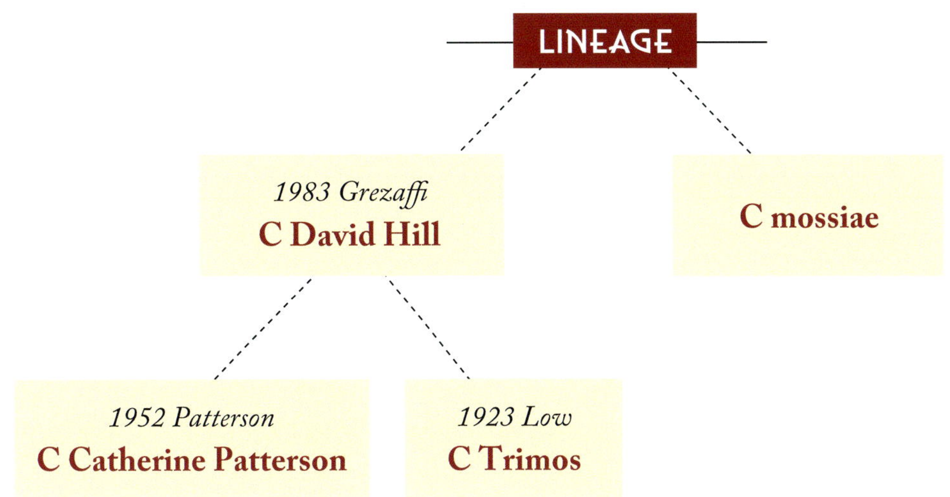

There are no known pictures of Pat Nixon's first namesake, the 1960 alba C Pat Nixon (Barbara Dane x Bebe White). Shown is the parent, C Bebe White. ARTHUR E. CHADWICK PHOTO

There are also no known pictures of Pat Nixon's second namesake, the 1969 semi-alba Lc Patricia Nixon, so we have remade it. Shown is the parent, Lc Lucie Hausermann.

ARTHUR E. CHADWICK PHOTO

PAT NIXON

★ ★ ★ ★ ★ ★ ★

Richard Nixon's victory in the 1968 Presidential election was the culmination of a political career that had seen the Californian rise through the ranks of the House of Representatives, Senate, and Vice Presidency. His wife, Pat, was always at his side, attending his speeches, handing out flyers, and working the crowds through each of his eight campaigns. She and Dick were characterized as a team – at a time when most political wives stayed in the background.

Nixon's wife, the former Pat Ryan, was nicknamed 'Pat' by her father when she was born on the eve of St. Patrick's Day. She met her husband while acting in an amateur theatre group. He informed her that night that they would one day be married. Three years later, they were married and she proudly wore an orchid at the ceremony.

As the wife of the President, Pat Nixon traveled to 78 countries – more than any First Lady at the time. She accompanied her husband to China in 1972 and, while the President was in meetings, Pat mingled with everyday citizens. For this, she won the hearts of people worldwide.

Her personal cause as First Lady was volunteerism. She said, "Our success as a nation depends on our willingness to give generously of ourselves for the welfare and enrichment of the lives of others."

First Lady Pat Nixon's love of gardening began in her childhood and continued as First Lady. In 1971, she opened the magnificent gardens of the White House to the public – a bi-annual tour that continued for decades. The Richard Nixon Presidential Library in Yorba Linda, California has extensive gardens with themes that were designed by Mrs. Nixon. Included is the feature "First Lady's Garden", which contains sizable plantings of the Pat Nixon Rose, as well as

ORCHIDS
of DISTINCTION

EDWARD A. MANDA
INCORPORATED
130 MAIN STREET
WEST ORANGE, N. J.

Orchids a Specialty
LARGEST COLLECTION OF
VARIETIES

Pat Nixon's first namesake was bred in 1960 by Manda Orchids of West Orange, New Jersey. They had previously named First Lady Lou Hoover's cattleya in 1929.

COURTESY OF THE AMERICAN ORCHID SOCIETY

One of the important intermediary hybrids of C Pat Nixon, C Irene (mossiae x Suzanne Hye), was bred in England by J. Gurney Fowler in 1914. Aside from having an outstanding orchid collection, he was Chairman of the RHS Orchid Committee.

COURTESY OF THE ORCHID WORLD

the roses of Lady Bird Johnson, Betty Ford, Rosalynn Carter, Nancy Reagan, and Barbara Bush.

Like her predecessor Jacqueline Kennedy, Mrs. Nixon also had two namesake cattleyas. The first one, C Pat Nixon (Barbara Dane x Bebe White) was named while her husband was running for President against John Kennedy in the very close 1960 election. Joseph A. Manda & Son of West Orange, New Jersey, who had previously named a cattleya after First Lady Lou Hoover in 1929, chose a classic white hybrid for the candidate's wife.

While there are no known surviving plants today, the flowers of C Pat Nixon must have been outstanding. Its ancestry glistens with well shaped albas dating back to the 1902 primary hybrid, C Cappei which was made from the two round-flowered and long-lasting Colombian species, C trianaei and C schroederae. There is one RHS award for C Cappei – an Award of Merit in 1918 when exhibited by Armstrong & Brown.

Noteworthy breeders combined two more species to C Cappei and the result was Pat Nixon's direct parent, C Barbara Dane which was awarded a First Class Certificate by the American Orchid Society when exhibited at the 1948 National Capital Orchid Society show. At the

C Pat Nixon has an ancestry of well shaped albas including C trianaei. Shown is 'Broomhill' which originated in England in the collection of Sir Mervyn E. M. Buller of Broomhill, Spratton, Northampton.

ARTHUR E. CHADWICK PHOTO

Another important alba species in C Pat Nixon is C gaskelliana. Shown is a painting of an early un-named variety from The Orchid Album circa late 1800's. COURTESY OF THE ORCHID ALBUM

The orchid collection of J. Gurney Fowler contained many awarded varieties including C labiata 'Mrs. E. Ashworth' FCC/RHS from 1896. A division of this plant currently resides in the Chadwick collection.

ARTHUR E. CHADWICK PHOTO

time, orchid judges were quite jaded by round whites having been exposed to hundreds of near perfect C Bow Bells. It was reported that C Barbara Dane 'Perfection' was a tetraploid (double the normal number of chromosomes) which gave it an extra advantage.

The other direct parent of Cattleya Pat Nixon is C Bebe White (Joan Manda x White Empress) from 1938, which was bred by the legendary cut flower grower Thomas Young Orchids of Bound Brook, New Jersey. The cross was so floriferous that an entire exhibit of C Bebe White was shown at the 1947 New York International Flower Show. C Bebe White was also a widely used stud plant during the 1940s.

C Bebe White would not be possible without its grandparent, C Irene (mossiae x Suzanne Hye) from 1914 as bred by J. Gurney Fowler. His estate in South Woodford, Essex was called Glebelands and was an *"old fashioned garden full of noble trees, flowering shrubs, and hot house plants."* He was strictly a hobbyist but had an entire range of rather elaborate greenhouses.

A typical greenhouse was 70 feet long by 20 feet wide with canvas blinds above the glass for shading and a water drip system along the ridge to keep it cool in the summer. The potting material was generally osmunda fiber top dressed with a mixture of peat and sphagnum moss which worked well for he garnered many awards. The *Orchid World* journal of 1912 wrote *"the orchid houses are well filled with choice exotic specimens selected by one who has been an admirer of all things rare and beautiful in horticulture."*

While his main interest was odontoglossums, Mr. Fowler's collection of pedigree cattleya species was awe inspiring and included large plants of C labiata 'Mrs. E Ashworth' FCC/RHS (1896), C labiata 'Princess of Wales' FCC/RHS (1899) and C schroederae 'Fowler's' AM/RHS (1904). Mr. Fowler was also Treasurer of the Royal Horticultural Society and Chairman of the RHS Orchid Committee.

Most English estate owners delegated their hands-on orchid duties to the head gardener and staff but Mr. Fowler was actively involved in the collection. Between 1895 and 1915, he registered nearly 60 new orchid hybrids from a wide range of genera. His cattleya crosses were mostly second and third generation hybrids but there were some lesser known primaries such as C Alfred Fowler (granulosa x trianaei) and C Phyllis (lueddemanniana x schroederae).

His most important hybrid, however, was C Irene which was simply 75% mossiae and 25% gaskelliana. The unlikely result was a perfectly round white flower that was recognized twice by the RHS judges with rare First Class Certificates.

Sadly, Cattleya Pat Nixon faded into obscurity after Richard Nixon lost the 1960 election.

Hausermann Orchids in Villa Park, Illinois was a massive operation. Shown is one of their greenhouses that was used for cut flowers. COURTESY OF HAUSERMANN ORCHIDS

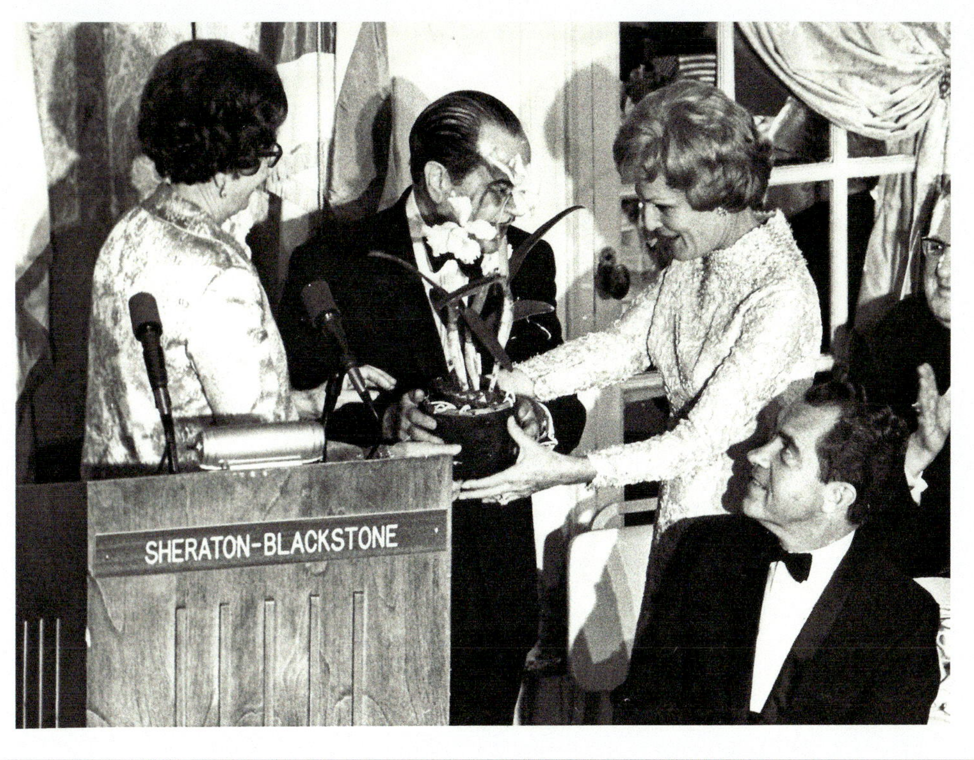

In 1969, First Lady Pat Nixon was presented with her second namesake cattleya, a semi-alba, in Chicago by businessman Clement Stone. The hybrid had been bred locally by Hausermann Orchids.

COURTESY OF HAUSERMANN ORCHIDS

Two years later, he ran for Governor in his home state of California and lost that election too and it was generally thought that his political career was over. However, he mounted a comeback and ran for President again in 1968.

This time he won and Pat Nixon became the new First Lady of the United States. Within a year, she had a second orchid named for her – a semi-alba from a different breeder – and she was actually presented with a blooming plant.

Wealthy Chicago businessman and philanthropist W. Clement Stone had donated millions of dollars to Nixon's campaign and the new President and his wife were visiting the Chicago area in 1968. Mr. Stone, who was an orchid fancier, contacted the local commercial grower, Hausermann Orchids, to see if they had a cattleya that could be named and presented to Mrs. Nixon on short notice. Hausermann found a lovely semi-alba hybrid (Lucie Hausermann x Stephen Oliver Fouraker) in bloom that had not yet been named from their cut flower greenhouses and arranged to have the plant transported to the Sheraton Hotel for a reception with the Nixons. It was here that Mr. Stone personally presented the new Nixon namesake orchid to the First Lady in front of her husband and a packed room.

Hausermann Orchids was founded in the Chicago suburb of Villa Park, Illinois in 1920 by Carl Hausermann, who grew sweet peas, roses, and gardenias for cut flower production. His son,

There are no known plants of the semi-alba, Lc Patricia Nixon (Lucie Hausermann x Stephen Oliver Fouraker), in existence today. Shown is the parent, Lc Lucie Hausermann (Alesia x Pegi Mayne) as bred by Patterson Orchids in 1965. ARTHUR E. CHADWICK PHOTO

The other parent of Mrs. Nixon's second namesake is the famed stud, Lc Stephen Oliver Fouraker (Pegi Mayne x Enid), as bred by Lines Orchids in 1961.

ARTHUR E. CHADWICK PHOTO

Four of the earliest semi-alba primary hybrids appear in Lc Patricia Nixon including C Fabia (labiata x dowiana) as bred by Veitch in 1894.

ARTHUR E. CHADWICK PHOTO

Edwin, began converting the operation over to cattleyas in the mid-1930s. By the time First Lady Pat Nixon visited Chicago, the company was producing over 400,000 cattleya blooms annually.

Hausermann's was a textbook family business with relatives working nearly all the jobs. In 1969, Edwin Sr. was President, and his brother-in-law, Ernest Finney was Vice President. Edwin's son, Gene, was in pot plant sales and his other son James was head grower. The cut flower department was headed by Roy Hausermann (Edwin's cousin). Paula Hausermann (Edwin's wife) worked in the lab. Lea Hausermann (One of Edwin's four daughters) did the office work.

By 1969, the lineage of cattleya hybrids was starting to get complex and it was common to have six or more generations of breeding within a single cross. Such is the case of Mrs. Nixon's semi-alba which is comprised of six different species and a dozen intermediary hybrids. Aside from the complexity and color differences of the two Nixon hybrids, there was the issue of botanical names.

The Royal Horticultural Society allows multiple hybrids for the same person as long as the names are different enough that they can't be confused. Mrs. Nixon's first namesake is called Pat Nixon while her second namesake is Patricia Nixon. The names are similar but different – Pat vs. Patricia.

The semi-alba, Lc Patricia Nixon (Steven Oliver Fouraker x Lucie Hausermann), was registered in 1969 by Hausermann Orchids. One of the parents, Lc Lucie Hausermann, was named for the company founder's wife by Patterson Orchids of Bergenfield, New Jersey and was a successful cut flower well into the 1980s. The other parent, Lc Steven Oliver Fouraker, was bred by Lines Orchids of Signal Mountain, Tennessee in 1961 and became a well known stud plant of semi-alba hybrids with many notable offspring to its credit.

Four of the earliest semi-alba primaries appear in Lc Patricia Nixon including Lc Bella (L purpurata x C labiata) 1884, C Maggie Raphael (trianaei x dowiana) 1889, C Fabia (labiata x dowiana) 1894, and C Enid (mossiae x warscewiczii) 1898. With this kind of complexity, the seedlings could potentially produce flowers in any season. Hausermann bloomed the cross out and kept the most prolific varieties for cut flowers.

After the presentation, the newly famous Nixon plants returned to an unceremonious life in the production greenhouses and, over time, were slowly phased out as the latest hybrids came along. At least one plant escaped and, as late as the 1980s, Tom Fennell of the Orchid Jungle in Homestead Florida was using it as a stud. Given the historical significance of this First Lady hybrid, we are in the process of re-making the cross.

What will be remembered about Mrs. Nixon's two namesake orchids is that the timing of the two hybrids coincided directly with her husband's two runs at the White House. The 1960 alba hybrid faded into obscurity soon after Mr. Nixon lost the election. The 1969 semi-alba hybrid was actually presented to the First Lady and its Chicago grower, Hausermann, still remains in business today. Mrs. Nixon's elation upon receiving her namesake orchid speaks volumes of her love for flowers. ✯

PERSONAL LIFE

Thelma Catherine Ryan was born in 1912 in Ely, Nevada. Her nickname "Pat" came from her father, citing her Irish heritage and birth date of March 16, the day before St. Patrick's Day. Her mother passed away from cancer when she was just 12 years old, and young Pat took over many duties around the house. She worked odd jobs before her marriage to Richard Nixon and is quoted as saying *"I never had time to think about… who I wanted to be, who I admired, or to have ideas… I had to work."*

She graduated with a Bachelor's degree in merchandising and accepted a teaching position in Whittier, California, where she met her future husband. They wed in 1940 and had two daughters, Julie and Tricia.

Prior to being First Lady of the United States, she was Second Lady from 1953 to 1961. She championed many charitable causes during her time in Washington, including volunteerism in local communities. Having grown up in poverty, her story resonated with the nation's citizens and invoked hope surrounding the American Dream. ✭

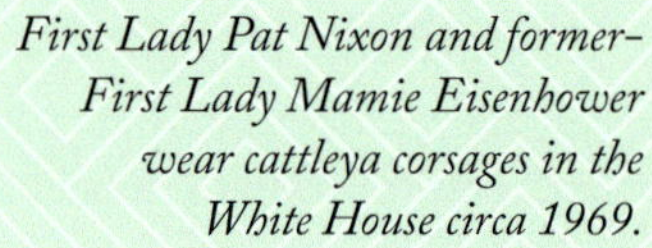

First Lady Pat Nixon and former-First Lady Mamie Eisenhower wear cattleya corsages in the White House circa 1969.

COURTESY OF THE NIXON PRESIDENTIAL LIBRARY

Pat Nixon was fond of wearing cattleya corsages. Here, she and her husband at a campaign stop in 1952.

COURTESY OF ALAMY/RBM VINTAGE IMAGES

C PAT NIXON

(1960 Manda)

COMPOSITION

- C labiata.................... 25%
- C trianaei.................. 25%
- C mossiae.................. 20%
- C lueddemanniana 13%
- C gaskelliana............ 11%
- C schroederae............. 6%

LINEAGE

1932 Dane
C Barbara Dane

1938 Thomas Young
C Bebe White

C labiata

1922 Moore
C Phoebe Snow

1937 Manda
C Joan Manda

1924 Armacost
C White Empress

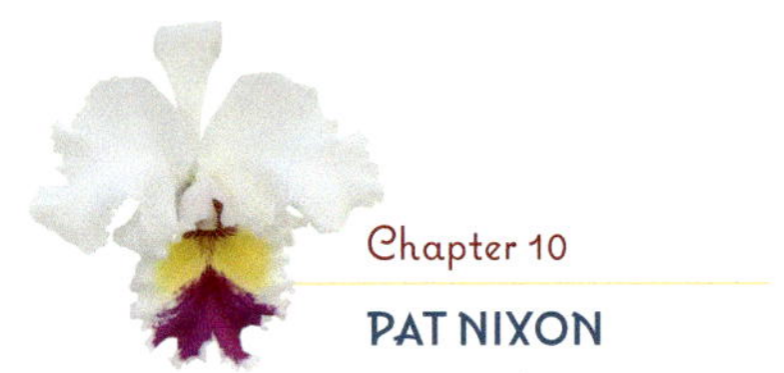

LC PATRICIA NIXON

(1969 Hausermann)

COMPOSITION

Species	%
C warscewiczii	31%
C mossiae	25%
C trianaei	16%
C labiata	12%
C dowiana	12%
L purpurata	3%

LINEAGE

1961 Lines
Lc Stephen Oliver Fouraker

1965 Hausermann
Lc Lucie Hausermann

1956 Patterson
Lc Pegi Mayne

1898 Veitch
C Enid

1932 Charlesworth
C Alesia

1956 Patterson
Lc Pegi Mayne

PAT NIXON

Cattleya trianaei alba is influential in Pat Nixon's 1960 namesake. This variety, 'Joe' from Joe Grezaffi, has been grown into a specimen and has 17 flowers. ARTHUR E. CHADWICK PHOTO

The darker variety of Lc Betty Ford, 'York' AM/AOS, became the public favorite. It was awarded several decades after its introduction and is still in production at Hausermann.

ARTHUR E. CHADWICK PHOTO

BETTY FORD

Betty Ford and her husband, Gerald, were eagerly looking forward to retirement following his thirteen terms as a Congressman from Michigan. The plan changed following a series of unlikely events, which elevated Mr. Ford first to Vice President and then to President. Following that eight month period, Betty Ford found herself First Lady of the United States.

Elizabeth Ann Bloomer Warren 'Betty' Ford championed a number of important causes during her short tenure at 1600 Pennsylvania Avenue. She was an outspoken advocate for women's rights and lobbied passionately for the Equal Rights Amendment (ERA). Within a few weeks of her husband taking office, she announced to the world that she had breast cancer – a disease which was not being discussed publicly. Her candor with this personal health issue led many women to seek testing and potentially life-saving treatment. Mrs. Ford became a symbol of the changing times and, in 1975, *Time* magazine named her Woman of the Year.

Following her White House years, Mrs. Ford gained more prominence when she founded and chaired the California-based Betty Ford Clinic in 1982 for substance abuse. As before, she opened up her personal life for the benefit of others. Today, the treatment center has seen tens of thousands of patients from all walks of life, including such celebrities as Elizabeth Taylor, Mickey Mantle, and Mary Tyler Moore.

Coming off its success with Pat Nixon's 1969 namesake cattleya, Hausermann Orchids of Villa Park, Illinois (now called Orchids by Hausermann) jumped at the chance to present another First Lady with one of its hybrids. Mrs. Ford was a flower enthusiast and was scheduled

PHOTO COURTESY OF THE GERALD R. FORD PRESIDENTIAL LIBRARY

Not just anyone can effortlessly wear a bright orange dress but Mrs. Ford's white cattleya corsage pulls the ensemble together. Here, she and the President appear at the 1976 Republican Presidential Convention.

COURTESY OF THE GERALD R. FORD PRESIDENTIAL LIBRARY

When it came time to present Mrs. Ford with her namesake cattleya, the hybrid was no longer in bloom so Roy Hausermann gave her a picture of the flower. She was all smiles.

COURTESY OF ORCHIDS BY HAUSERMANN

to appear at the 1982 Allied Florists Convention in Denver, Colorado. Though she had left the White House six years earlier, the former First Lady was a big draw for the annual event, which was being held at the posh Hilton Hotel.

As soon as it was announced that Mrs. Ford would attend the springtime convention, Hausermann looked through its stock and found a big dark purple hybrid which had not yet been named. They promptly registered the cross as Laeliocattleya Betty Ford (Nigrescent x Barbara's Delight). As the date for the event approached, however, none of the plants were blooming. Faced with having no flowers for the presentation, company representative Roy Hausermann decided to use a framed picture of the namesake to show the former First Lady. As can be seen from the photograph of the presentation, Mrs. Ford was all smiles and loved the gesture.

Betty Ford's namesake cattleya would not be possible without a number of early hybrids such as C Lord Rothschild (dowiana x gaskelliana) from 1893, that were made by the legendary Frederick Sander at his St Albans, England nursery. Grandson, David Sander, wrote *"His fame was such that, in 1885, a letter from South America addressed simply, 'Sander, Orchid King, England,' found him with no trouble."* Today, the Sander name survives in the countless species and hybrids that the founder introduced - most notably *Vanda sanderiana*.

Sander was determined to discover as many new species from the jungles around the world as he could. He sent explorers to tropical forests for months at a time in the hopes of introducing to the public something that had never been seen before. The prices he got at the weekly London auction houses were nothing short of astounding.

When he wasn't discovering new species, Sander was breeding new hybrids. He joined James Veitch and half a dozen other pioneers by introducing primary hybrids – two species put

Betty Ford's namesake cattleya would not be possible without a number of early hybrids made by Frederick Sander. Shown is one of his exhibits from 1914. COURTESY OF ORCHID WORLD

One of Sander's greatest achievements is the glamorous 1880s publication, Reichenbachia. Shown is C percivaliana from A. A. Chadwick's library. ARTHUR E. CHADWICK PHOTO

together – and leading biologist, H. G. Reichenbach, remarked sarcastically that *"All Orchidic England is now engaged in the procreation of mules."* It was controversial at the time to create something other than what Mother Nature intended.

To court wealthy clients, Sander launched a series of glamorous oversized periodicals called *Reichenbachia*, which portrayed orchid flowers life size. He commissioned well known artist Harry Moon (who would later be his son-in-law) to paint the orchids and even installed a state-of-the-art lithograph printing press to make copies. These were all very expensive and almost bankrupt the business.

There were four volumes with 192 paintings and the Imperial Edition weighed a whopping forty four pounds per volume. Volume 1 was dedicated to Queen Victoria; Volume 2 to Augusta Victoria, German Empress and Queen of Prussia; Volume 3 to Maria Feodorovna, Empress of Russia; and Volume 4 to Henriette, Queen of the Belgians. These royals were Sander's clients.

Sander's main orchid nursery at St Albans, England, was the largest in the world but he built another in Bruges, Belgium which was many times bigger and included shrubs, bay trees, and other non orchidaceous plants. There were 240 glasshouses in total. Sander traveled between the two locations regularly to check on things.

Frederick Sander is credited with making the 1893 primary hybrid, C Lord Rothschild (dowiana x gaskelliana). Shown is a photograph of the 1912 award painting, 'Albescens' AM/RHS, originally in color by Nellie Roberts. COURTESY OF ORCHID WORLD

Of course, this success couldn't continue forever and there were numerous downturns in his fortune, not the least of which was World War I which took most of his workers and fuel. Sander passed away in 1920 at age 73 but left an astonishing legacy that was carried on by his kids and grandkids. As the "Official Orchid Grower" to Queen Victoria, Frederick Sander's reputation was cast in stone and, even today, he is known as "The Orchid King."

Lc Betty Ford was destined to have a rich dark purple color because one of its parents is Lc Nigrescent (C Nigritian x Bonanza), which has an impressive background of some of the darkest hybrids ever made. The driving force for this color is Cattleya Fabia (dowiana x labiata) which appears four times in the lineage. Primary hybrids of Cattleya dowiana usually produce dark flowers, but with C labiata, this color is deeper and more intense than with other cattleya species. Only C Leda (dowiana x percivaliana) is as dark. The Royal Horticultural Society awarded a number of extremely dark C Fabia's including 'Memoria Lord Roberts' AM/RHS (1916) as shown by the Orchid King himself, Frederick Sander.

Cattleya Fabia was first made by James Veitch & Son's breeder, John Seden in 1894. The hybrid was one of Seden's earliest crosses, probably because the blooming season of the two parents overlapped (dowiana in August and an early labiata in September). Unfortunately, C

Gene Hausermann (center), shown here in 1978, estimates that his company has sold 20,000 Betty Ford namesakes since its introduction in 1982.

COURTESY OF ORCHIDS BY HAUSERMANN

Fabia did not get much acclaim at the time because, as Veitch underwhelmingly described it in his *Hortus Veitchii* in 1906, the flowers were "light rosy-pink with a lip approaching that of *Cattleya labiata*".

Remakes of the cross, however, produced the wonderful dark-colored flowers that made C Fabia famous. By 1946, C Fabia had been registered as a parent in over 200 crosses. The primary flowered in September which was the beginning of the fall social season and was widely grown commercially during the cut flower era of the 1930s, 40s and 50s in the United States. Thomas Young Orchids in Bound Brook, New Jersey grew entire greenhouses of C Fabia during this period.

Lc Nigrescent is a great dark hybrid because of its Fabia-based parent, C Nigritian (Fred Sanders x Nigrella), which included an unusually dark C Mrs. Pitt 'Charlesworth' AM/RHS (dowiana x loddigesii) in its ancestry. C Nigritian 'King of Kings' AM/AOS also proved to be an excellent parent for dark cattleyas. The three generation trio of Nigrescent (1959) – Nigritian (1945) – Nigrella (1934), whose root name is derived from the African river, Niger, proved unbeatable for the striking blackish purple Betty Ford.

The other parent of the Ford namesake, Lc Barbara's Delight (Aristocrat x Winter Belle), is built on the queen of well-shaped species, C trianaei, and was named after Gene Hausermann's sister, Barbara. This richly-colored purple hybrid was cut flower stock at Hausermann for many years and was registered the same year as Lc Betty Ford. In other words, Hausermann had to register two hybrids simultaneously in order to get Lc Betty Ford: Nigrescent x (Aristocrat x Winter Belle).

Hausermann cloned the two best varieties of the Lc Betty Ford and made them available to the public. The first was the same flower shown to Mrs. Ford, 'Winter Delight', medium lavender with a two-tone yellow/purple throat. The second was 'York', a dark purple with an even darker throat, named after nearby York Township.

'Winter Delight' was heavily promoted in the Hausermann catalog and, as late as 1992, was featured on the back cover. 'York' was also listed and, for many years, both varieties were sold in

There were two varieties of Lc Betty Ford cloned by Hausermann. Initially, 'Winter Delight' was heavily promoted and even appeared on the back cover of their catalog. COURTESY OF ORCHIDS BY HAUSERMANN

Chapter 11

BETTY FORD

Lc Betty Ford gets much of its color from the 1959 dark pare Lc Nigrescent. Shown is 'Dr. Walter Davis' AM/AOS.

ARTHUR E. CHADWICK PHOTO

Lc Betty Ford gets its great shape and long lasting qualities from C trianaei, the National Flower of Colombia. Shown is 'Powhatan'.

ARTHUR E. CHADWICK PHOTO

all sizes, ranging from young plants in 2" pots to specimens in 8" pots. The company had also grown and was now approaching 160,000 square feet of greenhouse space.

Despite its fame and early success, 'Winter Delight' was eventually phased out in favor of 'York'. Hobbyists sought the rich coloring and extremely vigorous 'York' which when grown well produces 4-5 large flowers per pseudobulb and multiple leads in a pot.

One of the fascinating characteristics of 'York' is that, although this variety is normally a November/December bloomer, bud formation can be delayed by using a technique that is rarely utilized today – the addition of lights. Back in the cut flower days, commercial nurseries might speed up or delay the natural blooming times of plants to coincide with the demand for corsages – usually holidays and dances. Only a few cattleya species can have their flowering season altered significantly. C labiata and some of its hybrids are controllable by light because in the jungle, the Brazilian species starts to bloom when the days get shorter (September in the United States).

Lc Betty Ford comes from a long line of dark species including C labiata. Shown is a specimen plant from A. A. Chadwick's collection. ARTHUR E. CHADWICK PHOTO

Growers discovered that a single incandescent light bulb, which turned on at dusk, effectively created longer daylight and could delay a C labiata hybrid for several months. Over time, a formula was developed that calculated the exact number of light bulb hours needed to gain the desired delay in blooming time. Growers could refer to a chart posted in the greenhouse and set their timers accordingly.

Betty Ford's namesake is heavily influenced by C labiata and variety 'York' responds very well to light. Thus, Hausermann, which grows thousands of 'York' each year, is able to spread out the blooming season from November to April. As a result, 'York' remains one of Hausermann's best sellers along with such staples as Lc Irene Finney and Blc Hausermann's Holiday.

Lc Betty Ford 'York' is by far the most widely circulated of all the first lady hybrids. Gene Hausermann estimates that his company has sold over 20,000 of them. It is common to see the plant on orchid society show tables around the country during the winter months – usually with a blue ribbon attached. In 2009, 'York' received an Award of Merit from the American Orchid Society – 27 years after the hybrid was first registered.

In her 1978 autobiography, *The Times of My Life*, Mrs. Ford wrote, *"I am an ordinary woman who was called on stage at an extraordinary time."* She was that rare celebrity who was down to earth and on par with the everyday person. *"People identified with me, they knew I was no different from them."*

She was also unapologetically candid and wasn't afraid to make waves. *"I'll move to the White House, do the best I can, and, if they don't like me, they can kick me out."* It turns out the public did like her but they couldn't quite forgive her husband for pardoning Richard Nixon.

Betty Ford's legacy of empowering women will continue for generations but it's her namesake cattleya that touches each of the thousands of orchid hobbyists who grow it. Her maiden name was, after all, Bloomer. ✯

PERSONAL LIFE

Elizabeth Anne Bloomer was born in 1918 in Chicago. She began working at a young age, ready to pursue a career and move to the city. Her first marriage to William Warren was short and she married Gerald Ford in 1948. He was beginning his first campaign for the U.S. House of Representatives. The pair has four children together.

Betty Ford was First Lady of the United States from 1974 to 1977. During her time in the White House, she advocated for many progressive ideas and movements, including equal rights, breast cancer awareness, and support for those suffering from substance abuse. She was also passionate about the arts with a keen interest in dance. She is generally considered one of the most influential women of the late twentieth century. ✯

LC BETTY FORD

(1982 Hausermann)

COMPOSITION

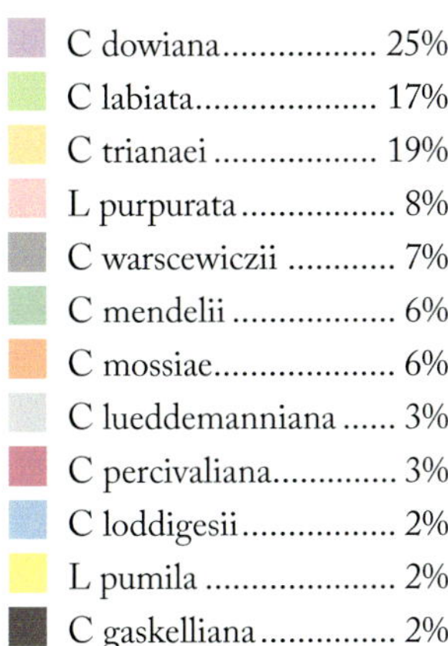

Species	%
C dowiana	25%
C labiata	17%
C trianaei	19%
L purpurata	8%
C warscewiczii	7%
C mendelii	6%
C mossiae	6%
C lueddemanniana	3%
C percivaliana	3%
C loddigesii	2%
L pumila	2%
C gaskelliana	2%

LINEAGE

1892 Hausermann
Lc Barbara's Delight

1959 Abbott
Lc Nigrescent

1957 Rivermont
Lc Aristocrat

1938 Low
Lc Winter Belle

1949 Bracey
Lc Bonanza

1945 Sander
C Nigritian

Rosalynn Carter accepted her namesake cattleya from a Venezuelan grower, Abraham Jesurun in 1977.

COURTESY OF THE CARTER LIBRARY

ROSALYNN CARTER

★ ★ ★ ★ ★ ★ ★

"Your thoughtful gesture of naming this lovely orchid after me will remain a symbol of the ties that bind our countries."

– Rosalynn Carter 1977 *(following her trip to Venezuela)*

In 1953, Jimmy Carter left a promising Navy career to run the family peanut farm in Plains, Georgia. Ten years later, he scored his first political victory by winning a seat in the State Senate. By 1971, he was Governor. His humble beginnings contributed to the public's perception of Carter as a Washington outsider and helped him win the White House in 1976.

His wife, Rosalyn, had no intention of being a traditional First Lady. She attended Cabinet meetings, national security briefings, and played a key role in the 39th President's signature achievement, a Middle East peace agreement. The Carters held the negotiations with the President of Egypt and the Prime Minister of Israel, as well as their wives which helped to create a more relaxed atmosphere.

In May of 1977, Mrs. Carter traveled as the President's official envoy to Latin America. She met with the presidents and prime ministers of seven countries. In preparation for the two week trip, Mrs. Carter took Spanish lessons and was briefed on the weighty issues of the day – from

Orchid collecting in the early 1900s meant traversing South American rivers by steam boat.

THOMAS R. BOYD PHOTO

A bountiful find of C mossiae in Venezuela circa 1900.

COURTESY OF THE ORCHID WORLD

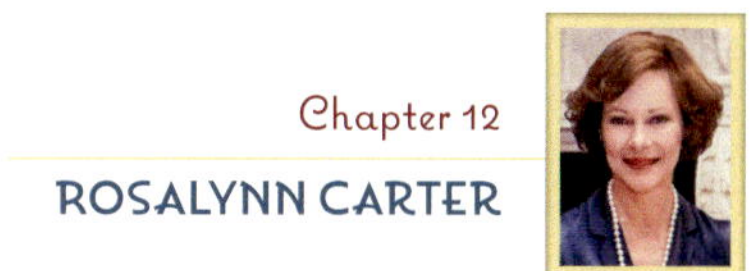

energy policy and nuclear weaponry to beef exports and financial aid. While other First Ladies had traveled abroad in support of their husband's agenda, none had engaged the issues directly.

The Carters had a special interest in Latin America and had traveled there many times prior to his presidency. The last stop on her historic trip was Venezuela, where Rosalynn met with President Carlos Andres Perez and his wife, Blanquita. After discussing important diplomatic topics, Mrs. Carter was escorted to a meeting of the North American Association of Venezuela, where she received a very special welcoming gift.

Venezuela is home to roughly 1,500 naturally occurring orchid species, including six large-flowered Cattleyas – gaskelliana, jenmanii, lawrenceana, lueddemanniana, mossiae, and percivaliana. The capital, Caracas, is a bustling city with well established commercial growers, such as famed orchidist Henrique Graf of Plantio De Orquidea. In the southeast corner of the city, just minutes from Graf's business, was a smaller grower, Urimare Nurseries (Viveros Urimare), owned by Dr Abraham Jesurun.

Jesurun was an accomplished grower and hybridizer, having registered over 50 cattleya crosses dating back to the 1960s. He used the best stud plants of the day from art shades like Slc Anzac and Lc Lee Langford to big purples like C Nigritian and Blc Norman's Bay. He named many of his hybrids after friends and family members.

Urimare Nurseries consisted of six greenhouses and a lab for seed sowing. Cattleyas were sold retail, wholesale, as cut flowers, and potted plants. Jesurun was well known in the area and presided over the local orchid society, Socieded de Orquideologia del Estado Miranda, for six years. Like many commercial growers, his business started out as a hobby. He split his time between orchids and running the two largest vegetable oil companies in Venezuela (Los Tres Cochinitos in Caracas and Aceite Diana in Valencia).

Abraham Jesurun was a savvy businessman. One of the top stories around the world that day was Rosalynn Carter visiting Venezuela. What better way to call attention to his orchid company than by naming a cattleya after the visiting wife of a newly elected American President – especially a First Lady who was trying to improve relations and the local economy.

The "Rosalynn Orchid", as it was referred to by her staff, was astounding. The flowers were a rich medium purple with dark orange 'eyes' in the lips and five flowers on the spike. The potted plant was wrapped in fancy gold foil and presented to Mrs. Carter by the grower himself, Abraham Jesurun and his wife, Gloria. The local Cub Scouts also gave cut cattleyas to the Carter entourage. As can be seen from the photograph, Mrs. Carter is smiling from ear to ear.

Afterwards, the historic plant was transported to Washington, D.C. aboard Mrs. Carter's plane. Rosalynn spoke first at a joint news conference, *"This morning in Venezuela, President Perez said...that...my visit to Latin America had opened new paths in inter-American relations."* Mr. Carter then joked, *"It's a much greater sacrifice for me to have her gone than the Vice President...or the Secretary of State."*

Undoubtedly, Mrs. Carter's namesake orchid, which accompanied her home, had also contributed to the warm feeling of the trip. She officially thanked Dr. Jesurun in a follow-up letter - *"Your thoughtful gesture of naming this lovely orchid after me will remain a symbol of the ties that bind our countries."* It could be said that her cattleya had become the official symbol of friendship between Venezuela and the United States.

The lineage of Cattleya Rosalynn Carter (Dinah x Dark Emperor) speaks volumes about

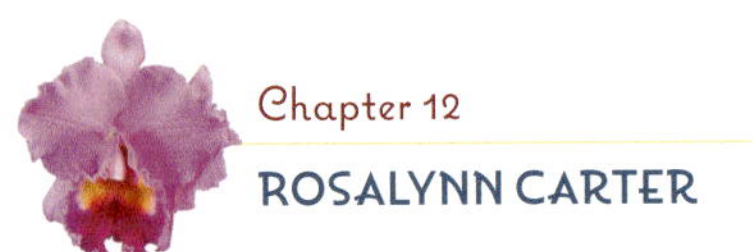

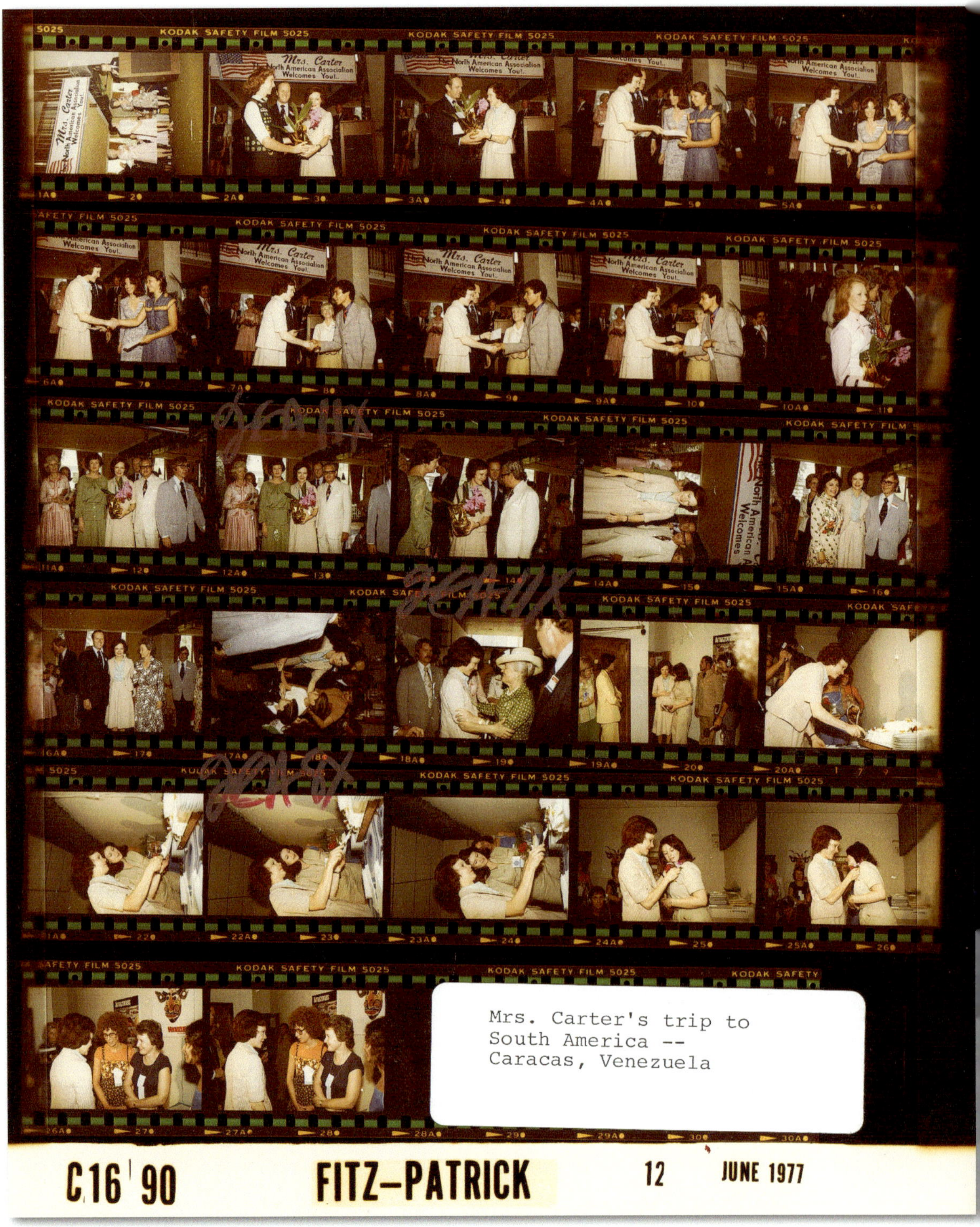

Mrs. Carter's trip to
South America --
Caracas, Venezuela

C16 90 FITZ–PATRICK 12 JUNE 1977

The Venezuelan orchid presentation was captured in a series of photographs and stored away for decades until we inquired about them. COURTESY OF THE CARTER LIBRARY

the quality of the hybrid. Jesurun had a number of fine stud plants dating back to the early 1900s including C Dinah (Dupreana x Elvina), first made by McBean's of Cooksbridge, Sussex, England in 1919. McBean's was an exhibitor at the very first Chelsea Flower Show in 1913 and is still in business today.

McBean's was highly regarded throughout England. *The Orchid World* visited the nursery in 1913 and reported that "*...the houses containing the extensive stock of orchids belonging to Messrs. J and A McBean are producing some of the finest examples of cultivated plants.*" Well grown plants are, in fact, the secret to exceptional blooming and McBean's excelled in both culture and awards.

McBean's was highly regarded throughout England. Shown is one of their cattleya houses circa 1913.
COURTESY OF THE ORCHID WORLD

"*Words fail to give a fair idea of the immense bulbs...*" The reporter then measured the foliage of some of the cattleya species - C schroederae, C mendelii, C warscewiczii and C mossiae - with a ruler and jotted down the dimensions. The lead bulb of one C schroederae was a whopping six inches in circumference.

By this time, McBean's was keen on making sibling crosses of species rather than importing cattleyas. The jungles were being depleted to the point that collectors were having trouble finding enough plants to make it worth the trip. This was in addition to the numerous perils already associated with jungle collecting.

Here is a firsthand account of what one collector encountered in neighboring Colombia while searching for C trianaei as revealed in a letter published in the *Journal of the North of England Horticultural Society*. It was 1909 and collector, Mr. Ryall, was sent to the Bogata area by the firm, Mansell and Hatcher, departing Southampton on a Royal Mail steamer. It would take a week or so to arrive at the ocean port of Barranquilla then an arduous trip up the Magdalena River over 500 miles on a smaller steam boat.

Ryall's first task was acquiring ten mules at the river base, Honda, which would carry the orchids back. He then had to locate wood and nails with which to build the packing cases. Construction would take place later at the collecting site after several more weeks of mule riding deep into the jungle.

Actual collecting took another three weeks and involved supervising locals who would scale the trees and cut the orchid plants off the bark, one by one, leaving as many roots as possible. Each evening, the plants would be tied up in bundles and carried to the campground.

Then the cases were constructed and plants carefully packed in layers with dried fern leaves (called bracken) leaving plenty of air space. Finally, the cases were marked with shipping numbers and loaded onto the mules for the lengthy journey back to Honda. At least from there, it was down river to Barranquilla.

This C schilleriana was typical of the fine jungle varieties at the turn of the century. COURTESY THE ORCHID ALBUM

We don't know the specifics but Mr. Ryall perished on his way back to England after three years abroad.

The Orchid World continued their tour of McBeans, *"We can see the wisdom of raising as many seedlings as possible from the same pod, for it is not until they bloom that one is able to discriminate between the good and bad varieties."* McBean's had both the greenhouse space and the patience to wait seven years to see the results. We, too, have experienced the joy when that first seedling blooms.

A multitude of growers collaborated on some of the other early hybrids in the Carter lineage. A. A. Peeters of Brussels, Belgium, exhibited the primary hybrid, C Dupreana (warneri x warscewiczii), in 1896 where it was described by the *Gardener's Chronicle* as *"larger than C warscewiczii and similarly colored."* The cross was registered by the legendary Firmin Lambeau of Villa Vogelsang (Birdsong House).

Breeder R. H. Gore played an important role in the Carter namesake. This 1949 catalog offered hundreds of cattleya varieties.

COURTESY OF R. H. GORE

C Dupreana was a promising hybrid and it became a popular stud plant for early summer dark purple hybrids. Its parent, C warneri, from Brazil, was one of the first cattleyas to receive a First Class Certificate from the RHS, when S Rucker exhibited it in 1866. The other Dupreana parent, C warscewiczii, from Colombia, has been heavily awarded and 'Low's' variety FCC/RHS from 1910 is one of the best for dark color.

C Elvina (schilleriana x trianaei) does not sound like a hopeful cross, given the notable shortcomings of C schilleriana in terms of flower size and typical color. However, it was used on occasion to increase the flower count and to keep the foliage compact. In addition, there are several very dark varieties including 'Pitt' FCC/RHS (1900) and 'Westfield' AM/RHS (1905).

The *Gardeners Chronicle* of 1896 described the grand introduction of C Elvina, *"J Veitch and Sons of the Royal Exotic Nursery in Chelsea received a gold medal for a remarkably fine group which would be praiseworthy at any season of the year. Among the plants...was the new Cattleya Elvina, a dwarf plant bearing large flowers, the sepals and petals of which were of that light purple..."* Sadly, this Elvina did not inherit the dark color of C schilleriana but there was one awarded variety the same year that was dark.

The other parent of C Rosalynn Carter, C Dark Emperor (Nigritian x Nigrella), was bred by Robert Gore of Fort Lauderdale, Florida in 1957. Aside from having a sizable cattleya business called the Orchid House, he was a trustee of the American Orchid Society and chaired the committee that established the AOS judging point system. He traveled the world and had one of the largest collections of C trianaei in existence – with 285 named varieties.

C warneri 'Brazilian Springtime' AM/AOS is a fine variety that originated in the jungles of Brazil.

ARTHUR E. CHADWICK PHOTO

C warscewiczii 'Powhatan' is a fine dark variety from the collection of A. A. Chadwick.

ARTHUR E. CHADWICK PHOTO

C trianaei 'Party Time' bloomed every New Year's Eve for 50 years in the collection of A. A. Chadwick.

ARTHUR E. CHADWICK PHOTO

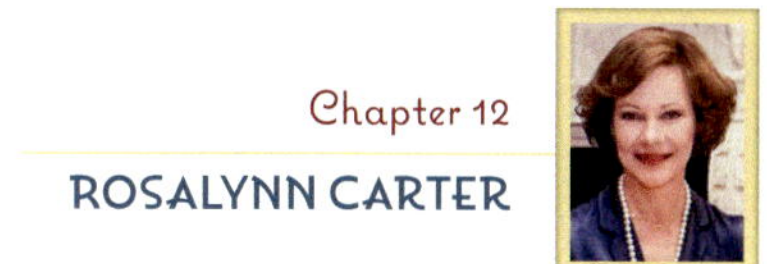

His mail order catalog of 1949, entitled "A Cavalcade of Orchids," would leave any hobbyist breathless. *"We have collected choice stock from all parts of the world and have spared no effort to build a collection of world recognition"* begins the listing. It then lists nearly 600 different varieties of lavender cattleya species and hybrids – each divided by blooming season. The Carter parent, C Dinah, is described as a *"good stud."*

Of the over 100 cattleya crosses that Gore registered during his lifetime, C Dark Emperor is arguably his greatest accomplishment. The hybrid garnered three AOS awards shortly after being named – 'El Portal', 'Mariner', and the well-known 'Black Caesar' which was described as having *"three intensely dark deep purple flowers of fine form, substance, and medium size on one spike."* It was promoted as a stud in full page color ads in the AOS Bulletin.

In 2015, Mrs. Carter wrote us a letter thanking us for the article of her namesake orchid that appeared in Orchids magazine. *"I thought the article was well done – and the photographs were beautiful."* She is a big fan of orchids and has them all over her house.

What will be remembered about Rosalynn Carter's namesake cattleya is that this is the only First Lady hybrid to have been bred outside the United States. Except for the presentation photographs of the Venezuela trip, there are no known images of the stunning flowers. The breeder's entire orchid collection was given away upon his death and it is unclear if any plants of Cattleya Rosalynn Carter exist today. Given the historical significance of the hybrid, we are in the process of remaking the cross.

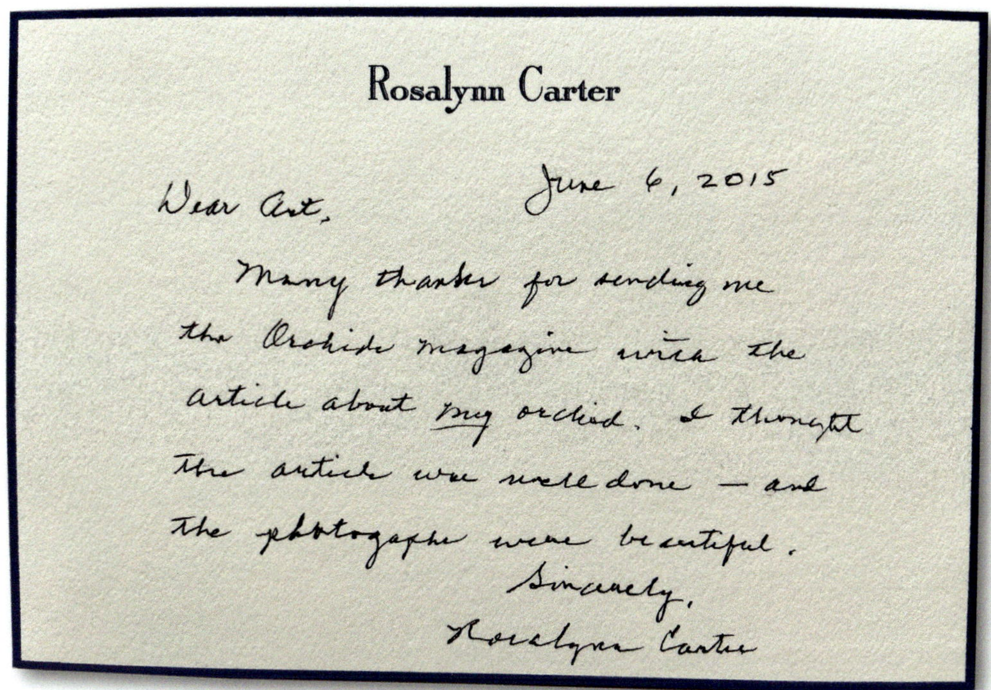

Rosalynn Carter

June 6, 2015

Dear Art,

Many thanks for sending me the Orchids magazine with the article about <u>my</u> orchid. I thought the article was well done – and the photographs were beautiful.

Sincerely,
Rosalynn Carter

Mrs. Carter wrote us a letter in 2015 after receiving a copy of Orchids magazine which contained our article about her namesake cattleya.

ARTHUR E. CHADWICK PHOTO

For her entire adult life, Rosalynn Carter was passionate about mental health. She served on the Board of Advisors of Habitat for Humanity and was co-founder with her husband of the Carter Center – a partnership with Emory University that is guided by a fundamental commitment to human rights. The former First Lady was the author of five books and a recipient of the Presidential Medal of Freedom. She passed away in November 2023 at the age of 96. ✯

Mrs. Carter was honored with her namesake Phalaenopsis by the breeder Gemstone Orchids in 1996.

COURTESY OF THE AMERICAN ORCHID SOCIETY

Mrs. Carter is fond of other tropical flowers including Birds of Paradise.

COURTESY OF THE CARTER LIBRARY

PERSONAL LIFE

Eleanor Rosalynn Smith was born in 1927 in Plains, Georgia. She was one of four children and helped her mother raise her three younger siblings after her father's passing when she was 13. Eleanor lived in poverty during her childhood but was mostly unaware of the fact, remaining close with the Plains community.

She graduated salutatorian of her high school and went on to pursue college, but had to drop out due to financial struggles and family obligations. Eleanor met Jimmy Carter, then a student at the US Naval Academy, in 1945 and the pair were wed in July of 1946. Eleanor and Jimmy have four children together - three sons and one daughter. ★

Rosalynn Carter wore a cattleya corsage on her wedding day.

COURTESY OF THE CARTER LIBRARY

C ROSALYNN CARTER

(1977 Jesurin)

COMPOSITION

- C dowiana................. 23%
- C trianaei.................. 17%
- C labiata..................... 17%
- C warscewiczii 12%
- C warneri.................. 12%
- C schilleriana 12%
- C loddigesii................. 5%
- C mossiae..................... 1%

LINEAGE

1919 McBeans
C Dinah

1957 Gore
C Dark Emperor

1906 Lambeau
C Dupreana

1896 Veitch
C Elvina

1945 Sander
C Nigritian

1934 Sander
C Nigrella

A. A. Chadwick took this photograph in 1950 of a greenhouse full of imported C trianaei. Notice how every flower is different. This was important because no two women wanted to wear the same looking corsage. One of the endearing qualities of this species is the seemingly endless number of subtle color variations in existence. No other species offers this excitement. This photo is also noteworthy because after it was taken, the plants were thrown out to make way for the "modern" hybrids. Sadly, the practice of "upgrading" greenhouse stock from species to hybrids was commonplace as growers tried to produce as many flowers per square foot of bench space as possible. Cattleya trianaei usually only makes two flowers per lead whereas many winter hybrids can make double that. However, just think what those C trianaei would be worth today! A. A. CHADWICK PHOTO

One of the first First Lady hybrids to ever get awarded was in 1970 with Lc Nancy Reagan 'Regal Lady' HCC/AOS when exhibited by the breeder, Rod McLellan.

COURTESY OF THE AMERICAN ORCHID SOCIETY

NANCY REAGAN

★ ★ ★ ★ ★ ★ ★

Nancy Davis Reagan was First Lady of the United States from 1981 to 1989. She ushered in an elegance and formality into the White House which had not been seen in years. Her favorite color was red, which she wore so often that the fire-engine shade became known as "Reagan Red." She and her husband, the 40th U.S. President Ronald Reagan, were inseparable and she was one of his closest advisors.

The former Nancy Davis was a successful Hollywood actress who appeared in twelve movies between 1949 and 1958. Her mother had also been an actress in the early days of film. It was only fitting that Nancy would marry a leading man and president of the Screen Actors Guild. The newlywed couple appeared together in one motion picture, *Hellcats of the Navy* (1957).

Soon after, Mrs. Reagan left her acting career to raise children. She then embarked on a political journey that saw her husband serve two terms as Governor of California and two terms as President of the United States.

Her major initiative as U.S. First Lady was the "Just Say No" anti-drug awareness campaign, which sought to encourage children to resist recreational drug use. Mrs. Reagan traveled the country promoting the idea - visiting rehabilitation centers, appearing on numerous talk shows, and recording public service announcements. Over 5,000 Just Say No clubs were founded in schools and a $1.7 billion drug enforcement law was passed on Capitol Hill. The popular slogan "Just Say No" became part of American culture.

Chapter 13

NANCY REAGAN

Nancy Reagan was fond of all flowers especially orchids. Here, she holds a bouquet of cymbidiums.

COURTESY THE REAGAN PRESIDENTIAL LIBRARY

In 1968, during Mr. Reagan's first term as Governor of California, local South San Francisco grower Rod McLellan named a cattleya for Nancy Reagan. A glamorous Hollywood couple now occupied the Governor's mansion and McLellan sought to get in on the action. The company could not have predicted that Mr. Reagan would one day become President of the United States.

Fifteen years earlier, the same South San Francisco firm enjoyed great success with another political wife, U.S. First Lady Mamie Eisenhower. This time, however, McLellan was targeting local hobbyists who were familiar with Mrs. Reagan and might buy her namesake plant because they liked her. At their spring open houses during peak cymbidium season, McLellan offered enormous displays of Lc Nancy Reagan seedlings in bloom for their walk-in clients. By one account, "*...there must have been 100 of them in the sales house.*"

Rod McLellan Company had humble beginnings dating back to the mid 1800s when the grandfather, David McLellan, moved to California during the Gold Rush and started a dairy farm. To entice his clients to pay promptly, he would include complimentary cut flowers with their milk delivery. It wasn't long before there were also substantial orders for flowers.

The next generation was led by Edgar and the company became the E. W. McLellan Co. Edgar passed in 1938 and it became the Rod McLellan Co. Rod had the foresight to get a botany degree from Stanford and thoroughly understood plants.

One of the first things Rod did was to acquire a large number of orchids from England during World War II. He divided the plants and used them for both cut flowers and pot plants. Among his many "firsts" was shipping cut flowers by plane, introducing the "orchid spa" or boarding, and the creation of SuperSoil potting media.

The Reagan hybrid was heavily promoted by McLellan in their catalog. The description says it all.

COURTESY OF ROD MCLELLAN CO.

The Rod McLellan showroom was breathtaking and clients traveled from all over the country to visit.

COURTESY OF ROD MCLELLAN CO.

Rod McLellan Co was a massive operation. This greenhouse held thousands of seedlings.

COURTESY OF ROD MCLELLAN CO.

By the late 1960s, the Rod McLellan Company and their "Acres of Orchids" were in full swing. Every month, they ran full-page advertisements in the AOS Bulletin – going head to head with such heavy-hitters as Stewarts, Vacherot & Lecoufle, Kensington, Rivermont, and Dos Pueblos. Each McLellan ad promoted a different genus: intergeneric oncidiums, miltonias in spike, novelty phal hybrids, complex paphs in bud, yellow cattleya seedlings. And who can forget the amazing Wonder-Lizer instant plant food and accompanying Model 100 Waterfeeder?

One parent of the Reagan namesake is Lc Walter Slagle (Mary Rose x Walter Winchell) from 1960. There are over a dozen awarded varieties including 'Lavish' AM/AOS and the entire cross received a rare Award of Quality.

COURTESY OF AMERICAN ORCHID SOCIETY

The new Nancy Reagan cattleya was destined to be great. Both of the parents were stars in their own right and McLellan picked the perfect color for her namesake flower. The lineage comprised many generations and was complex - with 11 species in the background. The majority of the breeding influence was from C dowiana, labiata, and trianaei, which bloom in the summer, fall, and winter respectively. Surprisingly, Nancy Reagan is a spring bloomer.

There was one flower quality award given to the hybrid. McLellan exhibited 'Regal Lady' HCC/AOS in March of 1970. This variety became one of the first of the first lady cattleyas to be awarded by the American Orchid Society.

McLellan advertised the new Reagan hybrid in their early 1970s catalog with a striking photograph. The caption reads, *"Lc. Nancy Reagan...excellent flower with outstanding parents (Lc. Walter Slagle 'Lavish' x C. Nigritian 'Sudan') – Practically all of our Walter Slagle plants have been outstanding. We hope to enhance the color with the addition of C. Nigritian."*

The other parent of the Reagan namesake is C Nigritian (Fred Sanders x Nigrella) from 1945. Shown is 'King of Kings' AM/AOS.

DAVID TOYOSHIMA PHOTO

It would be challenging to "enhance the color" of Lc Walter Slagle, which had been given numerous flower quality awards in part because of its stunning reddish purple color. However, C Nigritian was a proven breeder of dark purples with dozens of first generation offspring to its credit. It would be a breeder's dream to combine these two parents.

McLellan was offering three sizes of Reagan seedlings: 5" for \$15-\$20, 6" for \$18-\$30, and 7" for \$20-\$40. The plants must have been quite large to be offered in seven inch pots.

Rod McLellan not only bred the Reagan namesake but also its parent, Lc Walter Slagle (Mary Rose x Walter Winchell), and heavily promoted the hybrid in its mail order catalogs. The judges thought highly of the hybrid and awarded over a dozen varieties.

Most impressive, however, was the Award of Quality (AQ/AOS) given to the entire Slagle cross. This honor is exceedingly difficult to obtain and hybridizers spend a lifetime trying to get one. Twelve plants must be in bloom at the same time and must collectively be an improvement on the parents.

Not many large-flowered cattleya hybrids have ever won an Award of Quality. Previous winners include such stalwarts as C Irene Holguin, Bc Mount Hood, and Lc Elizabeth Off. McLellan had previously received the coveted award a few years earlier with Lc Ann Follis so they knew what was involved.

The plants have to be selected well in advance, staked while the buds are in the sheath, then groomed to perfection before they leave the greenhouse. Each flower has to open nearly flawlessly. Even still, the element of luck was required.

McLellan catalogs from the late 1960s show a beautiful tiered grouping of seedlings in bloom with the caption *"Lc. Walter Slagle has now won the highest acclaim as the famous top exhibition colored Cattleya... a triumphant example of profound perfection..."* The company was never shy about self-promotion.

The ad continues, *"Many have flowers with extremely deep shades of deep red lavender, some have golden "eyes" or more prominent yellow in the throat."*

Of particular interest is the Slagle cross being listed as *"controllable"* which means that the blooming season can be delayed significantly by the use of artificial lights. Hausermann's uses a similar technique to get their November-blooming Lc Betty Ford to produce flowers through May. Hybrids which are heavily influenced by C labiata are often capable of being light controllable.

Both Nancy Reagan and its parent, Walter Slagle, have an unusually long lineage of purple breeding. However, there is one ancestor that makes them different from other flowers of their day - the 1899 primary hybrid, Lc Dominiana (L purpurata x C dowiana), which produced some offspring with a reddish/purple tone.

Lc Dominiana is one of the most fascinating of the early cattleya hybrids. It was originally made by John Dominy, foreman of the British orchid company Messr James Veitch and Sons. Dominy is credited with being the first person to make a cattleya hybrid. He did this in 1852.

Although Dominy was a good orchid grower, he was a poor record keeper and often failed to record important facts about his crosses. In the case of Lc Dominiana, he neglected to mention the parents he used. When Lc Dominiana flowered for the first time in 1877, Dominy and his boss, James Veitch, had to guess which species he had used. In Veitch's famous 1887 *A Manual of Orchidaceous Plants*, Veitch speculates that the parents of Lc Dominiana *"were proba-*

Lc Nancy Reagan gets its fine shape and longevity from C trianaei. Shown is a late 1800s dark variety as painted by J. Nugent Fitch for the Orchid Album.

COURTESY OF THE ORCHID ALBUM

Some of the dark species that contribute to the Reagan namesake include L purpurata. Shown is a flammea variety.

ARTHUR E. CHADWICK PHOTO

C labiata can impart both dark color and floriferousness into hybrids. Shown is 'Meadowlark' AM/AOS with six flowers.

ARTHUR E. CHADWICK PHOTO

bly Cattleya dowiana and Laelia purpurata", but Robert Rolfe, editor of *The Orchid Review*, after seeing the flowers, felt it was C dowiana *"with some Laelia – probably L crispa."*

The mystery was not solved until the cross was remade by John Seden, who succeeded Dominy at Veitch. Seden combined C dowiana and L purpurata and, when the seedlings flowered, the blooms were just like Lc Dominiana. In *Hortus Veitchii*, his history of the Veitch company in 1906, James Veitch wrote that Seden's cross *"clears up the uncertainty which previously existed as to the origin of Laeliocattleya Dominiana."* He then published a full-page picture of a fine variety next to his comments.

John Seden apparently liked Lc Dominiana and sought to improve its somewhat starry shape by crossing it with a nice, round Cattleya trianaei. The new hybrid was called Lc Rosalind, which bloomed in 1896. Veitch describes Rosalind as having *"rose-pink in the petals with darker rosy-purple in the lip."*

Darker varieties of Lc Dominiana came along in the early 1900s, which produced the reddish-purple that we sometimes see in hybrids such as Lc Walter Slagle and Lc Nancy Reagan. A number of these intensely colored Dominianas were recognized by the Royal Horticultural

Another dark species that contributes to the Reagan namesake is C lueddemanniana. Shown is a first bloom seedling from a cross made by A. A. Chadwick. ARTHUR E. CHADWICK PHOTO

Society during this time including 'Monkend' AM/RHS when exhibited in 1911.

Seden made a second rosy purple primary hybrid that helped to shape history and influence the Reagan namesake - this one in 1882 with Lc Callistoglossa (L purpurata x C warscewiczii). While many of these were light, blush, or semi-alba colored, there were a few intense magenta varieties such as 'The Dell' FCC/RHS (1906) and 'Low' AM/AOS. The latter received its award in 2023 when exhibited by Chadwick's.

McLellan made one cross with Lc Nancy Reagan – a 1981 hybrid called Blc Fancy Nancy (Lc Nancy Reagan x Memoria Crispin Rosales), which coincided with Mrs. Reagan's first year in the White House. Once again, a reddish-purple flower was bred with a big purple stud and offered for sale to the public. Despite the considerable availability of Fancy Nancy, Nancy Reagan, and Walter Slagle, few specimens are known to exist today.

What will be remembered about Nancy Reagan in the horticulture world is her obvious love of orchids. Her namesake cattleya was registered while she was First Lady of California but it goes down in the history books as being ahead of its time for she would later move to 1600 Pennsylvania Avenue. The reddish purple color of her flower is unique among the wives of United States Presidents. ✯

First Lady Nancy Reagan was presented with her namesake Dendrobium by the Singapore Botanical Garden.

COURTESY OF THE SINGAPORE BOTANICAL GARDEN

PERSONAL LIFE

Anne Frances Robbins was born in 1921 in New York City. After her mother married Dr. Davis in 1929, her name was formally changed to "Nancy Davis" and the family relocated to Chicago. Nancy and Ronald were wed in 1952 and have a daughter and a son.

Nancy Reagan was First Lady of California from 1967 to 1975 and was very involved in her husband's two presidential campaigns. Her "Just Say No" initiative was considered successful and is still being talked about today. She received the Presidential Medal of Freedom and the Congressional Gold Medal. ✯

Seden's second contribution to the Reagan namesake was in 1882 with the primary hybrid, Lc Callistoglossa (L purpurata x C warscewiczii). Shown is the famous stud, 'Low' AM/AOS, as exhibited by Chadwick's in 2023.

ARTHUR E. CHADWICK PHOTO

LC NANCY REAGAN

(1968 Rod McLellan)

COMPOSITION

Species	%
C dowiana	30%
C labiata	20%
C trianaei	20%
C purpurata	6%
C warscewiczii	6%
C mendelii	5%
C lueddemanniana	3%
C loddigesii	3%
C mossiae	2%
C lawrenceana	1%

LINEAGE

1960 McLellan
Lc Walter Slagle

1945 Sander
C Nigritian

1938 Alexander
Lc Mary Rose

1952 Patterson
Lc Walter Winchell

1934 Sander
C Fred Sander

1934 Sander
C Nigrella

Cattleya dowiana grows naturally in Costa Rica. On a recent trip, we were taken to the jungle where a wild plant was in bloom. These particular flowers last 22 days which is quite long for the species. The local tour guide explained through a translator that he personally watches over the plants in this area to make sure that they are not stolen. Tourism is important in his country and he wants to be able to show visitors the beautiful flowers every year. First timers to the cloud forests might be surprised to find that the orchid blooms are not without serious imperfections. Insects, bacteria, bad weather and even monkeys have damaged the flowers and leaves. No orchid judge would even consider it for an award! ARTHUR E. CHADWICK PHOTO

Barbara Bush's namesake cattleya was bred by Lenette Greenhouses and named by Chadwick's in 2004. The semi-alba hybrid is capable of making five large flowers on a stem. Shown is 'First Lady' AM/AOS which was awarded in 2023.

ARTHUR E. CHADWICK PHOTO

Mrs. Bush tweaks the floral arrangements of the White House Florist.

COURTESY OF THE GEORGE H W BUSH PRESIDENTIAL LIBRARY

Mrs. Bush is presented a bouquet of orchids at the Singapore Botanical Gardens.

COURTESY OF THE GEORGE H W BUSH PRESIDENTIAL LIBRARY

BARBARA BUSH

★ ★ ★ ★ ★ ★ ★

"My mother was a big Garden Club of America member and would have loved this orchid!"

– Barbara Bush 2015

Barbara Pierce Bush's signature white hair and friendly persona endeared her to the American public for decades as her husband embarked on his numerous positions within the federal government. Prior to becoming the 41st President of the United States, George H.W. Bush was Vice President, Director of the CIA, Ambassador to the United Nations, and Liaison to the People's Republic of China.

As First Lady, Mrs. Bush adopted literacy as her signature cause. She had witnessed her son, Neil, struggle with dyslexia as a child and sought to empower families with the necessary tools to read. *"Family is unquestionably the most important part of my life. My wish is for every parent and child to experience the joy of reading and a lifetime of learning."* In 1989, she launched the Barbara Bush Foundation for Family Literacy.

Barbara Bush is no stranger to orchids. While the Bushes were on diplomatic trips to Asia, the Singapore Botanic Garden named and presented two orchid hybrids bearing her name. In

The entrance to a warm greenhouse at Messrs. Stuart Low & Co., Bush Hill Park, Enfield, England circa 1913. Low would later breed Blc Apparition, one of the parents to the Bush namesake.

COURTESY OF THE ORCHID WORLD

The Schroeder family was wealthy and active in orchids for several generations. Each year, they donated a silver cup for a winning exhibit. Shown is the 1912 Cup for Best Grouping of Hybrids at the Royal International Horticultural Exhibition.

COURTESY OF THE ORCHID WORLD

1982, she received Aranda Barbara Bush and, in 1992, Phalaenopsis Barbara Bush. The Singapore Botanic Garden is on the cutting edge of orchid technology and names their hybrids after foreign dignitaries and celebrities who visit the gardens.

In 2003, Owens Orchids in Pisgah Forest, NC, registered Odontocidium Barbara Bush after getting written permission from Mrs. Bush. Blooming plants were then sent to her home in Texas. The Owens family is distantly related to former President Jimmy Carter's family which helped facilitate the deal. Their orchid nursery had been in business since the early sixties.

It was the cattleya of 2004, however, that stole the show. Blc Barbara Bush (Lc Josephine Robinson x Apparition) launched Mrs. Bush into the orchid history books as she became part of a tradition of consecutive First Ladies having namesake cattleyas dating back to the Wilson administration.

The cross was named by Chadwick's but made by a small grower from North Carolina, Lenette Greenhouses. The business was founded in the late 1960s by Ken Griffith and his wife, Eleanor.

We made numerous trips to Lenette to buy their "dug-ups" or seedlings recently graduated from growing trays. They specialized in art shade phalaenopsis, particularly yellows, but were also known for cattleya species and hybrids. Clients who timed their visit just right might even get invited to dinner.

Their grower was Lee Potts who was a knowledgeable thirty-something responsible for setting up exhibits and working the show circuit. For most of the 1990s, while we were involved with area orchid shows, we were likely to be situated next to Lenette in a shopping mall or garden center.

One parent of the Bush namesake is Lc Josephine Robinson (Pegi Mayne x Cynthiana) from 1961. Shown is 'Lines' AM/AOS.

COURTESY OF THE AMERICAN ORCHID SOCIETY

Legendary grower Gene Crocker, of Carter & Holmes in Newberry, South Carolina, speaks fondly of his friend Ken Griffith. *"When I met him, he was my barber in Kannapolis, NC and he was growing orchids at his home. He had a greenhouse full of cymbidiums and sold the flowers at Easter. It was good to be able to talk orchids while I got my hair cut."*

Ken eventually gave up barbering and grew orchids full time. Over four decades, Lenette registered hundreds of crosses and kept two long hoop houses – a shady one for phalaenopsis and a bright one for cattleyas. *"The semi-albas were a passion of mine,"* Ken said.

And what a semi-alba cattleya it is. The parentage shows a heavy C warscewiczii and mossiae influence so the flowers are large and well presented. There isn't a specific blooming season as the seedlings bloom throughout the year.

One of the parents is Lc Josephine Robinson (Pegi Mayne x Cynthiana) which was made by Lines Orchids in 1961 and represented the culmination of Lines' outstanding breeding with semi-albas. Variety 'Lines' AM/AOS was one of 16 stud plants featured in their June 1965 AOS *Bulletin* article, on semi-alba breeding (along with two varieties of C Bess Truman). Owner John Lines described this cattleya as *"a very fine strong-growing semi-alba. The snow-white sepals and petals, combined with a beautifully proportioned lip, make this beautiful variety the queen of the*

In 1896, Baron Schroeder purchased all the specimens of a new cattleya species that was discovered and, shortly thereafter, it was named after his wife. C schroederae is a lasting reminder of the impact that the Schroeder family had on orchids. Shown is A. A. Chadwick's best seedling, 'Chadwick'.

ARTHUR E. CHADWICK PHOTO

Most varieties of Blc Barbara Bush are fall bloomers and C labiata is partly responsible. Shown is an 1880s fine variety, 'Foleyana'. COURTESY OF THE ORCHID ALBUM.

group."

Josephine Robinson is also a great example of "east coast" breeding. One parent, Lc Cynthiana was made by Rivermont Orchids of Signal Mountain, TN and the other parent, Lc Pegi Mayne (and grandparent, Lc Eugenia) was made by H. Patterson & Sons of Bergenfield, New Jersey. The early 1960s was a bountiful time for First Lady hybrids as Rivermont made Lc Jacqueline Kennedy, Manda made C Pat Nixon, Patterson made C Jacqueline Kennedy and Lines made C Bess Truman.

Lines received two awards from the American Orchid Society for Lc Josephine Robinson – 'Atlanta' AM/AOS in 1961 and the heralded 'Lines' AM/AOS in 1964 – and both had compliments on the lip coloring. 'Atlanta' is described as *"Lip deep purple edged with fine white ruffled border."*

Scott McCandless, who was the fourth generation owner at Lines, was able to locate John Lines' original handwritten notes for Lc Josephine Robinson 'Lines'. The lip is described as *"royal purple all the way around, faint white fringe on front, two medium gold eyes in the throat, burnt gold lines inside."* The plant had four large flowers at the time.

L purpurata provides much of the vigor and floriferousness to the Bush namesake. Shown is the fine semi-alba 'Cindarosa' AM/AOS which was awarded to Fennell's Orchid Jungle in 1988.

ARTHUR E. CHADWICK PHOTO

Much of Lc Josephine Robinson's outstanding traits can be derived from a long forgotten 1917 hybrid, Lc Schroderae (Bella x C Maggie Rafael) which appears on both sides of the parentage. The hybrid is a reminder of the huge impact that the Schroeder family had on orchid history.

Baron Sir Henry John William Schroeder (1824-1910) had one of the finest collections in all of Europe in the late 1800s. His estate, known as The Dell, sported 12 large orchid greenhouses including two that were devoted to just fine cattleya varieties. The Dell collection was so impressive that it was given a four page feature in the very first issue of *The Orchid Review* in 1893.

Baron Schroeder was a wealthy merchant banker and when a new cattleya species was discovered in 1896, he purchased all the specimens. Botanist H. G. Reichenbach named the new species for the Baron's wife, and called it Cattleya schroederae. The Baroness, he said, *"is so well known as an enthusiastic lover of orchids."*

When the Baron died, his son Baron H.W. Bruno Schroeder, took over the collection. He was a member of the Royal Horticultural Society's orchid committee and an active hybridizer. Bruno must have felt that one cattleya hybrid named after his family wasn't enough so, in 1917, he registered a new hybrid with the exact same name – Lc Schroederae (There was an identical name in 1892 - C trianaei x L jongeana and the RHS differentiates them with the date of registration – Lc Schroederae (1917) and Lc Schroederae (1892)). Of course, this was in addition to earlier family efforts - C Baroness Schroeder (trianaei x dolosa) from 1892 and the natural hybrid, C Schroederiana (dolosa x bicolor).

Lc Schroederae turned out to be a very successful white with colored lip cross. It earned many awards from the Royal Horticultural Society including 'Magnifica' FCC/RHS in 1919 and 'Gloriosa' FCC/RHS in 1920. In addition, the fine varieties went on to produce dozens of new hybrids for breeders worldwide.

The other parent of Blc Barbara Bush is Blc Apparition (Nanette x C Enid) and was made by Stuart Low & Co of Great Britain in 1949. The word, apparition, is derived from the French and means "supernatural" or "unexpectedly wonderful". The hybrid is a classic example of English breeding in that the entire lineage, with one exception, can be traced to commercial nurseries in Great Britain: Low, Sander's, McBean's, and Veitch. The French firm, Messieurs C Maron & Fils of Brunoy, intervened with Bc Mrs. J. Leemann in 1902.

"Rarely does one see such immense number of interesting orchids as are cultivated by Messrs. Stuart Low & Co., in their Bush Hill Park Nurseries, Enfield," writes a reporter for the Orchid World in 1913. *"Amateurs, of course, expect to see Colombian species, such as C mendelii, well represented, but here they may be seen in thousands, houses 100 feet in length being entirely devoted to their cultivation."* Low's was a prominent nursery in England for over a century and, even today, hobbyists are reminded of their importance wherever the 'Low' variety name is used such as Lc Callistoglossa 'Low' AM/AOS or Blc Norman's Bay 'Low' FCC/RHS.

Apparition made its way across the Atlantic where it was used as a stud plant by other growers besides Lenette including Joseph Redlinger of Homestead, Florida who bred Blc Memoria Judy Garland (x C Sonja Altenburg) in 1985. Another Florida nursery, Tom Ritter's Tropic 1 Orchids in Kissimmee, exhibited Apparition 'Sara' in 1966 and received a Highly Commended Certificate from the American Orchid Society. Once again, the judges raved about the coloring - *"Three large white flowers with petunia-purple lips, on one spike. Labellums edged in white. Flat flowers, well held."*

Blc Barbara Bush is the only First Lady hybrid to contain C quadricolor in the lineage. This Colombian species is rarely used in breeding for a number of reasons. Most obviously, the flowers remain 'cupped' on nearly all varieties. No other species does this. The buds begin opening just like a normal cattleya but then, for reasons unknown, never fully open. The flowers harden off in a half-open or bell-shaped position which makes it difficult to fully appreciate the beauty. In addition to having cupped flowers, the inflorescence often hangs downward, which leaves the viewer to crouch down in order to see inside.

Wild orchid collectors have traditionally passed up the opportunity to take native quadricolors from the trees due to their less than desirable characteris-

Colombians are proud of their C quadricolor and even issued a stamp to celebrate the species in 1947. Back then, it was called C chocoensis having come from the Choco region of the country. ARTHUR E. CHADWICK PHOTO

A number of fine semi-alba species can be found in the lineage of the Bush namesake including C trianaei. Shown is the historic stud, 'Snow', from the A. A. Chadwick collection. ARTHUR E. CHADWICK PHOTO

One of the most widely used hybrids in semi-alba cattleya breeding is C Enid alba (mossiae x warscewiczii), first made by Veitch in 1898. The Bush namesake is heavily influenced by C Enid. ARTHUR E. CHADWICK PHOTO

tics. Likewise, the cut flower industry wanted nothing to do with the species. As a result, there remain sizable populations of these cattleyas growing in the jungles while other species have gone practically extinct. Thus, the often ridiculed cupped flowers have turned out to be a survival mechanism.

For over 150 years, C quadricolor was called C chocoensis after the Choco region of Colombia. There is even a postage stamp from the country celebrating the species. Historical records show that the very first discoverers in 1849 used the name quadricolor after noticing the four shades in the throat – lavender, purple, yellow, and white. Early breeders were eager to make new hybrids and, despite its flaws, C quadricolor was a willing participant. The petals are wide and the four colors in the throat attractive. In addition, the flowers last nearly as long as the workhorse, C trianaei. By 1945, there were several dozen primary and early crosses using C quadricolor – including C Annette (x warscewicziii) in 1919.

The early Sander's hybrid registration books were particularly informative because they often listed the varieties of each parent. In the case of C Annette, the pod was held by C quadricolor alba and the pollen came from C warscewiczii 'Frau Melanie Beyrodt' or 'F.M.B.' The warscewiczii semi-alba stud is one of the most prolific breeder plants of all time but the C

The Bush namesake is the only First Lady cattleya to contain C quadricolor. Most breeders avoided this species due to the cupped nature of the flowers and the tendency to hang down. Shown is 'Alban'.

ARTHUR E. CHADWICK PHOTO

Lc Canhamiana (L purpurata x C mossiae) from 1885 was a widely used stud plant well into the 20th century. It even made the cover of Orchids magazine (then called the AOS Bulletin) in 1946. ARTHUR E. CHADWICK PHOTO

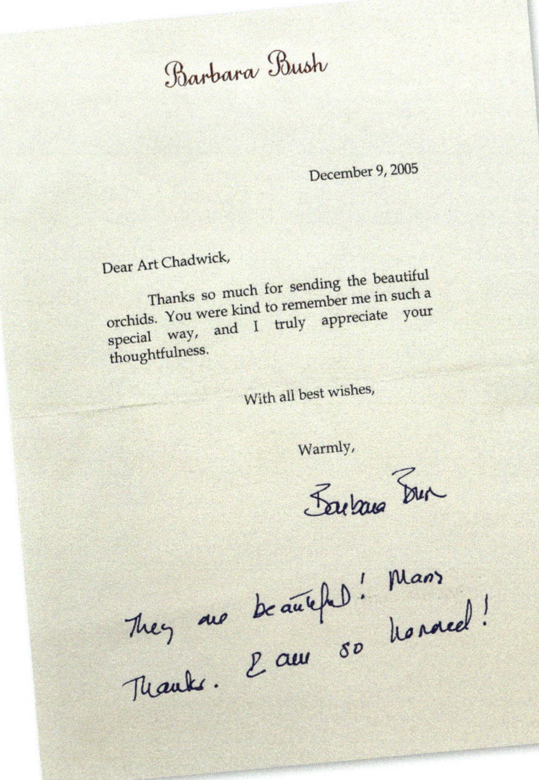

Barbara Bush

December 9, 2005

Dear Art Chadwick,

Thanks so much for sending the beautiful orchids. You were kind to remember me in such a special way, and I truly appreciate your thoughtfulness.

With all best wishes,

Warmly,

Barbara Bush

They are beautiful! Many Thanks. I am so honored!

Mrs. Bush sent us a lovely note in 2005 after we sent her a box of namesake flowers.
ARTHUR E. CHADWICK PHOTO

In 2005, Mrs. Bush spoke in Richmond for the Virginia Literacy Foundation. Coincidentally, her namesake orchid was about to bloom just thirty minutes away. COURTESY OF THE VIRGINIA LITERACY FOUNDATION

quadricolor was relatively new.

The only award of C Annette was a semi-alba in 1924 – given an FCC/MNEOS (Manchester and North of England Orchid Society). The judges wrote *"Four large white flowers, the labellum purple."* The next generation was wildly successful as Blc Nanette (C Annette x Everest) had dozens of registered offspring by 1960.

In 2005, Mrs. Bush was scheduled to appear in Richmond at the Virginia Literacy Foundation – an organization that she helped start while at the White House. As luck would have it, her namesake cattleya was happily growing just thirty minutes away at our Powhatan greenhouses and was about to bloom – a process that only happens once a year. Would the buds open in time for her arrival?

The answer was, sadly, no. The buds opened a few days after she left so we shipped a box of freshly cut Bush namesakes to her home in Houston, Texas. She responded immediately with a lovely hand-written note, *"They are beautiful. I am so honored!"*

About a decade later, Mrs. Bush and her daughter-in–law, Laura, were scheduled to appear in Austin, Texas at the Lyndon B. Johnson Presidential Library as part of the series "The Enduring Legacies of America's First Ladies." As luck would have it, her namesake cattleya was in glorious full bloom so we shipped a box of her namesake flowers directly to the event while I attended in the audience. There was discussion among the library staff about placing the flowers on stage with the two first ladies which would have really shown them off. Instead, the flowers were used to decorate the waiting room. Unforunately, the Bushes arrived with not a moment

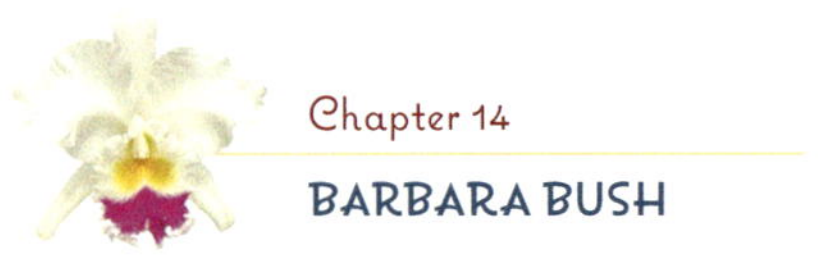

to spare and went straight on stage.

Alas, presenting cattleyas is not for the faint of heart.

Barbara Bush was First Lady of the United States from 1989 to 1993 and Second Lady of the United States from 1981 to 1989. Among her children are George W. Bush, the 43rd President of the United States and Jeb Bush, the 43rd Governor of Florida.

Barbara Pierce was born in New York City and grew up in Rye, New York. She met George H. W. Bush at the age of sixteen at a Christmas dance and they married three years later. They had six children. The Bushes lived in numerous cities around the country and even several years in China.

Mrs. Bush is the author of ten books including two for children - *C. Fred's Story* and *Millie's Book*. She passed away in 2018 at the age of 92. ✯

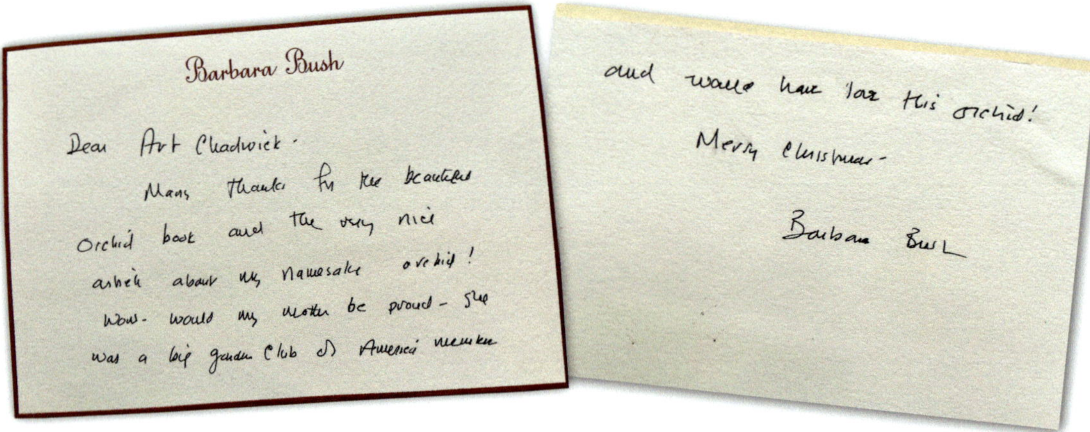

Barbara Bush

Dear Art Chadwick -
Many thanks for the beautiful orchid book and the very nice article about my namesake orchid! Wow - would my mother be proud - she was a big Garden Club of America member and would have loved this orchid!
Merry Christmas -

Barbara Bush

"My mother was a big Garden Club of America member and would have loved this orchid!" writes Barbara Bush in a second note to us after our article about her namesake hybrid appeared in Orchids *magazine.*

ARTHUR E. CHADWICK PHOTO

PERSONAL LIFE

Barbara Pierce was born in 1925 in Manhattan, NY and met her future husband at the age of 16. The pair became engaged right before he went to serve in World War II as a Navy pilot and were married upon his return. They have six children.

During her time as First Lady, she advocated for family literacy as her cause, and in her words, *"the most important issue we have"*. She received countless awards and honorary degrees. Mrs. Bush is one of two women in U.S. history to have been both a wife to and mother of a President. ✯

Barbara Bush was fond of flowers and was often seen with them.

PHOTO COURTESY OF
GEORGE H.W. BUSH PRESIDENTIAL LIBRARY

BLC BARBARA BUSH

(2004 Chadwick/Lenette)

COMPOSITION

Species	%
C warscewiczii	28%
C mossiae	25%
L purpurata	13%
C dowiana	9%
C trianaei	9%
C quadricolor	6%
C labiata	6%
B digbyana	3%

LINEAGE

1961 Lines
Lc Josephine Robinson

1949 Low
Blc Apparition

1956 Patterson
Lc Pegi Mayne

1950 McDade
Lc Cynthiana

1898 Veith
C Enid

1932 Low
Blc Nanette

Blc Hillary Rodham Clinton 'First Lady' HCC/AOS (Meditation x C Kittiwake) was bred by Carmela Orchids in 1993. It was awarded, cloned, and distributed throughout the United States.

ARTHUR E. CHADWICK PHOTO

HILLARY RODHAM CLINTON

★ ★ ★ ★ ★ ★ ★

Hillary Rodham Clinton was anything but a traditional First Lady. She was visible and outspoken with a resume that included being an attorney for the Children's Defense Fund and a professor of law at the University of Arkansas. She viewed politics as the *"art of making possible what appears impossible."*

Her husband, Bill, was the 42nd U.S. President, serving two terms from 1993 to 2001. In his first year of office, she chaired the Task Force on National Health Care Reform – a challenging position which brought her both praise and disdain. In 1996, she called on all Americans to collectively take responsibility for their children and published a book to that effect, *It Takes a Village*. By her husband's final year as President, she had moved her residence to New York and was running for the U.S. Senate.

In the fall of 1992, an unnamed cattleya seedling (Blc Meditation x C Kittiwake) was on a delivery truck en route to an upscale florist in Delaware. The buds had been wrapped in cotton for protection during the trip, but were now starting to open. The truck was being driven by A. A. Chadwick (Art Sr.), who took one look at the flowers and said, *"I'm keeping this one!"*

He enjoyed the flowers and suggested that we re-bloom the plant the following year. The timing coincided with the 1993 Eastern Orchid Congress which was held in Raleigh, North Carolina. We featured the semi-alba in our commercial display where it got the *Best Semi-Alba*

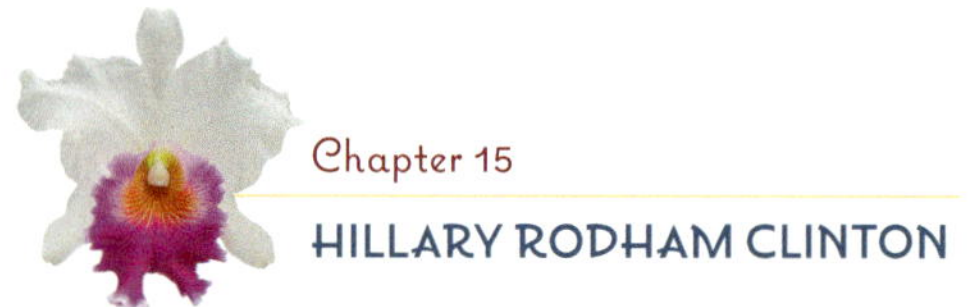

Cattleya in the show - no small feat given the dozens of exhibitors.

By now, we realized that this unnamed hybrid was very special so we contacted the breeder, Carmela Orchids, who graciously gave us permission to name the cross. At the time, the President of the United States was Bill Clinton and his wife, Hillary, had never had an orchid named after her. We (Art Sr. and Jr.) discussed the decades-old tradition of U.S. First Ladies having namesake cattleyas. Several of these women had actually been presented with the flowers. Perhaps we could not only name the hybrid after Mrs. Clinton, but also present it to her.

We set our sights on this lofty goal for the next time it would bloom - fall of 1994. Our exuberant letters to the White House were politely declined. Our senior U.S. Senator from Virginia, who was coincidentally an orchid client, followed up with a more official letter which was also turned down. Things were not looking good as the plant went in and out of bloom. The following year, however, through the efforts of the Lieutenant Governor of Virginia, we were given an opportunity.

In October 1995, the First Lady was scheduled to speak at the annual Kennedy-King dinner in Alexandria, Virginia. We were given front row seats to hear the slate of speakers, then ushered to a waiting room just before Mrs. Clinton took the stage. It was here that we experienced the bomb-sniffing dogs and the scrutiny of the Secret Service. Shortly after a thunderous applause from the stage (which sounded like a rock star was present), the door opened and in walked a long line of body guards followed by the First Lady.

Blc Hillary Rodham Clinton (Meditation x C Kittiwake) was bred by Carmela Orchids of Hakalau, Hawaii and named by Chadwick's. The company was founded by Yasugi Takasaki (right) and run by his sons, Gerritt (left) and Sheldon (center). COURTESY OF CARMELA ORCHIDS

In 1995, Art Chadwick Jr presented First Lady Hillary Clinton with her namesake cattleyas. The flowers were made into corsages, each with different colored ribbon. COURTESY OF THE WHITE HOUSE

We presented Mrs. Clinton with three flowers, each made into a fancy corsage with different colored ribbon. The First Lady was truly moved by our efforts and was focused as we explained the significance of the hybrid. She noticed that my wife was very pregnant and a discussion of baby names ensued. The meeting lasted only a few minutes but, according to her scheduler, this was quite a long period of time. Most "meet and greets" last a few seconds.

Gerritt Takasaki of Carmela Orchids is credited with making the cross, Blc Meditation x C Kittiwake, in the late 1980's. A small number of the seedlings were bloomed out at Carmela but most were sold to growers around the country. Gerritt could not have imagined that one of his hybrids would be in the hands of a First Lady.

Carmela Orchids was founded in 1960 in Hakalau, Hawaii by Yasuji Takasaki and his wife, Mitsuko. The company was named after their first daughter, Carmela, and all four of their children were involved in the business.

Mr. Takasaki had been a cultivation supervisor at a local sugar plantation in the mid 1940s and was dabbling with cut orchids as a side job. He purchased a planter box containing 90 Vanda Miss Joaquim for $800 from a friend. With the help of his family, he sought out to be *"the largest vanda grower in the territory of Hawaii."* By 1960, the company had three acres of Vanda Miss Joaquim production and *"picked 35,000 blossoms daily."*

The Clinton namesake is heavily influenced by C mossiae. Shown is a grouping of mostly C mossiae alba and semi-alba from the collection of J. Leemann, Esq., West Bank House, Heaton-Mersey, Lancashire circa 1913.

COURTESY OF THE ORCHID ALBUM

Sir Harry J. Veitch, F.L.S., V.M.H.
The Originator of the Royal Horticultural Society's Orchid Committee.

Sir Harry J. Veitch created the RHS Orchid Committee in 1889 as well as the Chelsea Flower Show. He was knighted in 1912. His company, James Veitch & Sons, made a number of primary hybrids found in Mrs. Clinton's cattleya. COURTESY OF THE ORCHID WORLD

By the end of the decade, Carmela Orchids was transitioning into potted plants. Mr. Takasaki purchased some cattleyas whose colorful flowers caught the attention of his two sons. The oldest son, Sheldon, graduated from the University of Hawaii with a degree in horticulture and became the company manager. The younger son, Gerritt, managed the tissue culture and seed germinating laboratory. Both sons traveled extensively to orchid shows throughout the U.S. and Japan putting in displays and selling at flower shows.

Over the years, Carmela Orchids built a reputation for high quality plants and offered hobbyists a chance to raise young seedlings from flasks and community pots. Their mail order catalogs contained pages of new and exciting cattleya and phalaenopsis crosses, many of which were shipped worldwide.

Blc Hillary Rodham Clinton has a long lineage dating back six generations and includes nine different cattleya species – predominately C dowiana, C warscewiczii, and C mossiae. Some of the earliest C warscewiczii primary hybrids from the late 1800s were influential including C Harold (x gaskelliana), C Hardyana (x dowiana), and C Enid (x mossiae). However, the best was yet to come.

The very next generation yielded a stunning semi-alba in 1912 called C Dionysius (Fabia x warscewiczii) as bred by wealthy hobbyist C. J. Phillips, Esq., of Sevenoaks estate. The "Glebe Collection", as it was called, was a relatively new venture and Mr. Phillips was acquiring a great many plants at auction houses and commercial firms. A reporter for *The Orchid World* wrote, *"The collection is fast assuming an important place in the history of Orchidology".*

Phillips was also making new hybrids in a wide range of genera, many of which were cattleyas. One entire greenhouse contained *"a large number of small pots filled with minute seedlings, mostly Cattleyas and Laelio-Cattleyas."* It takes years for seedlings to bloom and Phillips was investing heavily in the future.

The Royal Horticultural Society judges gave C Dionysius a First Class Certificate that year and noted that the varieties of the parents were C Fabia alba and C warscewiczii 'F. M. B.' The award painting by Nellie Roberts shows a flower with pure white sepals and petals and a rich magenta lip overlaid in classic dowiana gold veining. Superior parents increase the likelihood of outstanding results and Dionysius is a case in point.

C Dionysius plays into the first parent of the Clinton namesake, Blc Meditation (Bc Deesse x Lc Fedora) which was bred by Hawaiian backyard hybridizer, Bill Nishimoto in 1974. He gave the seed pod to commercial grower J. Milton Warne of Honolulu to germinate. Mr. Warne kept some seedlings to bloom out but sold many compots throughout the island. Blc Meditation became widely dispersed and was used extensively in breeding programs by other Hawaiian growers. Such well known plants as Blc Erin Kobayashi (x Blc Waikiki Gold), Blc Mahina Yahiro (x Bc Donna Kimura) and Blc Good News (x Lc Persepolis) were all bred in Hawaii using Blc Meditation as a parent. Over 100 offspring have been registered to date with Blc Meditation.

At first glance, the flower of Blc Meditation gives the appearance of being a large white with a classic oversized frilly 'brasso-type' lip. However, close inspection reveals a hint of purple in the very tip of the lip in many varieties. Thus, the hybrid was not a true alba which paved the way for some interesting white with colored lip breeding.

There has been speculation over the years about the Deesse variety that Nishimoto used

The French hybrid, Bc Deesse (Ferrieres x Lamartine) as bred by Vacherot & Lecoufle in 1947, imparts frilly lips into its offspring. Shown is 'Perfection' HCC/AOS. ARTHUR E. CHADWICK PHOTO

One parent of the Clinton namesake is Blc Meditation (Bc Deesse x Lc Fedora) from 1974 as bred by Bill Nishimoto. Shown is 'Silver Sword'. ARTHUR E. CHADWICK PHOTO

to make his famous Blc Meditation. Nishimoto has always claimed that he used '#47' which he acquired from Vacherot & Lecoufle via Beall Orchids in Washington State. Indeed, this variety was listed for sale in Alberts and Merkel Bros 1964-1965 catalog under the heading "Connoisseur Plants." Some islanders believe that he used variety 'Ranier' which looks similar.

Blc Meditation was wildly successful and remade many times by other growers. Sibling crosses of select varieties were also made. There are only two awards - 'King's Ransom' AM/AOS in 1983 and 'Lahaina Lipstick' AM/AOS in 1988. The most prized variety, 'Queen's Dowry', was never awarded, yet is considered to be the best breeder. Carmela used 'Queen's Dowry' to make Blc Hillary Rodham Clinton.

Bc Deesse is often given credit for the success of Blc Meditation, but the other parent, Lc Fedora, is also an impressive flower. Lc Fedora (Laguna x C Hardyana) was made in 1931 by Charlesworth & Company, Ltd, one of the great growers of England. World renowned for their Odontoglossum breeding, Charlesworth also pursued other genera including cattleyas and created such breakthroughs as Lc Luminosa, C Iris and Slc Anzac. Joseph Charlesworth started the company in 1880 in Heaton, Yorkshire, England (the same hometown as Art Sr.'s father).

The other parent of the Clinton namesake is C Kittiwake 'Brilliance' AM/ODC as bred by Armacost in 1948. ARTHUR E. CHADWICK PHOTO

Charlesworth bred three successive generations of semi-albas culminating in Lc Fedora with Lc Laguna in 1924, and C Tityus in 1912. In their 1933/34 catalog, Charlesworth offered several varieties of Lc Fedora for sale to the public including a rare albescens form for three pounds, three shillings.

The other parent of Blc Hillary Rodham Clinton is C Kittiwake (Brussels x Luegeae) which was bred by the California firm, Armacost & Royston in 1948. 'Arm-Roy' as they were called, was a massive operation in Los Angeles. Their monthly full page advertisements in the AOS Bulletin boasted the *Largest Breeders of Orchids in America.* They grew all genera, but cattleyas were their specialty.

Kittiwake was a valuable tetraploid stud plant at Armacost for decades. It was used to make such semi-alba classics as C Persepolis (x Pegi Mayne), C Ahmad Sheikhi (x Mem. Maggie Hood), and Blc Portage Glacier (x Bc Mount Hood). Kittiwake was never awarded by the American Orchid Society, but variety 'Brilliance' was given an Award of Merit by the Orchid Digest Corporation in 1962.

As late as 1979, Armacost was offering original divisions of C Kittiwake 'Brilliance' for $500 each. Their catalog glowingly described the plant as follows: *"Some orchids retail their worth because of their transcendent beauty. Some increase in worth as they are proven as breeders. C Kitti-*

C dowiana is often used in breeding to impart gold veining in the lips of the offspring. Shown is a fine variety from the late 1800's.

COURTESY OF THE ORCHID ALBUM

wake 'Brilliance' has both of these attributes and more…" Carmela used 'Brilliance' to make Blc Hillary Rodham Clinton.

Courtney Hackney's 2004 book, *"American Cattleyas: Species and Outstanding Hybrids that Define American Hybridizing"* praises C Kittiwake as well as one of its parents, C Luegeae. Charlesworth made C Luegeae in 1910 and it became a stud plant for dozens of hybrids for over half a century. The Orchid Digest Corporation recognized C Luegeae alba 'Fulfillment' with a Highly Commended Certificate after being exhibited by Roy Field in 1961.

The plant that was presented to Mrs. Clinton was given the variety name 'First Lady'. While the entire cross was high quality, there was one plant which stood out among the others. The radiant color of the lip is unique and the American Orchid Society judges described it as *"rose-purple, margins ruffled, picotee lilac, throat heavily veined saffron"* when they awarded a Highly Commended Certificate in 2005.

Variety 'First Lady' is a vigorous grower and blooms reliably every October with 2-4 large blossoms. The original plant has been split many times and there are divisions in private collections and on public display at The Smithsonian Gardens in Washington, DC.

C Fabia semi-alba (dowiana x labiata) from 1894 passes on its soft pastel lip and fall blooming time to the Clinton namesake. ARTHUR E. CHADWICK PHOTO

What will be remembered in the orchid world about Mrs. Clinton is the fact that she personally accepted her namesake cattleya – a nice gesture and a ceremony which was, at the time, rarely done. In addition, the best variety 'First Lady' was awarded by the American Orchid Society, cloned by the thousands and widely circulated among collectors – also a rarity. Lastly, the hybrid name includes her maiden name (Rodham) which is a first among First Ladies. ✯

A number of fine semi-alba C warscewiczii primaries can be found Blc Meditation including C Hardyana (x dowiana) from 1896.
ARTHUR E. CHADWICK PHOTO

The 1910 rarity, C Luegeae (dowiana x Enid) as bred by Charlesworth, is a true grandparent to Mrs. Clinton's hybrid. Shown is 'Fullfillment' HCC/ODC. ROY FIELD PHOTO

PERSONAL LIFE

Hillary Diane Rodham was born in 1947 in Chicago, Illinois. She met her future husband Bill Clinton while at Yale. Despite rejecting his proposals a handful of times, the pair was wed in 1975. They have one child, Chelsea.

During her time at the White House, she focused on healthcare reform - a difficult issue within the world of politics. While her plan was ultimately rejected, she did make progress. Hillary was very involved during her husband's Presidency, earning them the tongue and cheek title, "Billary".

Following her time as First Lady, Mrs. Clinton was a U.S. Senator of New York, U.S. Secretary State, and a U.S. Presidential candidate who won the popular vote. She is the author of numerous books. ✯

BLC HILLARY RODHAM CLINTON

(1993 Chadwick/Carmela)

COMPOSITION

- C dowiana 28%
- C warscewiczii 23%
- C mossiae 20%
- C gaskelliana 9%
- C trianaei 6%
- B digbyana 6%
- L purpurata 3%
- C labiata 2%
- C mendelii 2%

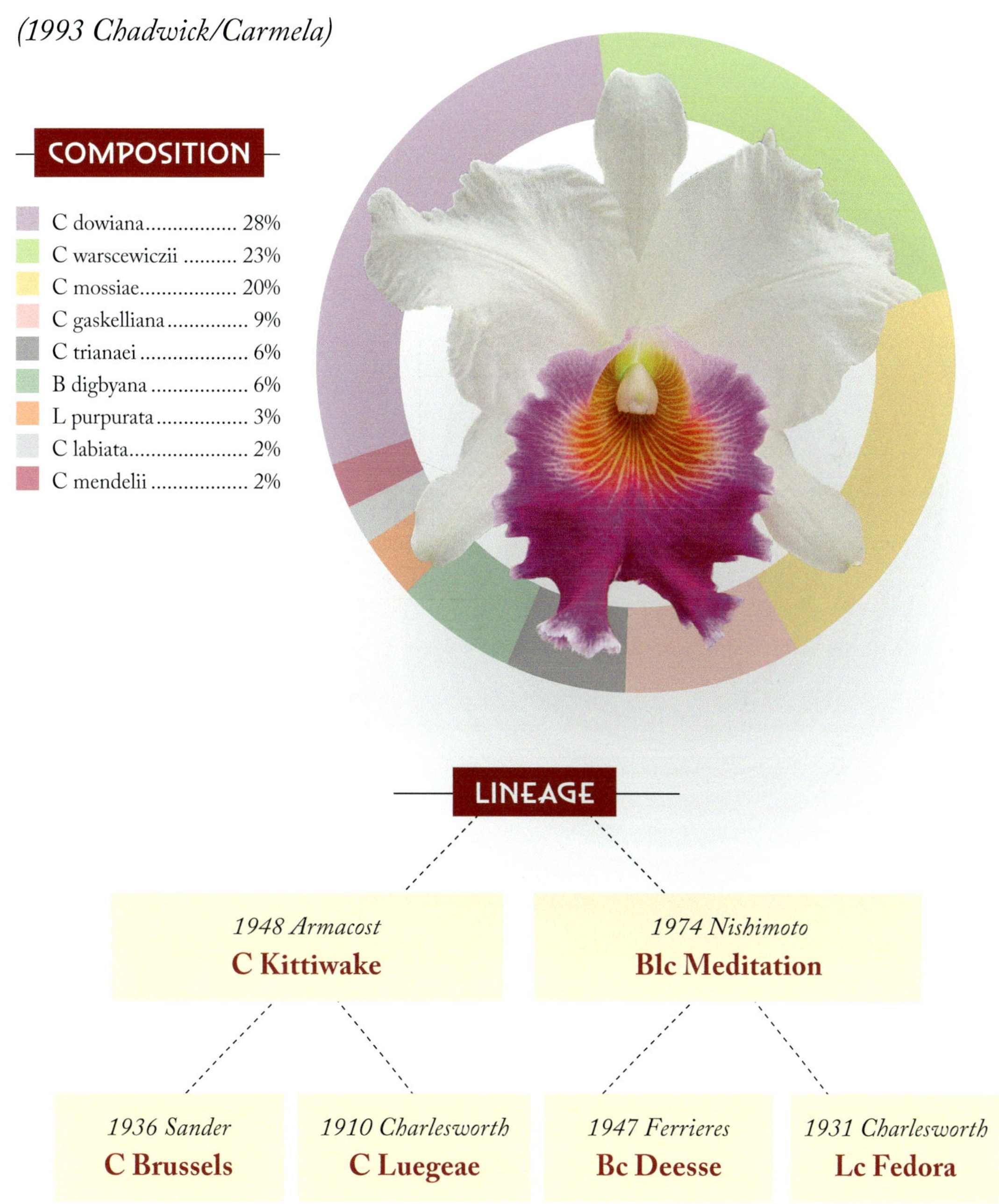

LINEAGE

1948 Armacost
C Kittiwake

1974 Nishimoto
Blc Meditation

1936 Sander
C Brussels

1910 Charlesworth
C Luegeae

1947 Ferrieres
Bc Deesse

1931 Charlesworth
Lc Fedora

Blc Laura Bush 'First Lady' AM/AOS (Good News x C walkeriana) has medium sized flowers with flared sepals and petals. It was given the flower quality award in 2013.

ARTHUR E. CHADWICK PHOTO

LAURA WELCH BUSH

★ ★ ★ ★ ★ ★ ★

"The lovely Laura Bush orchid is a centerpiece in our house!"
– Laura Bush 2016

The beginning of the 21st century brought the United States a new first lady, and with her, a new kind of cattleya.

Laura Welch Bush knew that she wanted to be a teacher since the 2nd grade. As a high school student, she read every chance she could. She earned an undergraduate degree in Education from Southern Methodist University and a graduate degree in Library Science from the University of Texas. Her first teaching job was at a public school in Dallas.

In 1977, Laura married George Walker Bush, the son of former Texas Congressman George H.W. Bush. She was not interested in politics and tried her best to avoid the spotlight.

After her husband became Governor of Texas in 1995, Mrs. Bush began promoting health, education, and literacy. She broadened these initiatives when he was elected the 43rd President of the United States. Her many accomplishments include organizing the National Book Festival and founding the Laura Bush Foundation for America's Libraries.

The cattleya named after Laura Bush is a departure from the big showy hybrids of the past

ABOVE PHOTO COURTESY OF THE WHITE HOUSE

and represents a trend in cattleya breeding toward smaller, more compact plants. Over most of the previous presidential administrations, the orchids named after U.S. First Ladies were the "classic" large flowered cattleyas - classic in that the blossoms measured 6-8" across and the foliage was upwards of 18" tall.

Blc Laura Bush (Good News x C walkeriana), however, is medium sized both in flowers and foliage thanks to the addition of the Brazilian species, C walkeriana as a parent. In its native country, this dwarf cattleya has countless color forms and varieties such that entire orchid shows are devoted to this one species.

The addition of C walkeriana as a parent gives the Bush namesake compact foliage compared to standard cattleyas. The species is native to Brazil.

ARTHUR E. CHADWICK PHOTO

When the collector, M. Gardener, first described Cattleya walkeriana in a 1843 *London Journal of Botany*, there was little doubt that it was a new species. It was so different in its flowering habit that it could not be mistaken for anything else. Unlike other cattleyas that bloom from the top of the pseudobulb, C walkeriana sends out a flowering stalk from the base of the previous pseudobulb which is unique in the orchid world.

Cattleya walkeriana was discovered by Gardener *"on the stem of a tree overhanging a small stream which falls into the Rio Sao Francisco, Brazil."* He named the orchid after Edward Walker who travelled with him and took care of the plants that were collected.

"The sight of huge clumps of C walkeriana, some in flower, perched on the very edge of the crevice and growing vigorously in the full morning sun with the magnificent cascading falls in the backdrop is a sight never to be forgotten" wrote explorer Jack Fowlie in his 1977 book, *The Brazilian Bifoliate Cattleyas and Their Color Varieties.* Indeed, C walkeriana is a magical plant when grown well and most hobbyists get their most vigorous bulbs when the rhizomes are mounted to slabs of bark or cork.

Cattleya walkeriana was such an unusual plant that it seems everyone wanted to describe it botanically. In 1847, John Lindley described a variation of C walkeriana as Cattleya bulbosa. Reichenbach described it as Epidendrum walkeriana when

C walkeriana likes to be on the dry side and grows best when mounted to bark slabs.

ARTHUR E. CHADWICK PHOTO

One of the earliest hybrids using C walkeriana is C Fitz Eugene Dixon (x Portia) from 1922 which was named after and bred by the second president of the American Orchid Society. Variety 'Ronaele' is his wife, Eleanor's, name spelled backwards. ARTHUR E. CHADWICK PHOTO

he was feverishly trying to redefine the genus Cattleya. He later changed it to Cattleya gardneriana in 1870 (Gard. Chron p 1473). Barbosa Rodrigues in his Genera et Species Novarum (vol. 1, pg.68 1877) called it Cattleya princeps. An array of botanical authorities from Rolfe, Veitch, and O'Brien in the UK to Du Boisson, Cogniaus, and Linden, however, stuck to the original name, Cattleya walkeriana, and all the rest faded away.

C walkeriana is shrouded in mystery for it is found living near two other species which look similar - C dolosa and C nobilor. To complicate matters, they all interbreed and natural hybrids can be found in the same general area. Thus, a real expert is often required to distinguish the true species, C walkeriana, from the many imposters.

One of the earliest hybrids using C walkeriana, C Fitz Eugene Dixon (x Portia), was bred by and named after the second President of the American Orchid Society in 1922. The hybrid is only half the height of its parent, C Portia, yet it still has clusters of medium-sized flowers. By the mid forties, there were over a dozen new hybrids registered with Walker's cattleya.

An important species in the lineage of Blc Good News is Laelia purpurata from Brazil. Shown is a fine variety from 1865 as painted by W. H. Fitch. COURTESY OF SELECT ORCHIDACEOUS PLANTS

It took breeders a long time to realize the true potential of C walkeriana. The fashion during the glamorous corsage days of the 40s, 50s, and 60s called for large flowered species such as Cattleya trianaei, mossiae, and labiata and plants with smaller blooms such as C walkeriana were relegated to novelty breeding.

As the orchid pot plant industry took hold of the U.S. in the 1970s, C walkeriana became more attractive. Since then, there have been hundreds of hybrids using C walkeriana and breeders show no sign of stopping. Some of the many popular crosses made using C walkeriana include Lc Love Knot (x L sincorama), Lc Mini Purple (x L pumila) and Bc Little Mermaid (x Maikai). C walkeriana has such good shape that there have been nearly one hundred AOS flower quality awards.

In its native country of Brazil, C walkeriana has two flowering seasons: March to May and October to December. The plant is noted for its dwarf foliage with pseudobulbs measuring only 2-6 inches high. The blossoms, on the other hand, are typically 4 ½ inches wide. The combination of small leaves, medium-sized flowers, and twice a year blooming has made C walkeriana an attractive choice for modern breeders whose clients have small growing areas.

Growers are advised to keep this species on the dry side as plants tend to rot with over-watering. As a result, a bark mix or mounting is recommended. C walkeriana has the reputation of being a 'shy bloomer' in that the conditions have to be quite favorable in order to get blossoms.

The other parent of the Bush namesake is Blc Good News (Lc Persepolis x Meditation) which was bred in 1988 by Carmela Orchids of Hakalau, Hawaii. Good News is a complex hybrid, containing ten species over six generations.

Some varieties of Blc Good News have prominent purple flares on the petals – a trait which can be traced to its parent, Lc Persepolis, and possibly all the way back to the species. C trianaei, C mossiae, and C gaskelliana are all known to have fine varieties with flaring on the sepals and petals and can be found in the lineage of Good News.

There have been four awarded varieties of Blc Good News including 'Hawaii' AM/AOS, which was exhibited by Carmela's at the Greater New York Orchid Society Show. Imagine the difficulty in shipping a fragile blooming cattleya from Hawaii to New York and have it arrive unblemished and ready to be inspected by a panel of judges. In addition, the plant had to compete with the thousands of other entries in the orchid show.

One of the interesting traits of Blc Good News is that there are varieties which bloom any time of the year. The four AOS awards were from April, July, September, and November.

The other parent of the Bush namesake is Blc Good News (Lc Persepolis x Meditation) from 1988 as bred by Carmela Orchids in Hakalau, Hawaii. Some varieties have flaring on the sepals and petals.

ARTHUR E. CHADWICK PHOTO

An important species in the lineage of Good News is Laelia purpurata which was described as *"one of the finest orchids in cultivation"* in1865 by Benjamin S. Williams, author of the Orchid Grower's Manual. When first introduced in England a decade earlier by Messrs. Backhouse and Son, of York, small plants of L purpurata sold for 25 guineas each. Soon, however, large quantities were imported by Messrs. Low, Veitch, and others and the price dropped to just a fraction of the original.

L. purpurata became *"a conspicuous feature in almost every mixed collection of orchids brought to our exhibitions"* says Williams. Even still, no two plants were alike which kept interest high. Given the large colorful blooms and tall foliage, L purpurata was widely grown for exhibition purposes and mature specimens could produce 40 to 50 flowers at a time. Clever growers could even stagger the blooms over a three month period – May, June, and July – if they owned early, mid-season, and late varieties.

Back then, guidelines for successfully importing L purpurata from Brazil were distributed to collectors which included shipping the plants after they had finished their new growths so that the bulbs wouldn't rot in transit. Upon arrival, *"they should be potted in small pots, each plant separately with a little moist moss and crocks and this will induce them to root."* We regularly use sphagnum moss and small clay pots when potting cattleyas at Chadwick's 150 years later.

Carmela bred Good News using the classic semi-alba stud, Lc Persepolis 'Splendor' AM/AOS (C Kittiwake x Pegi Mayne), which was made by Armacost in 1973. Armacost exhibited their Persepolis the following year where it just missed getting a First Class Certificate and was described as having *"sepals porcelain white; lip solid cerise with white edging and yellow striping in the throat."*

Armacost named the hybrid at the request of a wealthy Iranian client. The name, Persepolis, is the ancient capital of Persia and imposing ruins can still be found in Southern Iran.

One parent of Good News is Lc Persepolis 'Splendor' AM/AOS as bred by Armacost in 1973. It was widely used as a stud for semi-albas. ARTHUR E. CHADWICK PHOTO

C mossiae 'Ed Patterson' AM/AOS is a widely used stud plant from the 1960s that has distinct flaring on the sepals and petals. This species appears in the lineage of the Bush namesake.

ARTHUR E. CHADWICK PHOTO

C trianaei 'Splash' is a jungle plant from Colombia that has prominent flares on the petals. Fine varieties of this species can be found in the lineage of Blc Laura Bush and may contribute to the starburst look of the first lady cattleya. ARTHUR E. CHADWICK PHOTO

Carmela combined Persepolis with the classic Hawaiian stud, Blc Meditation (Bc Deesse x Lc Fedora) to make Good News. Most varieties of Meditation are pure white but variety 'Queen's Dowry' has a hint of purple in the throat and is known to breed semi-albas. 'Queen's Dowry' was used to make Good News.

Gerritt Takasaka of Carmela Orchids is credited with making the cross, Blc Good News x C walkeriana, in the 1990s. Carmela has a long history of breeding fine cattleya hybrids such as Blc Joann Yukimura, Blc Cornerstone, and Mem Anna Balmores.

The legendary founder of Carmela Orchids, Yasuji Takasaki, passed away in 2011 at age 95. Well into his 90s, he continued to work with the plants in his nursery and attend local orchid society events. At one meeting, he demonstrated the rigorous exercise program that enabled him to stay so fit. The Hilo Orchid Society honored Yasuji by naming a scholarship fund to the University of Hawaii after him.

It was a thrill at Chadwick's to bloom the seedlings from the then un-named cross, Blc Good News x C walkeriana. The flowers are all semi-albas but we were really taken by the occasional "starburst" pattern or purple flaring radiating along the petals and sepals. It gave the blossoms a "patriotic" look which seemed appropriate for the sitting first lady, Laura Bush, whose

Some of the Bush varieties have heavy flares in the sepals and petals including '#10'.

ARTHUR E. CHADWICK PHOTO

Mrs. Bush proudly accepted her namesake cattleya in 2006 at the United States Botanical Garden during the First Ladies Luncheon with the wives of U.S. Senators. COURTESY OF THE WHITE HOUSE

husband had been President during the tragic 9/11 events. Carmela kindly gave us permission to name the hybrid.

As the seedlings bloomed, we took note of the coloration. The degree of magenta flaring ranged from barely noticeable to heavy splashes on the sepals and petals. We set aside the very best variety and called it 'First Lady'.

Like the parent, C walkeriana, some of the Laura Bush seedlings bloom twice a year. It is obvious which plants took after the taller growing Good News and which stayed small like C walkeriana. In all cases, the flowers lasted a month or more and the flower count was 1-2 blossoms.

Each year in Washington, DC, there is a social event called the First Lady's Luncheon, in which spouses of the U.S. Senators have lunch with the sitting First Lady. In 2006, the United States Botanic Garden (USBG) hosted the event and the Executive Director, Holly Shimuzu, called us to see if we had any of the recently named Laura Bush seedlings in bloom.

Indeed, we did have one plant – a semi-alba with no flaring and I personally drove to Washington and left it with the garden staff. One of the nice things about having our nursery located in Richmond, Virginia is the close proximity to our Nation's Capital. The special cattleya was presented in a fancy bowl with small white phalaenopsis as accent plants and an engraved botanical nameplate. As can be seen from the photograph, Mrs. Bush is thrilled.

In 2013, we exhibited the very best Laura Bush seedling, 'First Lady', at an American Orchid Society judging event and it was given an Award of Merit. The breeder also got an award

for their 'Carmela' AM/AOS variety the previous year. It is always exciting when a First Lady hybrid is recognized by the horticultural authority.

As soon as we received the award for 'First Lady', we contacted Mrs. Bush's office with the fantastic news and offered to send her one of the namesake orchids. She was delighted and wrote us an appreciative note, *"Thank you for sending the lovely Laura Bush orchid to me. And congratulations on the prize it was awarded! George and I enjoyed its beautiful blooms here in our house in Dallas."* In addition, she emailed us a photo of her holding the blooming orchid.

Several years later, I had the pleasure of speaking to Mrs. Bush's garden club in Dallas. She was seated in the front and added insightful comments to the program. In one funny instance, she expressed a desire to have the best selling First Lady orchid hybrid of all time.

I joined her for lunch at the speaker's table and she couldn't have been friendlier. Then it was time for pictures. The Dallas Orchid Society kindly lent some showy cattleya plants for the event and Mrs. Bush posed so gracefully for all the shots.

Her love and knowledge of flowers cannot be overstated. While at 1600 Pennsylvania Avenue, she was a frequent visitor to the United States Botanical Garden, often with her family or garden club. She gave the ribbon cutting speech for the new National Garden in Washington.

Mrs. Bush is a longtime supporter of the Lady Bird Johnson Wildflower Center, founder of the conservation group, Texas by Nature, and is an honorary co-chair of the National Park Service's Centennial Celebration with Michelle Obama. Visitors to the George W. Bush Presidential Center can also enjoy her Urban Park, a 15 acre site filled with native prairie grasses and wildflowers. ☆

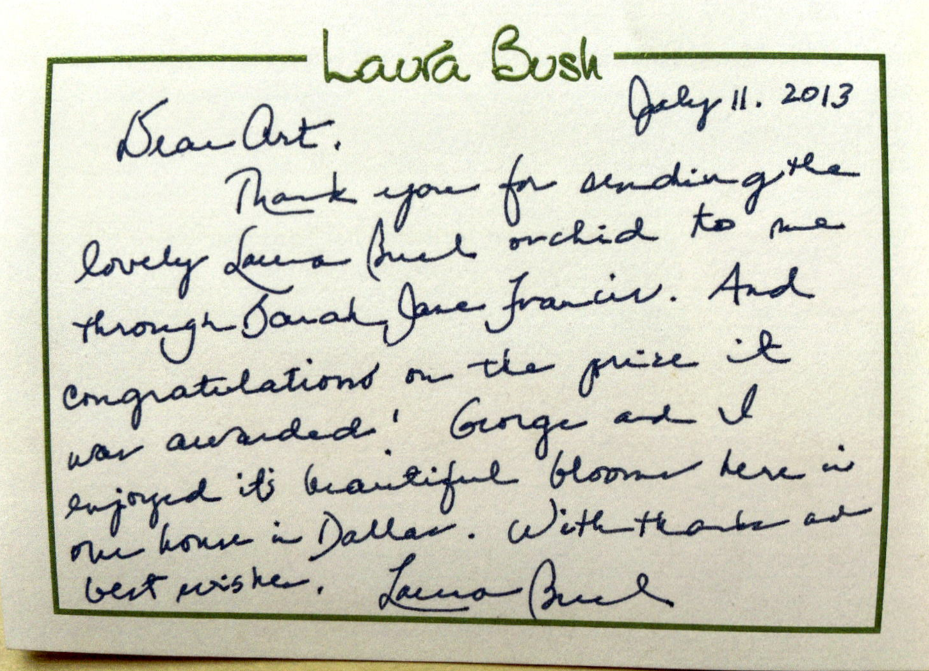

Laura Bush

July 11. 2013

Dear Art,

Thank you for sending the lovely Laura Bush orchid to me through Sarah Jane Francis. And congratulations on the prize it was awarded! George and I enjoyed its beautiful blooms here in our house in Dallas. With thanks and best wishes,

Laura Bush

Mrs. Bush wrote us a nice thank you letter after her namesake cattleya got an AOS award.

ARTHUR E. CHADWICK PHOTO

Following Art Chadwick's presentation to the Dallas Garden Club in 2016, Mrs. Bush posed for photographs with cattleya plants on loan from the Dallas Orchid Society. COURTESY OF LAURA BUSH

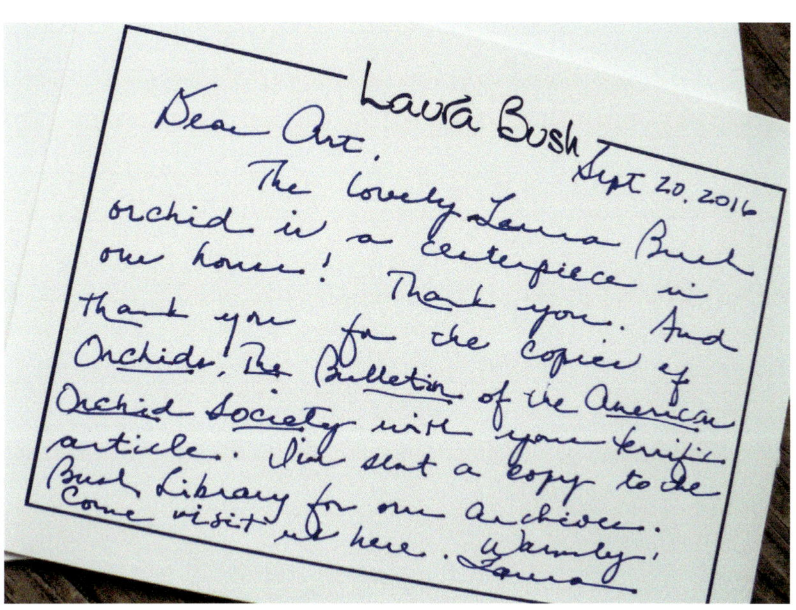

Laura Bush

Dear Art, Sept 20, 2016

The lovely Laura Bush orchid is a centerpiece in our house! Thank you. And thank you for the copies of Orchids, The Bulletin of the American Orchid Society with your terrific article. I've sent a copy to the Bush Library for our archives. Come visit us here. Warmly, Laura

Mrs. Bush wrote us a second letter after receiving a copy of Orchids *magazine with the article about her namesake cattleya.* ARTHUR E. CHADWICK PHOTO

PERSONAL LIFE

Laura Lane Welch was born in 1946 in Midland, Texas.

She and her husband have twin daughters - Jenna and Barbara. Prior to being First Lady of the United States, she was First Lady of Texas.

Mrs. Bush bears an extensive list of honors, accolades, and honorary degrees for her commitment to her worthy causes. In 2018, she received the Garden Club of America's Achievement Medal for her work "protecting our environment and national resources and her accomplishments in the fields of conservation, historic preservation, and civic improvement." ✯

Mrs. Bush holds her namesake cattleya at her home in Dallas shortly after it was awarded by the American Orchid Society.

COURTESY OF LAURA BUSH

BLC LAURA BUSH

(2002 Chadwick/Carmela)

COMPOSITION

Species	%
C walkeriana	50%
C dowiana	13%
C warscewiczii	12%
C trianaei	7%
C mossiae	6%
B digbyana	3%
C gaskelliana	3%
C labiata	3%
L purpurata	2%
C mendelii	1%

LINEAGE

1988 Carmela
Blc Good News

C walkeriana

1973 Armacost
Lc Persepolis

1974 Nishimoto
Blc Mediation

Lc Michelle Obama (Mini Purple x C trianaei) is a long lasting miniature that blooms in a spectrum of lavender hues.

ARTHUR E. CHADWICK PHOTO

Mrs. Obama is a gardening enthusiast and wrote a book about the subject while at the White House.

PHOTO COURTESY OF ALAMY

MICHELLE OBAMA

★ ★ ★ ★ ★ ★ ★

Michelle LaVaughn Robinson grew up on the South Side of Chicago and graduated from Princeton and Harvard Law School before meeting Barack Obama at her first full time job. She balanced her role as First Lady with raising two children, who were only 7 and 10 when her husband was elected.

She took on many causes during President Obama's eight years in office, including poverty awareness and supporting military families. Her passion, however, was fighting the relatively new problem of childhood obesity. To this effect, she promoted physical activity and healthy eating with a program called "Let's Move" which was *"about putting children on the path to a healthy future during their earliest months and years."* She appealed to elected officials, food manufacturers, and restaurant chains to make healthy food more accessible.

Her interest in horticulture was best exemplified by her 2012 book, *American Grown – the Story of the White House Kitchen*, which chronicled the vegetable, fruit, and herb garden that she planted in the White House's South Lawn. The Obama State Dinners emphasized domestically sourced flowers and often featured cut cattleyas and sprays of cymbidiums and phalaenopsis.

Mrs. Obama is the 17th consecutive first lady to have a cattleya named after her. We bred the compact hybrid, Lc Michelle Obama (Mini Purple x C trianaei) and presented the flowers to her in 2008 at Norfolk, Virginia's Harrison Opera House. She was campaigning for her

ABOVE PHOTO COURTESY OF MICHELLE OBAMA

Chapter 17

MICHELLE OBAMA

Mrs. Obama received her namesake cattleya in 2008 at the Harrison Opera House in Norfolk, Virginia. A grouping of five showy plants was supposed to be presented but the Secret Service allowed only two flowers. COURTESY OF MICHELLE OBAMA

One of the best varieties of Michelle Obama is this lovely shell pink. ARTHUR E. CHADWICK PHOTO

Masao Yamada used the diminutive species, Laelia pumila, in much of his breeding including his signature hybrid, Lc Mini Purple (x C walkeriana). Shown is a specimen, 'Tamara'. BAYARD SARADUKE PHOTO

husband and met us beforehand at a private reception. There were numerous politicians in attendance including the sitting governor of Virginia, Tim Kaine, who had previously presented Queen Elizabeth II with her namesake hybrid that we developed, when she visited Richmond in 2007.

Lc Michelle Obama is primarily a fall bloomer and we had five plants in flower on the day of her arrival. We displayed the cattleyas in a large bowl which turned heads as we walked through the crowded hallway of the opera house. It soon became obvious, however, that the Secret Service was not as excited about the orchids as we were.

Security was tight for the event and every attendee had to be screened. The orchid arrangement was, apparently, suspicious and required special bomb detecting equipment to be allowed into the reception. Unbelievably, the security team forgot to pack the equipment and, for a while, it looked as if there would be no presentation. As time grew near and after lengthy negotiations with the agents, I was allowed to pick two flowers from the arrangement for use in the presentation. This was not exactly the high impact statement that we were looking for.

Accompanying the now meager floral offering was the official RHS Certificate of Registration - framed, of course. Mrs. Obama was unaware of the preshow drama and was genuinely excited to receive her special orchid. We did the "Obama Bump" with our fists and she even held my hand during the photograph. She is almost as tall as I am.

The Obama namesake orchid was made possible by the breeding efforts of Reverend Masao Yamada, who hybridized one of the parents, Lc Mini Purple in 1965.

The Mini Purple parent was bred by the legendary Masao Yamada in Hawaii. He specialized in miniatures and used species like C luteola and L pumila which, at the time, were being overlooked.

COURTESY OF THE HONOLULU ORCHID SOCIETY

Yamada was born in 1907 on the Hawaiian island of Kauai. He was a practicing minister there when World War II began. He soon enlisted in the Army, where he became the first American of Japanese Ancestry (AJA) to be commissioned a chaplain. At the time, the United States was forcibly relocating many Japanese-Americans to interior camps.

In 1944, as part of the 442nd Battalion, he was sent to Europe where, among other things, he ministered to hundreds of wounded men.

Author Michael Markrich, in his book, *Combat Chaplain: The Personal Story of the World War II Chaplain of the Japanese American 100th Battalion* writes that upon Yamada's return to Hawaii after the war, he *"gained recognition in the orchid world as both a grower and for his advanced breeding techniques."* Yamada was quite active in the local orchid societies and regularly gave lectures throughout the islands. Aside from cattleyas, he was versed on a wide range of genera including

One of the earliest Laelia pumila hybrids is depicted in the Orchid Album – Lc Blesensis (x C loddigesii) of 1892.

COURTESY OF THE ORCHID ALBUM

dendrobiums and vandas.

Always eager to educate, Yamada took his orchid knowledge internationally and became involved in the World Orchid Conferences. He spoke at both the 2nd WOC in Honolulu, Hawaii and the 5th WOC in Long Beach, California and wrote extensively about his travels to the 7th WOC in Medellin, Colombia in 1972, where he was responsible for putting together the Hawaiian grower exhibit. The highlight for him was the two day jungle tour to see Cattleya mendelii, which involved a harrowing canoe ride and climbing up 6,000 feet *"where it was hard to breathe."*

Legendary grower, Roy Tukunga, remembers meeting Yamada in the early 70s. *"My mentor, Dr. Yoneo Sagawa, took me and a few students on a field trip to meet the famous Reverend Yamada. He was retired and was working on miniature and compact cattleyas. Everyone was ignoring the smaller species."*

Over his lifetime, Masao Yamada originated hundreds of hybrids. Much of his breeding involved miniature cattleyas and he was particularly fond of the diminutive species, C luteola which he used to make hybrids such as C Mini Alabaster (x C Enid). He also had considerable success using another dwarf species, Laelia flava and, in 1963, registered Lc Rosemary Clooney (x C Rainbow Hill), which received a number of flower quality awards and became widely circulated.

Few hobbyists do their own flasking, let alone create a custom germination medium - but Yamada did both. His "Yamada Formula" became known throughout Hawaii and combined Gaviota orchid fertilizer, white granulated sugar, peptone, agar, Clorox, tomato juice, coconut water, and half-ripe bananas.

Arguably, his greatest accomplishment was the creation of Lc Mini Purple (L pumila x C

Yamada also used other lesser known species such as C luteola to breed his miniatures.

ARTHUR E. CHADWICK PHOTO

walkeriana).

Hobbyists everywhere know of the cute little cattleya which makes a purple flower or two and always seems to be in bloom. H & R Nurseries grew several varieties of Mini Purple over the years including 'Lea' AM/AOS in the 80s. *"The seedlings easily broke in multiple directions. As fast as you could put on a new growth, a flower would appear"*, recalls Tukunga.

Lc Mini Purple is one of the most heavily awarded primary hybrids of all time with dozens of AOS flower quality awards, particularly in the 1990s, as miniatures became popular. There is even a cultural award for 'Lea' CCM/AOS which boasted 15 flowers. The Mini Purple cross has been remade many times using different varieties of the parents.

One interesting direction that breeders have taken is remaking Mini Purple as a coerulea. H & R Nurseries cloned two blue varieties, 'H&R' and 'Blue Hawaii' AM/AOS which can be found in many collections today.

Lc Mini Purple is still a widely used stud plant with hundreds of registered hybrids. Blc Rosebud (x Ronald Hausermann) and Lc Secret Love (x Candy Tuft) are industry staples for

The Obama namesake usually produces one to three flowers but this variety made five. ARTHUR E. CHADWICK PHOTO

One parent of the Obama namesake is the popular, Lc Mini Purple (L pumila x C walkeriana), from 1965. The plant is often grown in a basket. Shown is 'Summit Rose'. KEITH DAVIS PHOTO

Lc Mini Purple is commonly found in collections today as a coerulea. Shown is 'Blue Hawaii' AM/AOS. ARTHUR E. CHADWICK PHOTO

Hawaiian growers and hobbyists continue to be drawn to small plants, which are easy to grow and can bloom twice a year.

Over the years, much has been written about Cattleya walkeriana, which played a major role in an earlier first lady hybrid, Blc Laura Bush (x Good News). Laelia pumila, however, is lesser known.

The species flowered for the first time in Europe in 1838, in a collection belonging to Englishman John Allcard. He had received specimens from British Guyana. Allcard had a drawing made of a plant in bloom and sent it to the leading botanist Sir William Hooker, who classified it as a new cattleya species. The given name was pumila from the Latin 'pumilus' meaning small, not apparent. It was then published in Hooker's *Botanical Magazine* in 1839.

Meanwhile, it became known that the plant was actually native to Brazil, not British Guyana, and it had been discovered several years earlier by Dr Gardner near Rio De Janeiro. None of this information made it to France, however, and, in 1842, plants arrived in Paris where a well versed collector, Morel, assigned the name, Cattleya marginata.

A decade later, Reichenbach moved the species to the Laelia genus and completed the unfinished description by Hooker – now over 700 words long.

Laelia pumila was first recognized by the American Orchid Society judges in 1963 and, since then, has had over 60 AOS awards. The most famous variety, 'Black Diamond' HCC/AOS, garnered a culture award in 2006 when it carried an astonishing 38 flowers and 31 buds. Many of the awarded varieties, however, have only one flower.

The first L pumila hybrids were made in the late 1800s and crafted by the big names of the day: Charlesworth, Veitch, Low, Sander, Cookson, Black & Flory, Maron, Pitt, Roebling, and McBean. Since that time, hundreds of different hybrids have been created as modern breeders try for compact plants.

Lc Mini Purple is, by far, the most decorated of all the L pumila crosses, but there have been other successes. Sl Orpetii (x coccinea) in 1901 and Slc Pink Doll (x Tangerine Jewel) in 1983 are two examples of heavily awarded progeny.

The idea of combining Lc Mini Purple with a large flowered cattleya species is a relatively new concept. The desired result is a larger Mini Purple with, perhaps, two to three flowers instead of just one. In the past twenty five years, we have seen Mini Purple bred with C warscewiczii, C mendelii, L tenebrosa, C lueddemanniana, C jenmanii, C maxima, C labiata, L purpurata, and C warneri. Missing, of course, is C trianaei.

How could breeders have missed using C trianaei? The thought of using this species is as old as hybridizing itself. Nearly a thousand different crosses have been made using the National Flower of Colombia. Not only is the shape of the flowers better than all other cattleya species, but the blossoms last an incredible six weeks.

Despite its great traits, C trianaei was not always in favor as a parent. Back in 1916, *The Orchid World* noted that *"it has comparatively weak color, oftentimes thinness of the sepals and petals,*

The early imported cattleya species, such as C trianaei, were grown by wealthy collectors in large greenhouses. Shown is part of the Blenheim Palace Collection as owned by the Duke of Marlborough in 1911.

COURTESY OF THE ORCHID WORLD

C trianaei 'Powhatan' is a well shaped, intensely colored variety and was used to make Lc Michelle Obama.
ARTHUR E. CHADWICK PHOTO

and rarely more than one flower on a stem." While all of this is still true, the first two points are not necessarily negatives. The soft pastel shades of C trianaei can be an asset and there are certainly fine pure white and semi-alba color forms. Thin texture has been found to not have a negative effect on flower longevity as this species lasts longer than all others. The low flower count can be a problem, however.

One of C trianaei's greatest virtues is its flower variability for there are literally an infinite number of possibilities in the wild. Consul F C Lehmann visited Colombia and reported to *Gardener's Chronicle* in 1883, *"Of the many hundreds of plants which were seen in bloom, I was unable to select two that had flowers of equal size and color, so great was the variation."* This trait was especially important during the cut flower era when no two women wanted to wear the same looking corsage.

An often overlooked asset of C trianaei is its vigor. *"No matter how small may be the back-bulb*

C trianaei is the National Flower of Colombia and blooms in the widest range of colors of any cattleya species. Shown is a typical variety, potted to illustrate size. ARTHUR E. CHADWICK PHOTO

that is severed from the plant, it quickly commences to make a new growth and rapidly increases in size" wrote *The Orchid World* in 1914. We found that using C trianaei as a parent in the Obama namesake yielded strong seedlings.

It was fascinating to watch the Michelle Obama seedlings mature. Some plants took after the pumila parent and stayed small (less that 10") while others approached medium size (up to 18"). None grew as tall as the trianaei parent.

We were particularly interested in those seedlings which broke multiple leads, as Roy Tukunga talked about, since these would give the biggest floral display. In most cases, the Obama namesake reaches maturity in a 3" pot.

With cattleya seedlings, it is not always easy to compare the flowers of multiple varieties side by side because the plants often bloom at different times and are, generally, short-lived. The Obama offspring, however, consistently last six weeks and mostly bloom in the fall so large groups of plants can be examined next to one another.

Neither Mini Purple nor C trianaei have many flowers, so it is not surprising that Michelle Obama tops out at three blossoms per stem. Most varieties produce one or two.

As expected, we saw the entire spectrum of lavender hues in the Obama seedlings since the parent, C trianaei, has the widest range of colors of all the naturally occurring cattleyas. We personally found the pale varieties to be the most attractive.

C walkeriana blooms in a range of lavenders including this very dark variety. In all cases, the plants are compact which lend them nicely to miniature breeding. KEN REYNOLDS PHOTO

The lip color also varied – with hues ranging from light to medium to dark purple with a white or yellow suffusion. Some were solid, others veined, or marbled.

It was a joy to create Mrs. Obama's hybrid, bloom the seedlings, and make a personal presentation. The flowers have been photographed, painted, and written about by admirers. It has also been rewarding to see other breeders remake the cross in just the short time since it was registered. ✯

Much has been written about C walkeriana whose semi-alba form was a parent in the First Lady hybrid, Blc Laura Bush (x Good News). In the case of Michelle Obama, walkeriana is a lavender grandparent. KEN REYNOLDS PHOTO

PERSONAL LIFE

As the first African-American First Lady of the United States, Mrs. Obama became a role model for young Black girls everywhere. She was able to maintain a private family life as "mom-in-chief" while still doing important duties as the President's wife. Her earliest initiatives were focused on improving the lives of children.

Mrs. Obama had a likeable social media presence that endeared her to millions and made a fashion statement with her sleeveless dresses. She also promoted exercise as a way to be glamorous and healthy. Even today, she maintains high marks with the public. ✯

LC MICHELLE OBAMA

(2008 Chadwick)

COMPOSITION

- C trianaei 50%
- C walkeriana 25%
- L pumila 25%

LINEAGE

1965 Yamada
Lc Mini Purple

C trianaei

L pumila

C walkeriana

Blc Melania Trump 'First Lady' received a Highly Commended Certificate from the American Orchid Society in 2018. The judges described the flowers as having orange-pink sepals and lavender-pink petals.

ARTHUR E. CHADWICK PHOTO

MELANIA TRUMP

★ ★ ★ ★ ★ ★ ★

"The President joins me in sending our best wishes for your continued success in sharing the magnificence of your exquisite flowers with your community and our Nation."

– Melania Trump 2018, Letter to Art

Melania Knauss Trump is the wife of the 45th United States President. Prior to marrying Donald J. Trump in 2005, she was a successful model working with major fashion houses in Milan and Paris and later appearing on the covers of dozens of magazines including *Vogue*, *Vanity Fair*, and *Glamour*. She also had her own watch and jewelry line.

The former Melanija Knavs was born in Slovenia (formerly Yugoslavia) where her mother was a fashion designer. She moved to New York City in 1996 and became a naturalized U.S. citizen in 2006. Over the years, she has been active in the American Red Cross as well as the American Heart Association.

In her role as First Lady, Mrs. Trump focused on the many issues affecting children. She launched BE BEST – an awareness campaign to encourage wellness, offset the negative effects of social media, and help to reduce opioid abuse.

One of the benefits of being associated with this First Lady project is that everyone goes

ABOVE PHOTO COURTESY ALMAY/MEDIAPUNCH

Trump Chef Stephen Kotarski took two blooming Melania plants back to the White House where they waited two weeks for the scheduled meeting. The purple one folded but Mrs. Trump was photographed with the orange-lavender-pink one.

COURTESY OF STEPHEN KOTARSKI

Our first attempt to present the Melania flowers was made in 2018 through Congressman Dave Brat. COURTESY OF DAVE BRAT

Our second attempt to present the Melania flowers was made in 2019 through Trump chef, Stephen Kotarski, who just happens to be an orchid aficionado. COURTESY OF STEPHEN KOTARSKI

out of their way to help the cause. No sooner had Mr. Trump been elected, than our clients began offering their connections in Washington and a streamlined way to give the new First Lady her namesake orchid.

In early 2018, one of the Trump seedlings received a prestigious flower quality award from the American Orchid Society. The Highly Commended Certificate or HCC/AOS designation moved the cattleya into an exclusive club of honored First Lady hybrids. Only seven other namesakes have been given similar accolades.

The fall of 2018 brought fresh political momentum to the project when our local Virginia congressman got involved. House member Dave Brat was so impressed with the Trump orchid that he sent a staffer to the White House with a vase of cut flowers along with an impassioned plea to formally accept them.

Shortly thereafter, former First Lady Laura Bush called Mrs. Trump to encourage the orchid presentation after hearing a garden club lecture, "First Ladies and their Cattleyas," given by the author. Mrs. Bush is quite familiar with orchids having accepted her own namesake in 2005 at the United States Botanic Garden. Just before Congress was scheduled to take its winter break, we received an email from the Office of the First Lady.

The timing was perfect because there were at least four varieties in bud that would be fully open after the New Year and she could choose her favorite. The colors ran the gamut and represented the natural variation in seed grown plants.

However, no sooner had we responded to the White House than the government shut down for the next 33 days and, with it, our hopes of presenting the orchids. The emails stopped

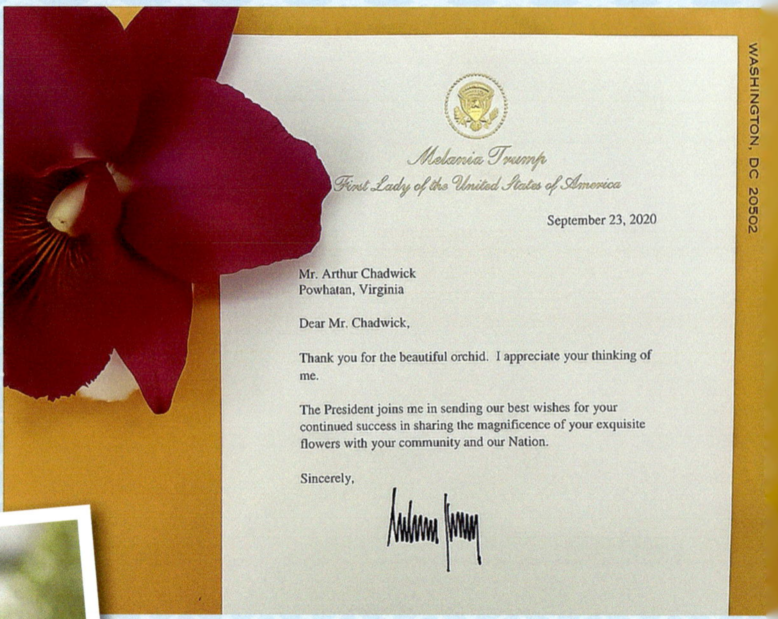

Chapter 18

MELANIA TRUMP

Melania Trump
First Lady of the United States of America

September 23, 2020

Mr. Arthur Chadwick
Powhatan, Virginia

Dear Mr. Chadwick,

Thank you for the beautiful orchid. I appreciate your thinking of me.

The President joins me in sending our best wishes for your continued success in sharing the magnificence of your exquisite flowers with your community and our Nation.

Sincerely,

WASHINGTON, DC 20502

Although the photographs of the orchid presentation were not released, Mrs. Trump did send us a thank you letter following a separate shipment of cut flowers. ARTHUR E. CHADWICK PHOTO

Melania Trump is the 18th consecutive First Lady to have a namesake orchid. She accepted her cattleya at the White House in 2019. COURTESY OF ALAMY/PAT BENIC

After the photographs, the author picked up the two Melania plants from the White House. It was April and the tulips and pansies were blooming. ARTHUR E. CHADWICK PHOTO

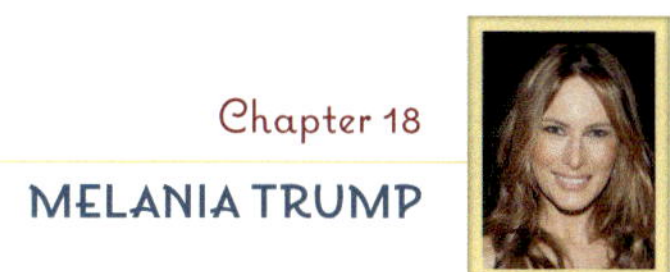

and one by one, the flowers folded until there were none left. Of course, we wouldn't let this one little mishap derail a Melania orchid presentation.

Several months later, in March, we had an interesting visitor at the greenhouse. He was a serious orchid hobbyist from out of town and was interested in bulbophyllums and other unusual genera. In passing, he mentioned that he was also the personal chef of the President's daughter Ivanka Trump and her husband Jarad Kushner.

Stephen Kotarski had been catering for the Trump family in New Jersey for a decade before moving to the District of Colombia. Upon hearing of our project, he immediately offered to assist and took two spring-blooming varieties of Melania Trump's hybrid back to Washington for consideration.

An official date was set for the presentation but it was nearly two weeks away and we wondered whether the flowers would still look fresh for the photograph. In the interim, the National Park Service was given the task of caring for the delicate orchids in their secret off-site greenhouse facility half an hour away. It was unseasonably warm during this period as the delicate cattleyas were shuttled back and forth through safety check points. The day before the scheduled event, one of the two plants folded.

On a Tuesday morning in early April, orchid history was made. First Lady Melania Trump sat down in the Green Room of the White House and was photographed with her namesake hybrid. The seedling that made the arduous journey was the same plant that had been awarded by the American Orchid Society the previous year – variety 'First Lady.'

The next day, I was summoned to pick up the plants from the White House grounds. The security was intense as I entered through the E Street gate and drove down East Executive Avenue. Massive barricades opened and closed and a dozen armed guards looked me over.

The gardens overlooking the east wing were lovely with perfectly manicured hedges and spring plantings of yellow tulips and blue pansies. Brick walkways led visitors around and pink dogwoods dotted the landscape. The White House itself is a formidable structure and I was honored to be in its presence.

Per Mrs. Trump's request, the cattleya that she was photographed with was taken across the street and donated immediately to the United States Botanic Garden which, at the time, was the repository for the First Lady orchid collection. The plants now reside at the nearby Smithsonian Gardens.

For the next few weeks, I eagerly looked in my mailbox for the promised 8" x 10" color photographs of the orchid presentation. I was envisioning her dress matching the flowers. When nothing came, I called the Office of the First Lady and was told that it was decided that the pictures would not be released.

Though disappointed, I contacted the Trump chef who had initially arranged the meeting and he assured me that there would be another opportunity. Sure enough, the next time we had a flush of Melania namesakes in bloom, we sent the cut flowers to her vacation house.

Shortly thereafter, we received a glowing thank you that read *"Thank you for the beautiful orchid. I appreciate your thinking of me. The President joins me in sending our best wishes for your continued success in sharing the magnificence of your exquisite flowers with your community and our Nation."*

Blc Melania Trump is the most complex of all the First Lady hybrids and contains a whop-

One parent of the Trump namesake is the big white C Bold Swan, which has C Bow Bells on both sides of its lineage. Shown is Bow Bells 'Anne Chadwick'.

ARTHUR E. CHADWICK PHOTO

The other parent of the Melania hybrid is the red stud, Blc Chia Lin (Oconee x Maitland), from 1989. Breeding with this plant yields unpredictable results. Shown is 'Super Gold'. ARTHUR E. CHADWICK PHOTO

The Chia Lin parent, Blc Maitland, comes from a long line of yellows including C Triumphans (dowiana x rex) from 1904. Shown is A. A. Chadwick's remake. ARTHUR E. CHADWICK PHOTO

ping 19 different species. In general terms, the cross combines a classic big white with an unpredictable art shade.

One parent of the Trump namesake is Cattleya Bold Swan (Old Whitey x Swan Lake). This lovely white hybrid has a lengthy ancestry and relies heavily on three of the work horses of the cut flower era - C mossiae, C gaskelliana, and C trianaei. Together, they provide big round flowers and exceptional vigor.

The legendary C Bow Bells is a grandparent on both sides of the lineage. It has been nearly 75 years, almost the length of a human lifetime, since a hybrid named Bow Bells burst upon the orchid stage. The year was 1945 and the stage was the September meeting of the Trustees of the American Orchid Society. At the meeting, Clint McDade of Rivermont Orchids exhibited five plants of a new white cattleya hybrid that had such outstanding flowers that one was awarded a First Class Certificate and the whole group received a rare Silver Medal of Excellence. Amazingly, four of the five plants were seedlings flowering for the first time.

The next appearance of C. Bow Bells was at the 1948 Miami Orchid Show where two more plants received First Class Certificates. Such accolades were unprecedented, and in one brief moment in the long history of cattleyas, this fragile flower had revolutionized the quality of white hybrids. It had become near-perfection by all judging standards and C. Bow Bells would go on to become one of the most awarded hybrids.

Cattleya Bow Bells was a product of the breeding program of the British orchid company Black & Flory who gave it its name and registered it with the Royal Horticultural Society in April 1945. Black & Flory was known for breeding fine cattleya hybrids and Clint McDade had purchased a large number of C. Bow Bells seedlings before any of them had flowered. When they began blooming in his greenhouses on Signal Mountain, Tennessee, he found he was sitting on a gold mine. McDade later described C. Bow Bells as *"a botanical phenomenon among orchid plants. All plants grown from this one seed pod are strikingly similar in having all the superior qualities desired in orchids. The plant itself is noted for its vigor... The wide petals and sepals have good form and carriage and the large wide lip has a ruffled edge."*

In addition to C Bow Bells, we find such fine stud plants as C Ethyl Bishop (1945), C Empress Bells (1952), and C Vesper Bells (1958) in the lineage of C Bold Swan. Vesper Bells carries genes of the tall growing species, C loddigesii, which tend to impart flatter, waxy flowers.

The other parent of Blc Melania Trump is the 1980s reddish stud, Blc Chia Lin (Oconee x Maitland). Over the years, there have been numerous AOS awards for this hybrid and the colors range from ruby red to red violet to fuchsia. It's truly a beautiful flower and few, if any, big reds today are an improvement.

As a breeder plant, Blc Chia Lin is wildly unpredictable given its colorful lineage that comprises sixteen species. Most influential is the naturally occurring yellow, C dowiana, which is always the prized plant in anyone's collection despite its reputation as being tricky to grow. (Experts recommend giving C dowiana warm nights, no cooler than 65° F.) We also find such unlikely cattleyas as L tenebrosa and C bicolor along with Epidendrum cinnabarinum – hardly the standards of big round flowers.

With so many generations of dissimilar plant combinations, it's hard to get a handle on the inner workings of the cross. The Oconee parent, from 1976, is heavy on dark purple breeding beginning with the earliest of primary hybrids, Lc Callistoglossa (L purpurata x C warscewiczii)

C Prince John (Hardyana x dowiana) from 1913 is rarely seen today but can be found in the lineage of Blc Maitland. Shown is A. A. Chadwick's remake.

ARTHUR E. CHADWICK PHOTO

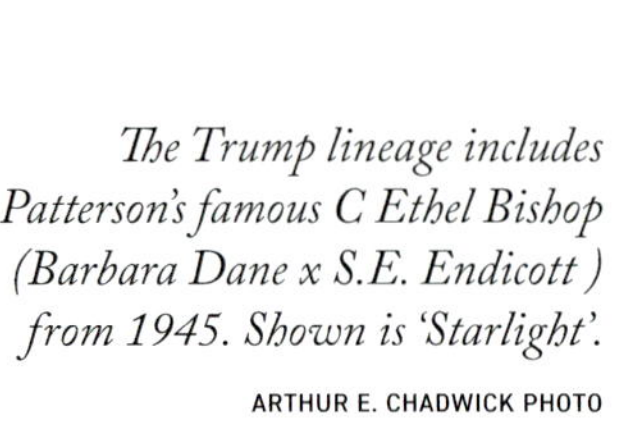

The Trump lineage includes Patterson's famous C Ethel Bishop (Barbara Dane x S.E. Endicott) from 1945. Shown is 'Starlight'.

ARTHUR E. CHADWICK PHOTO

from 1882 as well as the dark form of C Fabia (dowiana x labiata) from 1894. Experience has shown that breeding with C dowiana tends t darken the offspring of other purples.

The Maitland parent is also from the 70's and is not a particularly well-shaped yellow. The petals are narrow and fall forward but, variety 'Miles' HCC/AOS, which is named after the originator, has intense yellow color that can partly be attributed to the 1904 primary hybrid, C Triumphans (dowiana x rex).

Early breeders were enamored with C dowiana until they found out that it generally didn't produce hybrids that were yellow. The pigment in its sepals and petals is so genetically recessive that it disappears entirely when bred with any other large flowered cattleya. It wasn't until a strange new cattleya species was imported from the jungles of Peru in 1890 that C dowiana finally produced a yellow-petal large flowered hybrid. The secret ingredient that made everything work was Cattleya rex – a blossom whose creamy appearance resembled pale lemon overlaid with white.

Cattleya rex had been one of the most elusive species in the history of orchid collecting, and it was a wonder that it ever made it to Europe. It had been previously seen in the wild by the well known explorer Jean Linden when, as a young man in his 20s, he was traveling through South America for the Belgian government in the 1840s. It was seen again, 30 years later, by the orchid collector Gustav Wallis. In Linden's case, he was just surveying the plant life of Peru and Ecuador and was not in a position to bring back many epiphytes. Wallis, on the other hand, was in the business of gathering wild plants but found it impossible to extract the C rex specimens from the tops of the 70 foot tall trees and transport them alive through the dense jungle to a suitable port.

For years, other explorers tried to coax C rex out of the jungle, but all were unable to bring even one healthy plant back to Europe and the horticultural world. The biggest obstacle was the isolated rainforest area where C rex is endemic.

The Trump namesake contains 19 species and is heavily influenced by C mossiae, the National Flower of Venezuela. Shown is a greenhouse full of recently imported C mossiae circa 1913. COURTESY OF THE ORCHID WORLD

A key player in art shade breeding is L tenebrosa which blooms in yellow, bronze, and rust. Shown is a fine early variety as painted for the Orchid Album in the 1880s. COURTESY OF THE ORCHID ALBUM

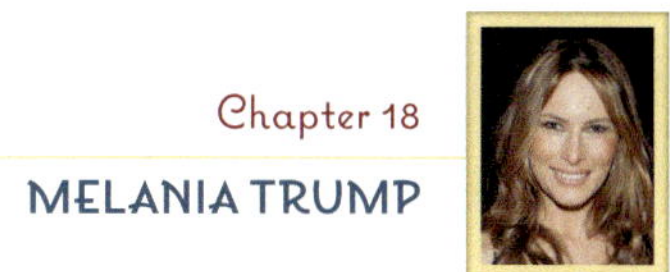

It wasn't until after a carefully planned effort by experienced plant collector Eric Bungeroth that a small number of C rex finally arrived in Liverpool, England in November, 1890. The orchids that survived were sold to Jean Linden's company L'Horticulture Internationale where a client named Charles Maron was the first to bloom a plant. He would later use C rex in hybridizing and crossed it with C dowiana to produce the primary hybrid Cattleya Triumphans.

Other exciting early hybrids found in Maitland include the yellow C Prince John (dowiana x Hardyana) from 1913 which produces deeply colored magenta lips and Bc Heatonensis (B digbyana x C Hardyana) from 1902 which offers Maitland a touch of frilly lip.

The Trump cross was named by Chadwick's and bred by Michael Sinn of Canaima Orchids in Atlanta, Georgia. Mr. Sinn is a world class hybridizer who is often sold out years before his seedlings bloom. He is originally from Venezuela and earned a degree in civil engineering there. But his true love is orchids. *"When my friends were going to the beach, I was going to the jungle looking for plants,"* he says.

A species that plays an important role in yellow breeding is the creamy C rex. Shown is a grouping from A. A. Chadwick's greenhouse. ARTHUR E. CHADWICK PHOTO

The Trump seedlings bloom in a wide range of colors including this apricot variety.

ARTHUR E. CHADWICK PHOTO

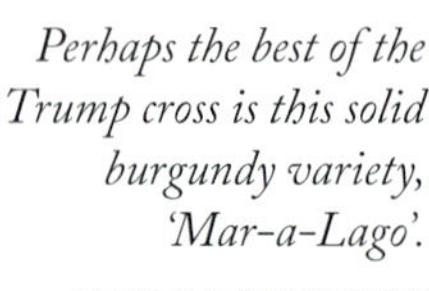

Perhaps the best of the Trump cross is this solid burgundy variety, 'Mar-a-Lago'.

ARTHUR E. CHADWICK PHOTO

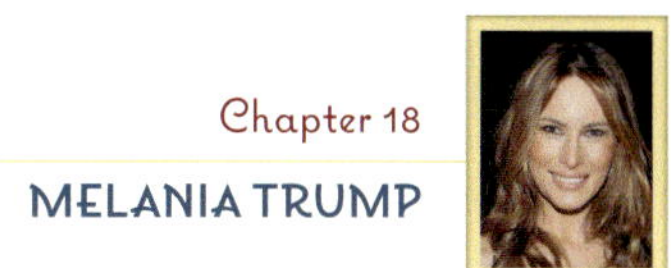

The first Trump seedlings to bloom at Chadwick's produced hues rarely seen in cattleyas - blush, apricot, burgundy, and rust. Later, some traditional colors such as pink and purple came along. The one trait that was consistent throughout was the vigor of the plants which all had robust leaves and strong inflorescences. The flowers are medium to large sized and appear mostly in the fall and winter.

What will be remembered about Mrs. Trump's namesake cattleya is that she personally accepted the flowers at the White House and was photographed with them. However, the pictures were not released which temporarily left the project in limbo. Fortunately, a follow-up shipment of cut flowers yielded a nice thank you note.

In addition, while nearly all previous First Lady hybrids are white, purple or a combination of the two, the Melania namesake can be found in a rainbow of colors.

Since her time at 1600 Pennsylvania Avenue, Mrs. Trump has kept a low profile. Time will tell if she re-engages with the public on her First Lady initiatives of children's issues or works with non-profits. She joined all living First Ladies for the funeral of former First Lady Rosalynn Carter. ✯

First Lady Melania Trump and Prince Harry at the INVICTUS GAMES in Toronto, Canada in 2017. A white phalaenopsis enhances the meeting. COURTESY OF ALAMY/EVERETT COLLECTION

PERSONAL LIFE

Since her time at 1600 Pennsylvania Avenue, Mrs. Trump has kept a low profile. Time will tell if she re-engages with the public on her First Lady initiatives of children's issues. She joined all living First Ladies for the funeral of former First Lady Rosalynn Carter. ✯

BLC MELANIA TRUMP

(2016 Chadwick/Sinn)

COMPOSITION

Species	%
C dowiana	24%
C mossiae	14%
C gaskelliana	12%
C trianaei	11%
C warscewiczii	6%
C labiata	6%
C loddigesii	5%
L tenebrosa	5%
C warneri	4%
C lueddemanniana	2%
B digbyana	2%
C bicolor	2%
C rex	2%
C percivaliana	2%
L purpurata	1%
C schroederae	.4%
C intermedia	.4%
C mendelii	.4%
L cinnabarina	.2%

LINEAGE

2015 Chadwick/Unknown
C Bold Swan

1989 Su Ping-ho
Blc Chia Lin

1969 Armacost
C Old Whitey

1964 Rivermont
C Swan Lake

1976 Carter & Holmes/Kirch
Blc Oconee

1970 Miles
Blc Maitland

One of the important hybrids in the Trump namesake is Blc Norman's Bay (Bc Hartland x Lc Ishtar) from 1946. Shown is the famous dark stud, 'Vesuvius'.

ARTHUR E. CHADWICK PHOTO

Jill Biden's namesake cattleya is a lovely shade of yellow green and was officially registered with the Royal Horticultural Society in 2013.

ARTHUR E. CHADWICK PHOTO

JILL BIDEN

★ ★ ★ ★ ★ ★ ★

"One [orchid] for my desk and one for my husband's."

– Jill Biden 2022

Until recently, most Americans rarely heard mention of Wilmington, Delaware. The state itself is tiny and bears the nickname "Small Wonder". My parents have lived there since 1960, growing orchids in their redwood greenhouses and raising a family.

Horticulturalists know the Wilmington area as a hotbed of plant activity with the famed Longwood Gardens just over the Pennsylvania line and the annual Philadelphia Flower Show a short drive up I-95. Even closer is the sprawling 1000 acre former DuPont estate known as Winterthur Museum, Garden & Library. Now Wilmington has a new attraction - the 46th President of the United States.

Joe and Jill Biden have been fixtures in Wilmington for as long as anyone can remember. They are regulars at the local grocery store, Janssen's Market, and most residents have had at least one sighting of the famous couple. My father once sat next to Mr. Biden in the barber shop.

Dr. Jill Biden, or Dr. B as her students call her, grew up about an hour north in Willow Grove, Pennsylvania. She met her future husband on a blind date while he was a freshman Senator and they married a few years later. For most of her adult life, she has been an educator – teaching at nearby public schools and technical colleges.

Chapter 19
JILL BIDEN

On January 20th, 2021, Jill Biden became First Lady of the United States. She also became the 19th consecutive First Lady to have a namesake cattleya hybrid. It all happened so quickly, it's almost as though there was a special orchid already waiting for her.

There was.

You see, we were clairvoyant and had named her hybrid ten years earlier while her husband was Vice President. In our line of business – naming orchids after First Ladies – you start to see a pattern, one of which is that Vice Presidents often become Presidents. George Bush Sr. Gerald Ford. Lyndon Johnson. And so on.

The Biden orchid, botanically known as Blc Jill Biden (Goldenzelle x Sea Swirl), was officially registered in 2013. It had been bred by The Orchid Trail of Morrisville, North Carolina and un-named until we got a hold of it. The lineage is well known in orchid circles.

The first parent, Blc Goldenzelle (Fortune x C Horace), is a product of the 1980s California breeding scene and is one of the most widely used stud plants in history with over 250 registered offspring. The American Orchid Society has granted prestigious flower quality awards to 30 different varieties of Goldenzelle.

Orchid historians debate the origin of Goldenzelle but the story goes that multiple members of the South Coast Orchid Society were active in breeding at this time and often used the same stud plants. Ultimately, orchid judge and modest commercial grower John Hanes submitted the application to the Royal Horticultural Society for registration but, generally speaking, it was a group effort. Ironically, Hanes spent most of his time with lady slippers.

One parent of the Biden namesake is the well known and highly decorated stud, Blc Goldenzelle (Fortune x C Horace) from 1982. Shown is variety 'High Noon'. ARTHUR E. CHADWICK PHOTO

Flandria, Ltd, was a massive operation in Bruges, Belgium. Shown are the greenhouses as featured in the December 1952 AOS Bulletin. PHOTO COURTESY OF THE AMERICAN ORCHID SOCIETY.

Long before Hanes was immortalized by the success of Blc Goldenzelle, he first made an impact in the orchid world by helping to create an international standard of judging – one that could be used at World Orchid Conferences. He later started a small business out of his home, mightily called Hanes Orchids of Distinction, in San Gabriel, California, where he made over 500 hybrids, mostly paphiopedilums. He and his wife, Tommie, who was also an AOS judge, were involved with all things orchid for over 60 years.

Goldenzelle delirium would not have been possible without the fine attributes of the parent, C Horace (trianaei x Woltersiana) – a 1938 tall growing and stately big purple credited to the Belgian firm, Flandria Ltd or "F" in the RHS registry. Flandria registered so many hybrids during its three decade (1929-1960) breeding spree that the Royal Horticultural Society got tired of writing the company name with every application and simply used the letter F. For modern day growers who aren't familiar with the abbreviation, it takes a little research to figure out who or what is being referenced.

Flandria was a massive operation with over a million square feet under glass and self described as "the largest horticulture company in the world." They grew much more than orchids and their 1920s catalog cover lists azaleas, palms, bay trees, anthuriums, ficus, philodendrons, bromeliads, and eurya. The nursery was founded in the east coast city of Bruges which became the epicenter of European orchids with major competitors Sanders and Vincke close by.

Flandria's secret to success, as far as orchid interests were concerned, was their 1929 purchase of Theodore Pauwel's nursery which was located just 50 miles west in Merelbeke and had been nearly destroyed by German bombers in World War I. The Pauwels catalog of "Orchidees" was written entirely in French and catered to the well-to-do. At the time, Belgium was divided into three social classes and each had its own language with French being the elite.

Theodore Pauwels began his career collecting plants in the wild before going into business

Orchid breeder, Theodore Pauwels and his wife, Liezie visit Nice, France in 1924 prior to his joining Flandria, Ltd. COURTESY OF ROGER BONTE

The secret to Goldenzelle's success as a stud is its parent, C Horace (trianaei x Woltersiana) - a 1938 masterpiece bred by Theodore Pauwels of Flandria, Ltd. Shown is 'Maxima' AM/AOS.
ARTHUR E. CHADWICK PHOTO

for himself in 1888. Pauwels experimented with a wide range of orchids and registered some of the earliest lady slipper hybrids including the legendary Paph Alma Gevaert (lawrenceanum x Maudiae) in 1911. The hybrid has been remade countless times and can be found in many collections today. His true love was cattleyas, however, and, fortunately, this is what Flandria specialized in.

By the time Pauwels moved to Bruges, he had amassed an impressive stud collection and went into overdrive with hybridizing. He brought with him his very best breeder plants - C Edithiae (Suzanne Hye x trianaei), Lc Robertiana (Saint Gothard x C Amabilis), and C Woltersiana (Queen Mary x Rajah), among others. There was plenty of greenhouse space at Flandria and a sizable staff to repot all the plants.

Biden grandparent, C Horace, relies on several primary hybrids including the 1888 C Empress Frederick (dowiana x mossiae). Shown is A. A. Chadwick's remake.

ARTHUR E. CHADWICK PHOTO

Beginning in 1929, Pauwels made hundreds of hybrids for Flandria. He crossed his three favorite studs with everything he could find and it was just a question of time before he hit the jackpot. C Horace (Woltersiana x trianaei) of 1938 was that jackpot.

C Horace is known for its "perfect" shape in that the flowers are big and round with overlapping petals and a 'closed' lip. The richly colored lavender blooms are not crowded and have plenty of space to fully open. The hybrid is typically a spring bloomer.

Recently, the American Orchid Society gave a flower quality award to C Horace 'Maxima' AM/AOS – 70 years after it was created.

Over the years, breeders everywhere have benefitted from Pauwel's efforts as we find C Horace as a parent in countless registrations. The resulting hybrids are the "Who's Who" of the cattleya world and include such classics as Lc Drumbeat (x Bonanza), Lc Melody Fair (x Stephen Oliver Fouraker), Lc Prism Palette (x Colorama), Blc Tribute (x Mem Crispin Rosales), and, of course, Blc Goldenzelle (x Fortune).

The other parent of Blc Jill Biden is Blc Sea Swirl (Greenwich x Mount Vernon) which produces flowers with an exotic greenish hue and originated in 1989 at the breeding program of Orchids by Hausermann in Villa Park, Illinois. Variety 'Whirlpool' AM/AOS was one of the best seedlings and soon cloned by the thousands. Hobbyists still grow it today.

Most greenish hybrids begin their lineage with the only large flowered species that comes close to green and that is the unforgettable chartreuse-colored B digbyana from Mexico. We find this species on both sides of Sea Swirl but what is a little unexpected is the addition of the tall growing bifoliate, C granulosa, from Brazil. In the wild, C granulosa grows in lowland areas that get routinely flooded during the rainy season and has to desperately hang on to shrubs and small trees to survive.

The 1902 primary hybrid, Bc Mrs J Leemann (B digbyana x C dowiana), imparts great color and frilly lips, and can be found on both sides of the Biden parentage.

ARTHUR E. CHADWICK PHOTO

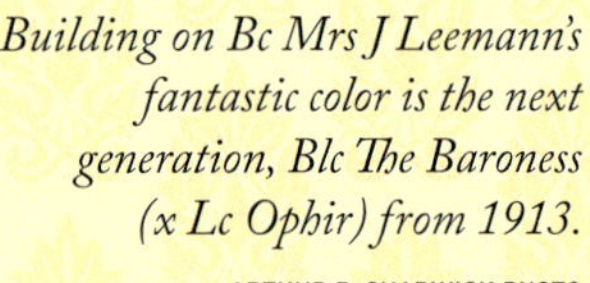

Building on Bc Mrs J Leemann's fantastic color is the next generation, Blc The Baroness (x Lc Ophir) from 1913.

ARTHUR E. CHADWICK PHOTO

Shortly after the Jill Biden orchid was named, the Vice President, himself, was scheduled to appear in Richmond, Virginia on a campaign trip. Politicians regularly visit the city because of its close proximity to the U.S. Capitol and have been nearly omnipresent during Virginia's recent two-plus decade run as a swing state.

We heard about the impending Biden visit from our client and political activist, Molly Payne, who saw our "Jill" hybrid in bloom at the greenhouse. We wondered if this might be a good time to, at least, present the flowers to the Vice President. Timing is critical with perishable orchids as there is only a narrow window when the petals are their freshest.

Spouses sometimes accompany politicians to campaign events and it was unclear if both Bidens would be in attendance. Our plan is always to give the flowers directly to the honoree, but, given the short notice, the Vice President might have to do. We cut the flowers, placed them in a water tube, and let our client take them to the rally where she presented the flowers on stage to a grinning Joe Biden amidst a throng of cheers.

He loved the orchids and took them back to Wilmington that night for his wife to enjoy. This is likely the only time in history in which namesake orchids have been transported on

An unlikely semi-alba appears in the Blc Sea Swirl lineage, Lc Jane Dane (Britannia x President Wilson) from 1937 which combines a big purple with a yellow. ARTHUR E. CHADWICK PHOTO

There are few yellow species in the cattleya family and breeders tried them all in the early days. Shown is L xanthina from A. A. Chadwick's collection which is a distant relative of the Biden namesake.
ARTHUR E. CHADWICK PHOTO

The bifoliate species, C granulosa, occasionally appears in the background of greenish hybrids. In this case, it's both a grandparent and great grandparent to Blc Sea Swirl. This late 1800's print appeared as plate 14 in the French publication, Dictionnarie Iconographique des Orchidees. COURTESY OF CHARLIE HARKNESS

Air Force Two, the official plane of the Vice President. Once again, Delaware lived up to its nickname, "Small Wonder", and the story could have ended there had it not been for a later development.

As fate would have it, Mr. Biden was elected President of the United States seven years later and, suddenly, his wife's namesake orchid was elevated to the ultra-exclusive First Lady's collection. It now became paramount that we make an official presentation directly to Dr. Biden.

In 2013, Jill Biden's orchid was first presented to her husband by our client and political activist, Molly Payne, when the Vice President visited Richmond, Virginia. PHOTO COURTESY OF MOLLY PAYNE

Although we have done this sort of thing many times over the years, there are no guarantees and, at the end of the day, we are only dealing with flowers. Security concerns and, now, pandemic restrictions severely limit how close the general public can get to elected officials. We clearly understand that Joe Schmoe can't just get an appointment with The White House.

A rare opportunity presented itself in 2022 as our local congresswoman and rising star, Abigail Spanberger, was up for re-election. She was quite familiar with our business and had actually visited our greenhouses a few years earlier. One day in July, I noticed a Jill Biden orchid coming into bloom with two big buds and I set it aside.

As the flowers opened, it was readily apparent that this was a particularly good blooming of this cattleya. The two flowers were nicely displayed and the color was incredible. I sent a picture to the Spanberger staff along with the message, "*Would Abigail have any interest in presenting Jill Biden's orchid? The flowers will be fresh for a week or two.*"

Congresswoman Abigail Spanberger visited our greenhouses in 2018 and, later, helped to set up the orchid presentation to First Lady Biden. COURTESY OF ABIGAIL SPANBERGER

This was a bold request given the fact that Ms. Spanberger has a full slate of important duties and the subject matter is merely flowers. I expected something along the lines of "*Thank you for your request. The flowers are lovely but Ms. Spanberger's schedule is full. We wish you the best with your endeavors.*" I went about my day and practically forgot about my superfluous request.

The next day, I got this response, "*Tell us more about your project. We might be able to help.*" Ever so cautiously, I explained what would be involved with an orchid presentation. I still thought it was a long shot given the myriad of factors involved, not the least of which is that the First Lady's schedule had to be open.

This greenish species appears in the early lineage of the Biden namesake – C bicolor alba as found in the turn-of-the-century rendition by John Nugent Fitch for the Orchid Album.

COURTESY OF THE ORCHID ALBUM

First Lady Jill Biden was presented two plants of her namesake cattleya on July 19, 2022 in the Vermeil room of the East Wing of The White House. ERIN SCOTT PHOTO, OFFICIAL WHITE HOUSE PHOTOGRAPHER

The day after, there was a flurry of incoming phone calls and emails from both the Spanberger office and the Office of the First Lady. "*I understand you have a highly perishable flower. We are trying to get this meeting expedited*", and my favorite, "*How exactly do these orchid presentations work?*"

A date of July 19th was set and following a lengthy security pre-check, it was now a waiting game. Would the flowers collapse in the summer heat or get eaten by a slug? These are things that orchid growers worry about.

My fears were allayed when a second Biden hybrid opened and it was just as lovely as the first. This variety had a slightly different lip color which would give us something to talk about – variations in orchid seedlings. Most importantly, I now had two chances to have something in bloom for the big day.

Originally, the presentation was scheduled to be outside in the First Lady's Garden but, due to the extreme heat, it was moved inside to the Vermeil room of the East Wing. This is the room that holds that rare Vermeil china and is adorned with portraits of former First Ladies: Lady Bird Johnson, Jacqueline Kennedy, Pat Nixon, Mamie Eisenhower and Lou Hoover.

The event was also supposed to be videotaped but an unplanned big league meeting with the First Lady of Ukraine, Olena Zelenska, took place right beforehand and required the equipment. I guess Ukraine takes precedence.

The security at the White House is intense. There were four vehicle barriers just to get to the East Wing. These are the kind in which a giant metal wall comes out of the ground.

At every barrier, I was given a more advanced security check. By the time I got inside the White House grounds, I was soaking wet from the heat.

The guards had been expecting the orchids, having requested pictures of the plants ahead of time. There were two 4" clay pots, each with a cattleya plant of 4 or 5 pseudobulbs and two flowers on top, wrapped in cotton. Nothing suspicious about that!

It was here that my box of orchids was taken away. It was to go through a separate security protocol. I was told of previous floral arrangements that got shredded by mistake in their X-ray machine.

While the poor orchids were getting the third degree, I was led across the grounds to the building that holds more than 500 White House staff members for the dreaded Covid screening. This was, in fact, my most feared scenario in which I fail the test and get thrown out. There is no plan B. It's back to the salt mines empty handed.

After ten circles in each nostril with a cotton swab, I was led down the hall and told "If you don't hear from us, it's good news." That all sounds lovely except that the patient is left in limbo and waiting for their phone to ring long after the nurse knows the results. Apparently, I passed the test although I never heard conclusively and, two days later, the top story in the world was "*President Tests Positive for COVID*".

Imagine the guilt I would have knowing that I gave the President Covid? Or, worse yet, what if he died from it? What started out as a footnote in botanical history suddenly had the real possibility of taking down the leader of the free world.

All these things passed through my mind as I waited patiently in the Vermeil room with other members of the First Lady team, including her scheduler, public relations staffers, and photographer. The White House Chief Floral Designer, Hedieh Ghaffarian, joined us as well. They had me practice my little speech a few times and do some role playing so that I was absolutely ready.

Then it was game time. Dr. Biden walked in the room. She was wearing a blue floral dress and yellow high heels - the colors of Ukraine – and was all smiles. I couldn't help but smile back. I said my little speech and we chatted about the variations in the two seedlings.

As we posed for photographs, I casually mentioned that I went to Tatnall, a prep school in Wilmington, Delaware just down the road from her house. Suddenly, I was her best friend, "*Hey Susan, he went to Tatnall! Small world!*"

From there, it was smooth sailing for the remainder of the 25 minute meeting. We walked around the room discussing the flowers that were in each of the first lady portraits. She mentioned that, one day, she too would have a portrait and wondered what flowers would be in hers. I, of course, mentioned orchids and she said, "*Maybe so!*"

At the end, she asked if I was taking the orchids back to Richmond and I reminded her that these were gifts to her. Then the bombshell: "*I'd like one on my desk and one on my husband's desk.*" Surely this must be the first time that a First Lady orchid sat in the Oval Office. ✯

PERSONAL LIFE

Aside from being a First Lady, Dr. Biden is a professor at the Northern Virginia Community College, where she teaches English and writing. She is also a mother, a grandmother, and a bestselling author. She previously served as Second Lady of the United States from 2009 to 2017. ✯

BLC JILL BIDEN

(2013 Chadwick/Orchid Trail)

COMPOSITION

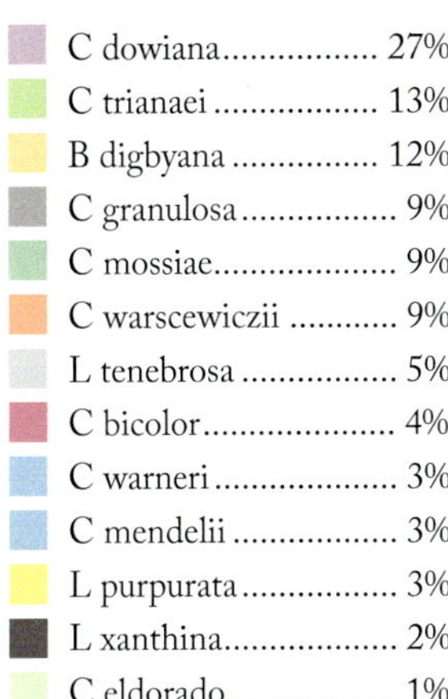

- C dowiana 27%
- C trianaei 13%
- B digbyana 12%
- C granulosa 9%
- C mossiae 9%
- C warscewiczii 9%
- L tenebrosa 5%
- C bicolor 4%
- C warneri 3%
- C mendelii 3%
- L purpurata 3%
- L xanthina 2%
- C eldorado 1%

LINEAGE

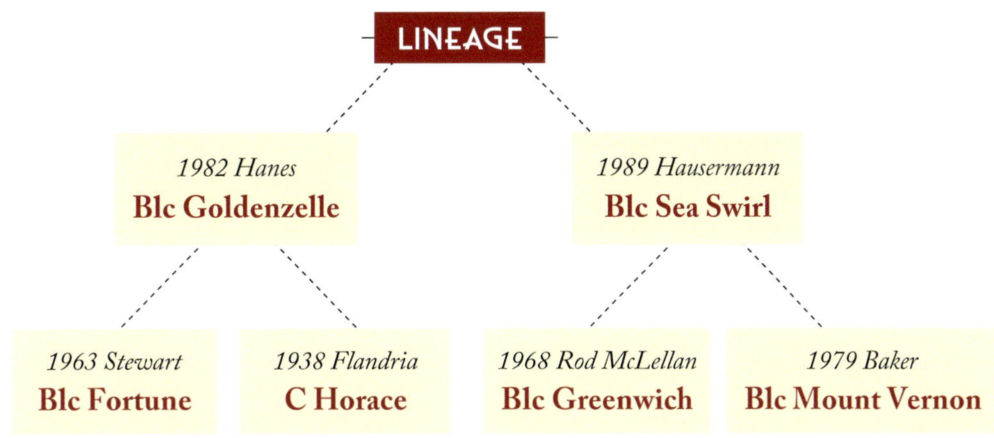

OTHER NOTABLE WOMEN AND THEIR ORCHIDS

MARGARET THATCHER

The Thatcher namesake was bred by Lenette Greenhouses in Kannapolis, North Carolina and named by Chadwick's just in time for her visit – Blc Margaret Thatcher (Lc Princess Margaret x Summer Bay).

ARTHUR E. CHADWICK PHOTO

Former British Prime Minister, Margaret Thatcher, was presented with a corsage of her namesake cattleya by Art Chadwick when she visited Richmond, Virginia in 2004. After it was pinned on, she walked up to a wall mirror and proclaimed, "Simply lovely!" She wore the flowers all day while touring the University of Richmond.

IAN BRADSHAW PHOTO

PRISCILLA PRESLEY

Ms. Presley's namesake cattleya was recently given an Award of Merit by the American Orchid Society. The hybrid, Lc Priscilla Presley 'Beverly Hills' AM/AOS (Bonanza x Altesse), had been used for cut flowers for many years before being named. ARTHUR E. CHADWICK PHOTO

The First Lady of Rock & Roll, Priscilla Presley, discusses orchids with Art Jr. at Graceland in 2019. Ten years earlier, we had named a big purple cattleya hybrid after her after finding out that she was an orchid enthusiast. Her love for cattleyas started when Elvis gave her 16 purple blooms on her 16th birthday.

COURTESY OF PRISCILLA PRESLEY

FARRAH FAWCETT/ALANA STEWART

Farrah Fawcett's cattleya was named with assistance from the Farrah Fawcett Foundation in Beverly Hills, California. The hybrid, Blc Farrah Fawcett (C Bold Swan x Goldenzelle), is a lovely fall blooming art shade.
ARTHUR E CHADWICK PHOTO

Alana Stewart is the President of the Farrah Fawcett Foundation as well as being her best friend. In addition, she is a First Lady of Rock & Roll having been married to Sir Rod Stewart. She enjoys her Farrah orchids as both cut flowers and blooming plants. COURTESY OF ALANA STEWART

LC EDITH BOLLING WILSON

C FLORENCE HARDING

BC GRACE COOLIDGE

BLC MRS HERBERT HOOVER

LC ELEANOR ROOSEVELT

C BESS TRUMAN

LC MAMIE EISENHOWER

C JACQUELINE KENNEDY (1961)

THE ORCHIDS OF THE FIRST LADIES

C LADY BIRD JOHNSON

LC PATRICIA NIXON

LC BETTY FORD

C ROSALYNN CARTER

LC NANCY REAGAN

BLC BARBARA BUSH

BLC HILLARY RODHAM CLINTON

BLC LAURA BUSH

LC MICHELLE OBAMA

BLC MELANIA TRUMP

BLC JILL BIDEN

THE CATTLEYA WHEEL

The *Cattleya Wheel* lets growers know when the different species bloom. In some cases, there are as many as four species in bloom at once.

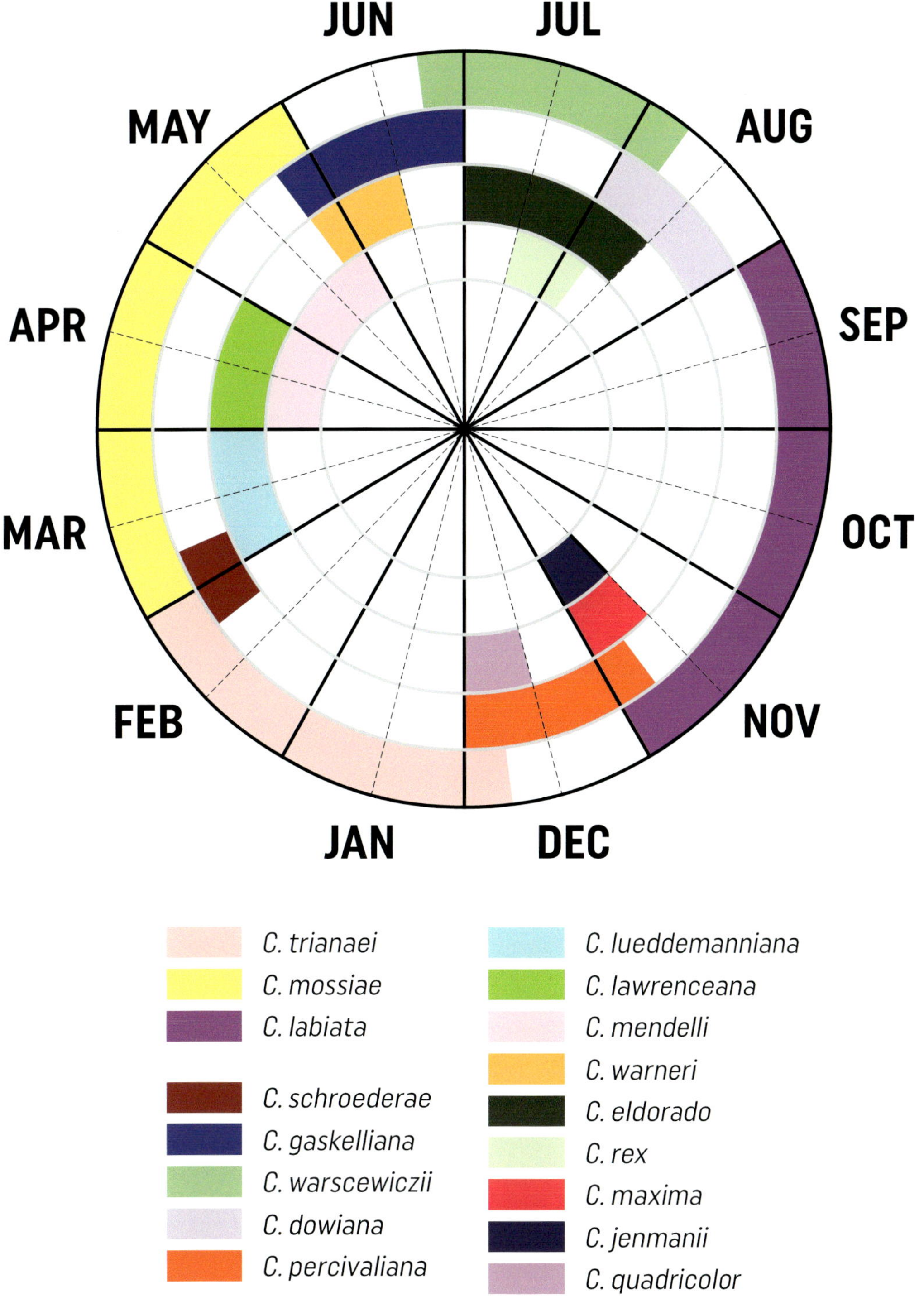

For nearly fifty years, the White House had extensive greenhouses attached.
COURTESY OF THE WHITE HOUSE HISTORICAL ASSOCIATION

ABOUT THE BACK COVER

Most people don't know that there used to be extensive greenhouses attached to the White House!

The idea of a "botanical house" was authorized by President Franklin Pierce and, in 1857, construction began under President James Buchanan. The first greenhouse was a simple wood framed building with glass sides and a glass passageway to the main residence. Staff and political figureheads enjoyed the lush greenery and radiant blooms inside.

President Abraham Lincoln would take guests into the charming space and give away lemons from a prized citrus tree. First Lady Mary Todd Lincoln adored the structure and was known to send floral arrangements and bouquets grown in the greenhouse to government officials and local hospitals around Washington. There was significant fire damage in 1867 and the structure was renovated to twice the original size.

In the 1870s, further expansion continued. Typical plants of the era including ferns, herbs, fruits, and of course, orchids. The rich greenery and flora was used in the kitchen and to decorate the White House all year round. Another expansion in the late 1880s added rose houses, a camellia house, a bedding plant house, and dedicated orchid houses.

During the Rutherford Hayes administration, *"must-see"* tours of the conservatory were given after White House formal dinners. First Lady Lucy Hayes loved the greenhouses and spent considerable time there. She was responsible for the *"extensive, expensive, avant-guard"* dinner service that showcased the fauna and flora of the United States, with much inspiration from the conservatory.

There was no lack of appreciation for the plants under President Chester Arthur, who was a bachelor and delighted in arranging the ferns and palms throughout the White House. In fact, after the gardeners had spent the afternoon decorating, *"they would find, the next morning, that the President had amused himself by changing everything completely"* wrote Demorest's *Family Magazine* in 1895.

A diplomatic dinner for Grover Cleveland's wife, Frances, required *"the best the conservatories can afford"* and she would confer with the head gardener as to which orchid to feature as décor. The steward then arranged the flowers, lamp shades, and ribbons on the table. If the popular lady slipper, Paphiopedilum insigne, was chosen, *"the table was massed with them, a corsage knot was placed besides the plate of each lady, while a single flower was provided as a boutonniere for each gentleman."*

During the Benjamin Harrison administration in the early 1890s, the conservatory was at its peak of beauty. His wife Caroline's preference was decidedly orchids and *"she took so great an interest in the collection that it was enlarged at her request."* In one photograph, an entire shelf is filled with blooming cattleyas.

Caroline Harrison was known to personally select floral bouquets from the greenhouses and send them all over Washington. She was an accomplished artist and as *"china-painting was almost her only diversion...she used some of the finest orchids as models."* She also created a famous portrait of one of the cattleyas in 1892. The piece was simply called "White House Orchid."

While the orchid was not identified, experts readily recognize the flower as C trianaei based on the shape of the blooms and by the plant having only single flowers on a stem. In addition, the sunburned and otherwise rough looking leaves indicate that this plant had been recently imported from the jungle (Colombia).

Her successor, First Lady Ida McKinley, was also known to regularly host guests in the conservatory.

To many horticulturalists' dismay, the entire greenhouse complex was demolished in 1902 to make way for the West Wing. ✯

Inside the White House greenhouses were tropical plants of all kinds including an entire shelf of blooming cattleyas.

COURTESY OF THE
WHITE HOUSE HISTORICAL ASSOCIATION

In 1902, the White House greenhouses were torn down to make way for the West Wing.

COURTESY OF THE
WHITE HOUSE HISTORICAL ASSOCIATION

BIBLIOGRAPHY

American Orchid Society. 1932 – 2002. *Bulletin*. Quarterly/Monthly of the American Orchid Society; re-named *Orchids* 2003.

American Orchid Society. 2003 – present. *Orchids*. Monthly. American Orchid Society.

Boyle, F. 1901. *The Woodlands Orchids*. New York: Macmillan.

Bush, Barbara. 1994. *Barbara Bush A Memoir*. Lisa Drew Books, New York.

Chadwick, A. A. and Arthur E. Chadwick. 2020. *The Classic Cattleya*s. 2nd edition. Powhatan, Virginia: Chadwick & Son Orchids, Inc.

Clinton, Hillary Rodham. 2003. *Living History*. Simon & Schuster, New York.

Dunsterville, G., and L. Garay. 1959. *Venezuelan Orchids Illustrated*, Vols. 1 – 6. Andre Deutsch.

Eisenhower, Julie Nixon. 1986. *Pat Nixon: The Untold Story*. 1986. Simon & Schuster, New York.

Ford, Betty. 1978. *The Times of My Life*. Harper & Row, New York.

Fowlie, J. A. 1977. *The Brazilian Bifoliate Cattleyas and Their Color Varieties*. Azul Quinta Press.

Gardeners' Chronicle, The. 1841 – 1901. Weekly Publication. London.

Hackney, C. 2004. *American Cattleyas*. Wilmington, North Carolina: Hackney.

Heymann, C. David. *A Woman Named Jackie*. Carol Communications, New York.

Kaufman, Scott. 2007. *Rosalynn Carter: Equal Partner in the White House*. University Press of Kansas, Lawrence, Kansas.

Kessler, Ronald. 2006. *Laura Bush: An Intimate Portrait of the First Lady*. Doubleday, New York.

Linden, J. 1885 – 1906. *Lindenia: Iconographie des Orchidees*. Ghent. Belgium: Linden.

Michaelis, David. 2020. *Eleanor*. Simon & Schuster Paperbacks, New York.

Miranda, F. 1996. *Orchids from the Brazilian Amazon*. Rio de Janeiro: Expressao e Cultura.

Obama, Michelle 2018. *Becoming*. Penguin Random House.

Orchid Digest Corporation. 1937 – present. *Orchid Digest*. Bimonthly/quarterly. Orchid Digest Corporation.

Paxton, J. 1834 – 1849. *Paxton's Magazine of Botany*. London: Orr and Smith.

Rolfe, R. A. and Hurst, C. C. 1909. *The Orchid Stud-Book*. Lawn Crescent, England: Frank Leslie & Co.

Rolfe, R. A. 1893 – 1920. The Orchid Review. London: West Newman.

Rogerson, W. P. 2004. *"Cattleya Species and their Culture." Orchid Digest* 68 (4):203.

Ronaele Manor Collection of Orchids, The. 1931. Elkins Park, Pennsylvania: Dixon.

Sale, Sara L. 2010. *Bess Wallace Truman: Harry's White House "Boss"*. University Press of Kansas, Lawrence, Kansas.

Sander, D. and W. J. Wreford. 1946 – 1960. *David Sander's One Table List of Orchid Hybrids*. David Sander's Orchids.

Sander, F. 1888 – 1894. *Reichenbachia: Orchids Illustrated and Described*. 4 vols. St. Albans, England: F. Sander and Company.

Sander's Complete List of Orchid Hybrids to 1 January 1946. St. Albans, England: Sanders.

Sander's List of Orchid Hybrids. 1961 – 2004. London: Royal Horticultural Society.

BIBLIOGRAPHY

Swinson, A. 1970. *Frederick Sander: the Orchid King.* London: Hodder and Stouchton.

Toulemonde, T. 2004. *The Colombian Cattleya*. Colombia: Toulemonde.

Veitch, J. 1887. *A Manual of Orchidaceous Plants*. Vol. 1, Epidendreae. Chelsea: Veitch.

Warner, R. 1865. *Select Orchidaceous Plants*. London: Crescent, Cripplegate.

Warner, R., and B. S. Williams. 1882 – 1897. *The Orchid Album*, 11 vols. London: Williams.

Williams, B. S., and H. Williams. 1894. *The Orchid-Grower's Manual.* 7th edition. London.

Wilson, Gurney F. L. S. 1910. *The Orchid World.* 6 vols. Haywards Heath, Sussex.

Withner, C. L. 1988. *The Cattleyas and their Relatives. Vol. 1*, The Cattleyas. Portland, Oregon: Timber Press.

Withner, C. L. 1989. *The Cattleyas and their Relatives. Vol. 2*, The Laelias. Portland, Oregon: Timber Press.

INDEX

A

B

C

INDEX

D

E

F

G

H

INDEX

I

J

K

L

M

N

S

T

FEBRUARY 3, 1947 AMERICAN ORCHID SOCIETY BULLETIN 117

Nature is a Mere Tyro

The best that Nature can do looks feeble beside the pampered perfection of an American-grown hybrid orchid. And the gap between species and hybrid broadens, as year after year the hybrid's beauty is enhanced, its value augmented.

Here at Thomas Young Orchids we are in the vanguard of those who, with patience and skill, are trying to "gild refined gold, to paint the lily."

THOMAS YOUNG ORCHIDS INC.

America's Foremost Growers

BOUND BROOK, NEW JERSEY

New York 1, N. Y., 804 Avenue of the Americas
Boston 16, Mass., 537 Tremont Street
Mayfield Heights, Ohio, Box Q
Chicago 5, Ill., 632 S. Wabash Avenue

SHIP YOUR SURPLUS FINE BLOOMS TO OUR NEAREST BRANCH. WE WILL SELL THEM FOR YOU

In the 1940s, cattleyas were in high demand and commercial growers ran ads touting their competitive advantages. In this piece, Thomas Young Orchids informs readers that the modern hybrids are so much better than the species.

COURTESY OF THOMAS YOUNG ORCHIDS

EARLY CORRESPONDENCE FROM MAJOR GROWERS AND A. A. CHADWICK

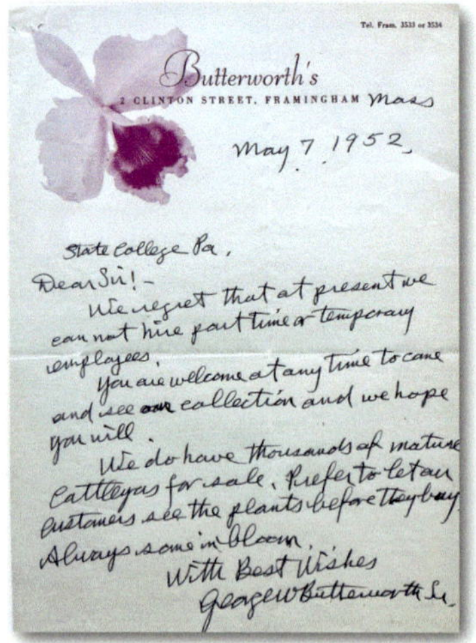

Tel. Fram. 3533 or 3534

Butterworth's
2 CLINTON STREET, FRAMINGHAM Mass

May 7 1952

State College Pa.

Dear Sir! –
We regret that at present we can not hire part time or temporary employees.
You are welcome at any time to come and see our collection and we hope you will.
We do have thousands of mature Cattleyas for sale. Prefer to let our customers see the plants before they buy.
Always some in bloom.
With Best Wishes
George W Butterworth Sr.

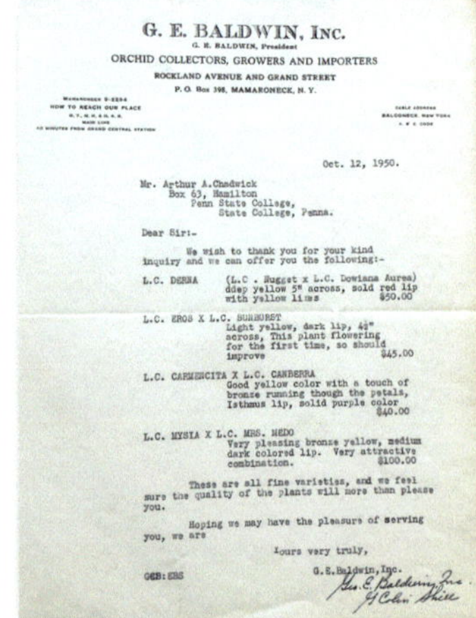

G. E. BALDWIN, INC.
G. E. BALDWIN, President
ORCHID COLLECTORS, GROWERS AND IMPORTERS
ROCKLAND AVENUE AND GRAND STREET
P. O. Box 398, MAMARONECK, N. Y.

Oct. 12, 1950.

Mr. Arthur A.Chadwick
Box 63, Hamilton
Penn State College,
State College, Penna.

Dear Sir:-

We wish to thank you for your kind inquiry and we can offer you the following:-

L.C. DERNA (L.C. Nugget x L.C. Dowiana Aurea) deep yellow 5" across, solid red lip with yellow lines $50.00

L.C. EROS X L.C. SUNBURST Light yellow, dark lip, 4½" across, This plant flowering for the first time, so should improve $45.00

L.C. CARMENCITA X L.C. CANBERRA Good yellow color with a touch of bronze running though the petals, Isthmus lip, solid purple color $40.00

L.C. MYSIA X L.C. MRS. MEDO Very pleasing bronze yellow, medium dark colored lip. Very attractive combination. $100.00

These are all fine varieties, and we feel sure the quality of the plants will more than please you.

Hoping we may have the pleasure of serving you, we are

Yours very truly,
G.E.Baldwin,Inc.

GEB:EBS

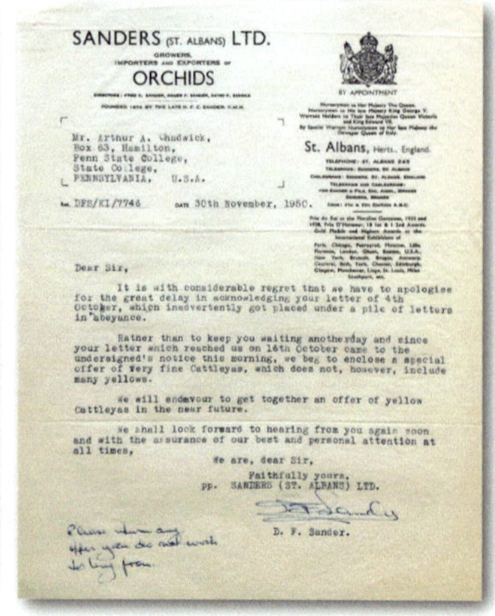

SANDERS (ST. ALBANS) LTD.
GROWERS, IMPORTERS and EXPORTERS of
ORCHIDS

Mr. Arthur A. Chadwick,
Box 63, Hamilton,
Penn State College,
State College,
PENNSYLVANIA. U.S.A.

St. Albans, Herts. England.

DFS/KI/7746 Date 30th November, 1950.

Dear Sir,

It is with considerable regret that we have to apologise for the great delay in acknowledging your letter of 4th October, which inadvertently got placed under a pile of letters in abeyance.

Rather than to keep you waiting another day and since your letter which reached us on 14th October came to the undersigned's notice this morning, we beg to enclose a special offer of Very fine Cattleyas, which does not, however, include many yellows.

We will endeavour to get together an offer of yellow Cattleyas in the near future.

We shall look forward to hearing from you again soon and with the assurance of our best and personal attention at all times,

We are, dear Sir,
Faithfully yours,
pp. SANDERS (ST. ALBANS) LTD.
D. F. Sander.

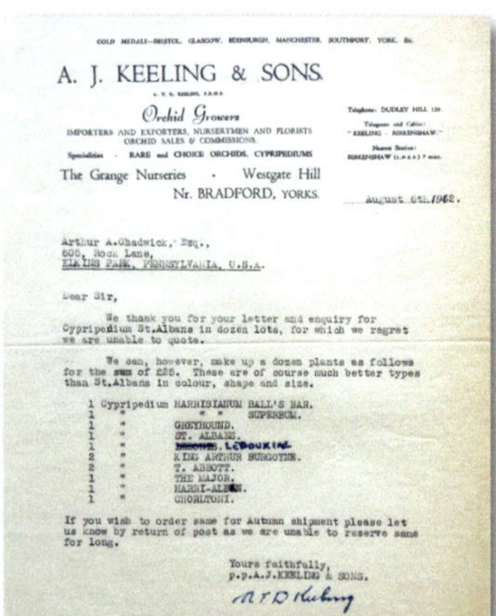

GOLD MEDALS—BRISTOL, GLASGOW, EDINBURGH, MANCHESTER, SOUTHPORT, YORK, &c.

A. J. KEELING & SONS.
Orchid Growers
IMPORTERS AND EXPORTERS, NURSERYMEN AND FLORISTS.
ORCHID SALES & COMMISSIONS.
Specialities · RARE and CHOICE ORCHIDS, CYPRIPEDIUMS
The Grange Nurseries · Westgate Hill
Nr. BRADFORD, YORKS.

August 6th,1962.

Arthur A.Chadwick, Esq.,
605, Rock Lane,
ELKINS PARK, PENNSYLVANIA, U.S.A.

Dear Sir,

We thank you for your letter and enquiry for Cypripedium St.Albans in dozen lots, for which we regret we are unable to quote.

We can, however, make up a dozen plants as follows for the sum of £25. These are of course much better types than St.Albans in colour, shape and size.

1 Cypripedium HARRISIANUM BALL'S VAR.
1 " " SUPERBUM.
1 " GREYHOUND.
1 " ST. ALBANS.
1 " LEBOUXIAE.
1 " KING ARTHUR BURGOYNE.
2 " T. ABBOTT.
1 " THE MAJOR.
1 " HARRI-ALBUM.
1 " CHORLTONI.

If you wish to order same for Autumn shipment please let us know by return of post as we are unable to reserve same for long.

Yours faithfully,
p.p.A.J.KEELING & SONS.

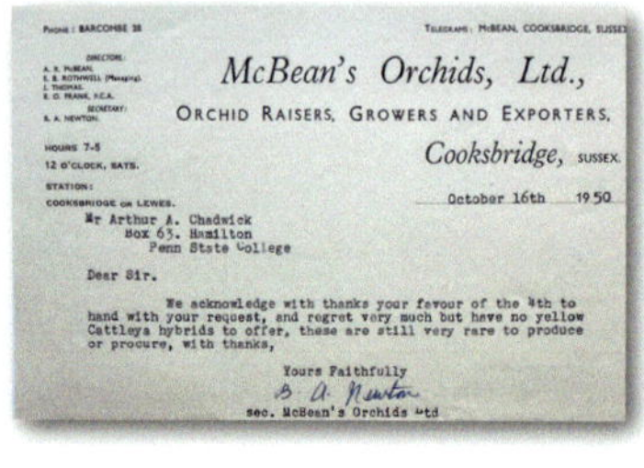

PHONE: BARCOMBE 38
TELEGRAMS: McBEAN, COOKSBRIDGE, SUSSEX

McBean's Orchids, Ltd.,
ORCHID RAISERS, GROWERS AND EXPORTERS,
Cooksbridge, SUSSEX.

HOURS 7-5
12 O'CLOCK, SATS.
STATION:
COOKSBRIDGE or LEWES.

October 16th 1950

Mr Arthur A. Chadwick
Box 63. Hamilton
Penn State College

Dear Sir.

We acknowledge with thanks your favour of the 4th to hand with your request, and regret very much but have no yellow Cattleya hybrids to offer, these are still very rare to produce or procure, with thanks,

Yours Faithfully
B. A. Newton
sec. McBean's Orchids Ltd

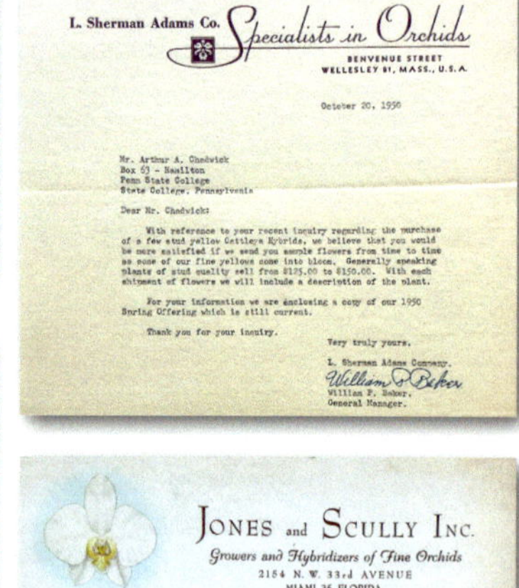

L. Sherman Adams Co. Specialists in Orchids
BENVENUE STREET
WELLESLEY 81, MASS., U.S.A.

October 20, 1950

Mr. Arthur A. Chadwick
Box 63 - Hamilton
Penn State College
State College, Pennsylvania

Dear Mr. Chadwick:

With reference to your recent inquiry regarding the purchase of a few stud yellow Cattleya Hybrids, we believe that you would be more satisfied if we send you sample flowers from time to time as some of our fine yellows come into bloom. Generally speaking plants of stud quality sell from $125.00 to $150.00. With each shipment of flowers we will include a description of the plant.

For your information we are enclosing a copy of our 1950 Spring Offering which is still current.

Thank you for your inquiry.

Very truly yours,
L. Sherman Adams Company.
William P. Baker,
General Manager.

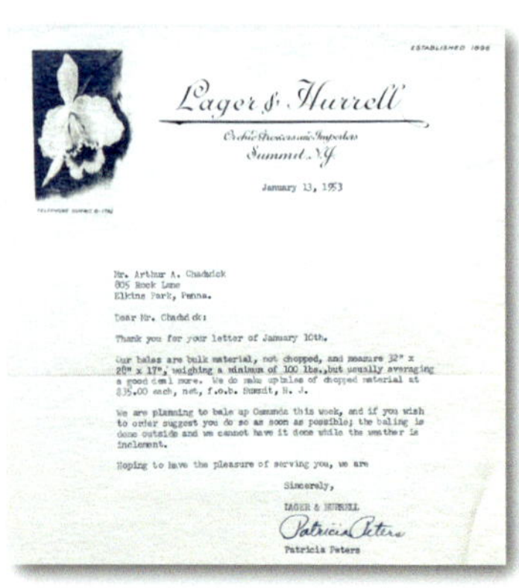

ESTABLISHED 1896

Lager & Hurrell
Orchid Growers and Importers
Summit, N.J.

January 13, 1953

Mr. Arthur A. Chadwick
805 Rock Lane
Elkins Park, Penna.

Dear Mr. Chadwick:

Thank you for your letter of January 10th.

Our bales are bulk material, not chopped, and measure 32" x 20" x 17", weighing a minimum of 100 lbs., but usually averaging a good deal more. We do make up bales of chopped material at $35.00 each, net, f.o.b. Summit, N. J.

We are planning to bale up Osmunda this week, and if you wish to order suggest you do so as soon as possible; the baling is done outside and we cannot have it done while the weather is inclement.

Hoping to have the pleasure of serving you, we are

Sincerely,
LAGER & HURRELL
Patricia Peters

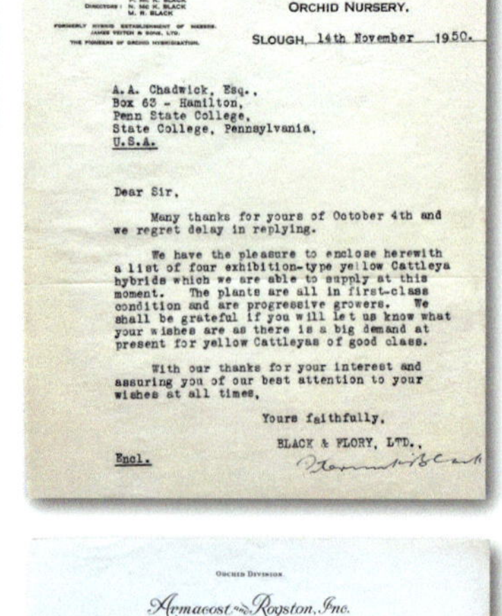

TELEGRAMS: ORCHIDS, SLOUGH
TELEPHONE: SLOUGH 22871
PASSENGER STATION: SLOUGH, G.W.R.
GOODS STATION: LANGLEY, G.W.R.

BLACK & FLORY, LTD.
ORCHID SPECIALISTS.

ORCHID NURSERY.

SLOUGH, 14th November 1950.

A.A. Chadwick, Esq.,
Box 63 - Hamilton,
Penn State College,
State College, Pennsylvania,
U.S.A.

Dear Sir,

Many thanks for yours of October 4th and we regret delay in replying.

We have the pleasure to enclose herewith a list of four exhibition-type yellow Cattleya hybrids which we are able to supply at this moment. The plants are all in first-class condition and are progressive growers. We shall be grateful if you will let us know what your wishes are as there is a big demand at present for yellow Cattleyas of good class.

With our thanks for your interest and assuring you of our best attention to your wishes at all times,

Yours faithfully,
BLACK & FLORY, LTD.,

Encl.

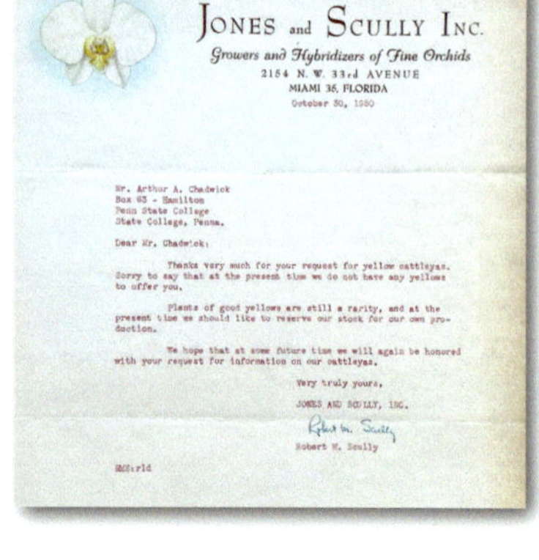

JONES and SCULLY INC.
Growers and Hybridizers of Fine Orchids
2154 N. W. 33rd AVENUE
MIAMI 35, FLORIDA

October 30, 1950

Mr. Arthur A. Chadwick
Box 63 - Hamilton
Penn State College
State College, Penna.

Dear Mr. Chadwick:

Thanks very much for your request for yellow cattleyas. Sorry to say that at the present time we do not have any yellows to offer you.

Plants of good yellows are still a rarity, and at the present time we should like to reserve our stock for our own production.

We hope that at some future time we will again be honored with your request for information on our cattleyas.

Very truly yours,
JONES AND SCULLY, INC.
Robert M. Scully

RMS:rld

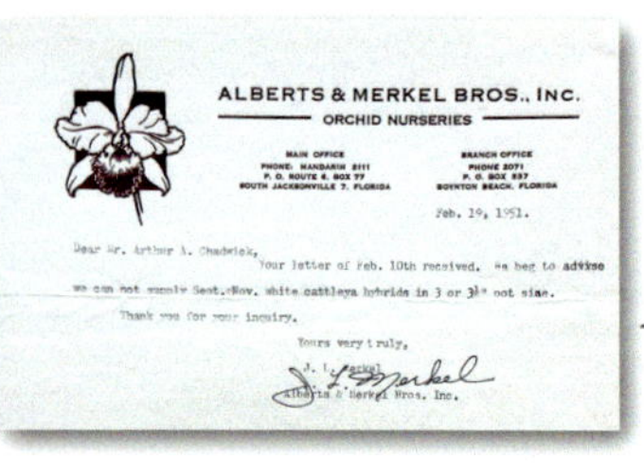

ALBERTS & MERKEL BROS., INC.
ORCHID NURSERIES

MAIN OFFICE
PHONE: MANDARIN 2111
P. O. ROUTE 4, BOX 77
SOUTH JACKSONVILLE 7, FLORIDA

BRANCH OFFICE
PHONE 2071
P. O. BOX 837
BOYNTON BEACH, FLORIDA

Feb. 19, 1951.

Dear Mr. Arthur A. Chadwick,
Your letter of Feb. 10th received. We beg to advise we can not supply Sept.-Nov. white cattleya hybrids in 3 or 3½" pot size.

Thank you for your inquiry.

Yours very truly,
J. L. Merkel
Alberts & Merkel Bros. Inc.

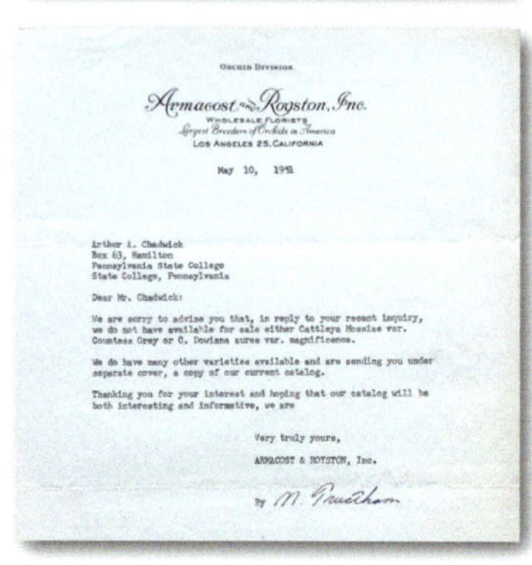

ORCHID DIVISION

Armacost and Royston, Inc.
WHOLESALE FLORISTS
Largest Breeders of Orchids in America
LOS ANGELES 25, CALIFORNIA

May 10, 1951

Arthur A. Chadwick
Box 63, Hamilton
Pennsylvania State College
State College, Pennsylvania

Dear Mr. Chadwick:

We are sorry to advise you that, in reply to your recent inquiry, we do not have available for sale either Cattleya Mossiae var. Countess Grey or C. Dowiana aurea var. magnificence.

We do have many other varieties available and are sending you under separate cover, a copy of our current catalog.

Thanking you for your interest and hoping that our catalog will be both interesting and informative, we are

Very truly yours,
ARMACOST & ROYSTON, Inc.
By M. Grantham

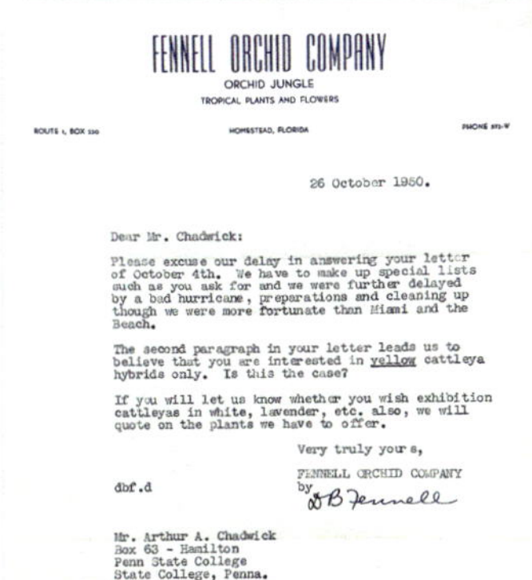

FENNELL ORCHID COMPANY
ORCHID JUNGLE
TROPICAL PLANTS AND FLOWERS
ROUTE 1, BOX 330 — HOMESTEAD, FLORIDA

26 October 1950.

Dear Mr. Chadwick:

Please excuse our delay in answering your letter of October 4th. We have to make up special lists such as you ask for and we were further delayed by a bad hurricane, preparations and cleaning up though we were more fortunate than Miami and the Beach.

The second paragraph in your letter leads us to believe that you are interested in yellow cattleya hybrids only. Is this the case?

If you will let us know whether you wish exhibition cattleyas in white, lavender, etc. also, we will quote on the plants we have to offer.

Very truly yours,
FENNELL ORCHID COMPANY
by D B Fennell

dbf.d

Mr. Arthur A. Chadwick
Box 63 - Hamilton
Penn State College
State College, Penna.

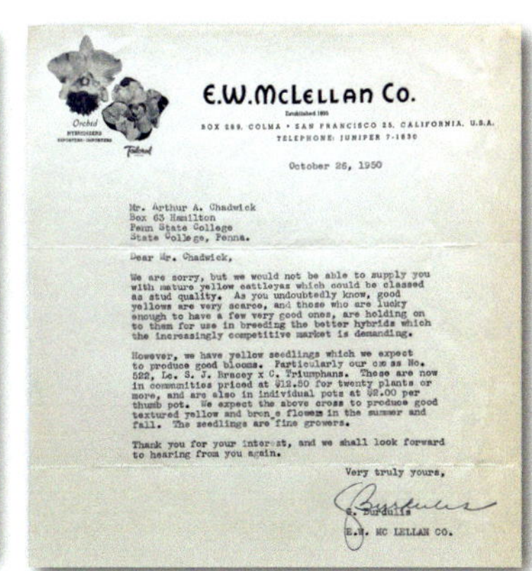

E.W. McLELLAN Co.
BOX 289, COLMA • SAN FRANCISCO 25, CALIFORNIA, U.S.A.
TELEPHONE: JUNIPER 7-1830

October 26, 1950

Mr. Arthur A. Chadwick
Box 63 Hamilton
Penn State College
State College, Penna.

Dear Mr. Chadwick,

We are sorry, but we would not be able to supply you with mature yellow cattleyas which could be classed as stud quality. As you undoubtedly know, good yellows are very scarce, and those who are lucky enough to have a few very good ones, are holding on to them for use in breeding the better hybrids which the increasingly competitive market is demanding.

However, we have yellow seedlings which we expect to produce good blooms. Particularly our cross No. 522, Lc. S. J. Bracey x C. Triumphans. These are now in communities priced at $12.50 for twenty plants or more, and are also in individual pots at $2.00 per thumb pot. We expect the above cross to produce good textured yellow and bronze flowers in the summer and fall. The seedlings are fine growers.

Thank you for your interest, and we shall look forward to hearing from you again.

Very truly yours,
G. Burdulis
E.W. MC LELLAN CO.

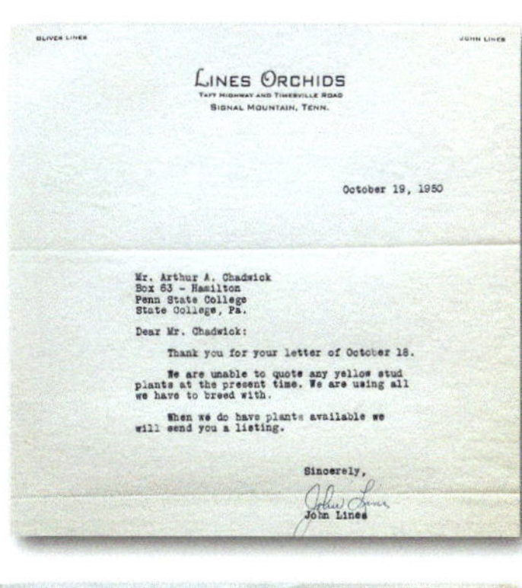

OLIVER LINES — JOHN LINES
LINES ORCHIDS
TAFT HIGHWAY AND TIMESVILLE ROAD
SIGNAL MOUNTAIN, TENN.

October 19, 1950

Mr. Arthur A. Chadwick
Box 63 - Hamilton
Penn State College
State College, Pa.

Dear Mr. Chadwick:

Thank you for your letter of October 18.

We are unable to quote any yellow stud plants at the present time. We are using all we have to breed with.

When we do have plants available we will send you a listing.

Sincerely,
John Lines

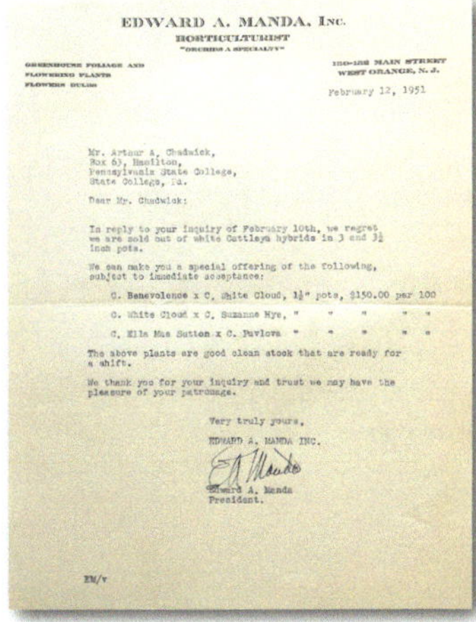

EDWARD A. MANDA, INC.
HORTICULTURIST
"ORCHIDS A SPECIALTY"
150-152 MAIN STREET
WEST ORANGE, N. J.

February 12, 1951

Mr. Arthur A. Chadwick,
Box 63, Hamilton,
Pennsylvania State College,
State College, Pa.

Dear Mr. Chadwick:

In reply to your inquiry of February 10th, we regret we are sold out of white Cattleya hybrids in 3 and 3½ inch pots.

We can make you a special offering of the following, subject to immediate acceptance:

C. Benevolence x C. White Cloud, 1½" pots, $150.00 per 100
C. White Cloud x C. Suzanne Hye, " " " " "
C. Ella Mae Sutton x C. Pavlova " " " " "

The above plants are good clean stock that are ready for a shift.

We thank you for your inquiry and trust we may have the pleasure of your patronage.

Very truly yours,
EDWARD A. MANDA INC.
Edward A. Manda
President.

EM/v

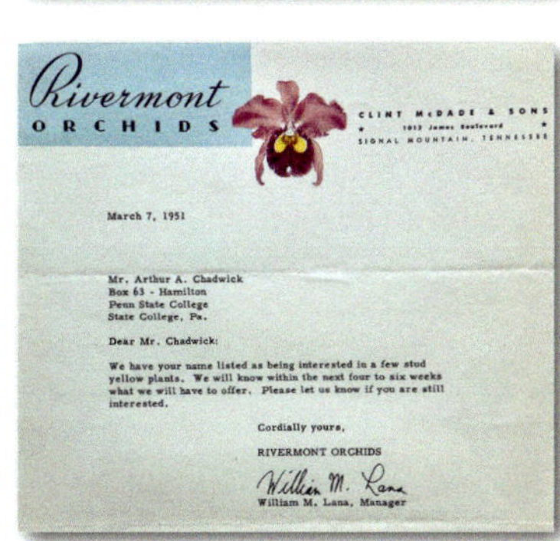

Rivermont ORCHIDS
CLINT McDADE & SONS
1013 James Boulevard
SIGNAL MOUNTAIN, TENNESSEE

March 7, 1951

Mr. Arthur A. Chadwick
Box 63 - Hamilton
Penn State College
State College, Pa.

Dear Mr. Chadwick:

We have your name listed as being interested in a few stud yellow plants. We will know within the next four to six weeks what we will have to offer. Please let us know if you are still interested.

Cordially yours,
RIVERMONT ORCHIDS
William M. Lana, Manager

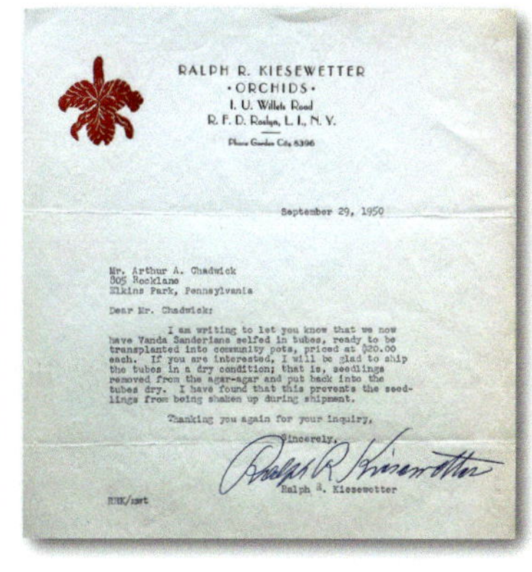

RALPH R. KIESEWETTER
• ORCHIDS •
I. U. Willets Road
R. F. D. Roslyn, L. I., N. Y.
Phone Garden City 8396

September 29, 1950

Mr. Arthur A. Chadwick
805 Rocklane
Elkins Park, Pennsylvania

Dear Mr. Chadwick:

I am writing to let you know that we now have Vanda Sanderiana selfed in tubes, ready to be transplanted into community pots, priced at $20.00 each. If you are interested, I will be glad to ship the tubes in a dry condition; that is, seedlings removed from the agar-agar and put back into the tubes dry. I have found that this prevents the seedlings from being shaken up during shipment.

Thanking you again for your inquiry,

Sincerely,
Ralph R. Kiesewetter

RRK/srt

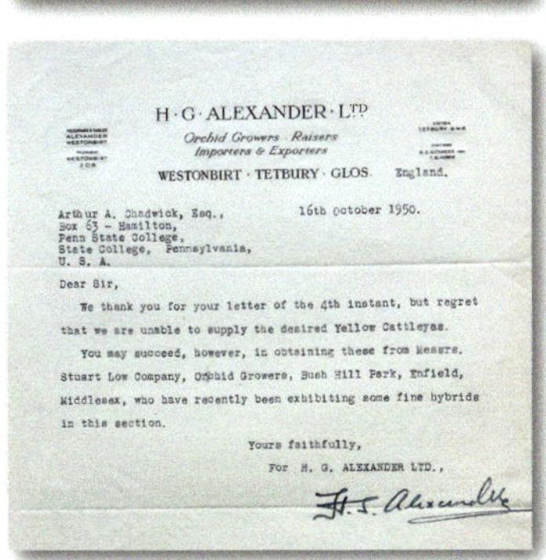

H · G · ALEXANDER · LTD
Orchid Growers · Raisers
Importers & Exporters
WESTONBIRT · TETBURY · GLOS. England.

Arthur A. Chadwick, Esq.,
Box 63 - Hamilton,
Penn State College,
State College, Pennsylvania,
U. S. A.

16th October 1950.

Dear Sir,

We thank you for your letter of the 4th instant, but regret that we are unable to supply the desired Yellow Cattleyas.

You may succeed, however, in obtaining these from Messrs. Stuart Low Company, Orchid Growers, Bush Hill Park, Enfield, Middlesex, who have recently been exhibiting some fine hybrids in this section.

Yours faithfully,
For H. G. ALEXANDER LTD.,
H. G. Alexander

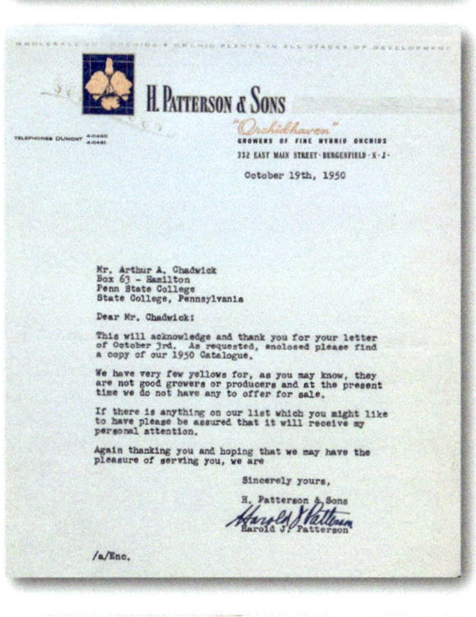

WHOLESALE CUT ORCHIDS • ORCHID PLANTS IN ALL STAGES OF DEVELOPMENT
H. PATTERSON & SONS
"Orchidhaven"
GROWERS OF FINE HYBRID ORCHIDS
332 EAST MAIN STREET · BERGENFIELD · N · J ·
TELEPHONES DUMONT 4-0460 4-0461

October 19th, 1950

Mr. Arthur A. Chadwick
Box 63 - Hamilton
Penn State College
State College, Pennsylvania

Dear Mr. Chadwick:

This will acknowledge and thank you for your letter of October 3rd. As requested, enclosed please find a copy of our 1950 Catalogue.

We have very few yellows for, as you may know, they are not good growers or producers and at the present time we do not have any to offer for sale.

If there is anything on our list which you might like to have please be assured that it will receive my personal attention.

Again thanking you and hoping that we may have the pleasure of serving you, we are

Sincerely yours,
H. Patterson & Sons
Harold J. Patterson

/a/Enc.

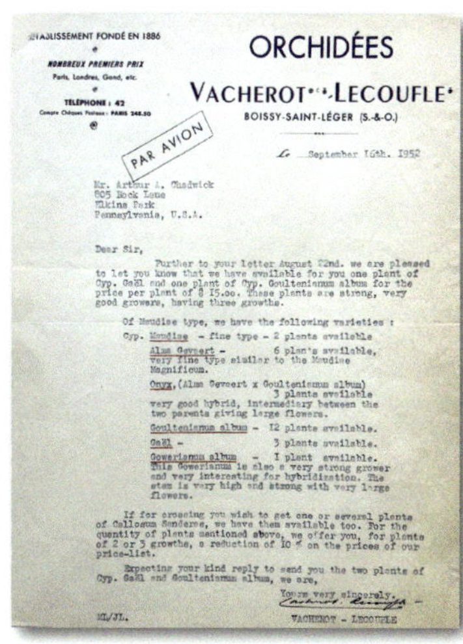

ÉTABLISSEMENT FONDÉ EN 1886
NOMBREUX PREMIERS PRIX
Paris, Londres, Gand, etc.
TÉLÉPHONE : 42
Compte Chèques Postaux : PARIS 248.50

ORCHIDÉES
VACHEROT & LECOUFLE
BOISSY-SAINT-LÉGER (S.-&-O.)

PAR AVION

Le September 16th. 1952

Mr. Arthur A. Chadwick
805 Rock Lane
Elkins Park
Pennsylvania, U.S.A.

Dear Sir,

Further to your letter August 22nd. we are pleased to let you know that we have available for you one plant of Cyp. Gaël and one plant of Cyp. Goultenianum album for the price per plant of $ 15.oo. These plants are strong, very good growers, having three growths.

Of Maudiae type, we have the following varieties :

Cyp. Maudiae – fine type – 2 plants available

Alma Gevaert – 6 plants available, very fine type similar to the Maudiae Magnificum.

Onyx, (Alma Gevaert x Goultenianum album) 3 plants available very good hybrid, intermediary between the two parents giving large flowers.

Goultenianum album – 12 plants available.

Gaël – 3 plants available.

Gowerianum album – 1 plant available. This Gowerianum is also a very strong grower and very interesting for hybridization. The stem is very high and strong with very large flowers.

If for crossing you wish to get one or several plants of Callosum Sanderae, we have them available too. For the quantity of plants mentioned above, we offer you, for plants of 2 or 3 growths, a reduction of 10 % on the prices of our price-list.

Expecting your kind reply to send you the two plants of Cyp. Gaël and Goultenianum album, we are,

Yours very sincerely,
VACHEROT - LECOUFLE

ML/JL.

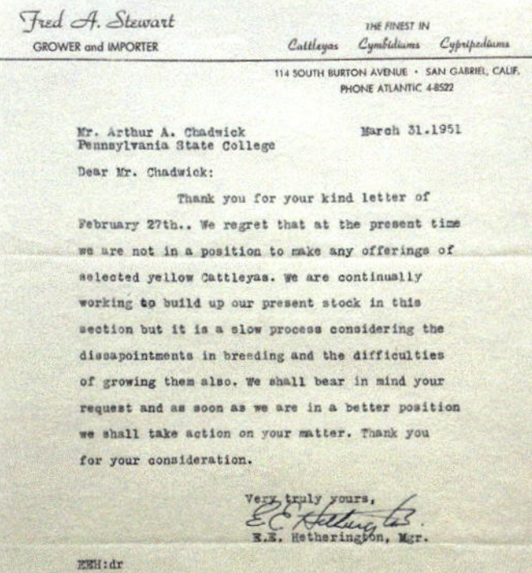

Fred A. Stewart
GROWER and IMPORTER
THE FINEST IN Cattleyas Cymbidiums Cypripediums
114 SOUTH BURTON AVENUE · SAN GABRIEL, CALIF.
PHONE ATLANTIC 4-8522

Mr. Arthur A. Chadwick
Pennsylvania State College

March 31.1951

Dear Mr. Chadwick:

Thank you for your kind letter of February 27th.. We regret that at the present time we are not in a position to make any offerings of selected yellow Cattleyas. We are continually working to build up our present stock in this section but it is a slow process considering the dissapointments in breeding and the difficulties of growing them also. We shall bear in mind your request and as soon as we are in a better position we shall take action on your matter. Thank you for your consideration.

Very truly yours,
E.E. Hetherington, Mgr.

EEH:dr

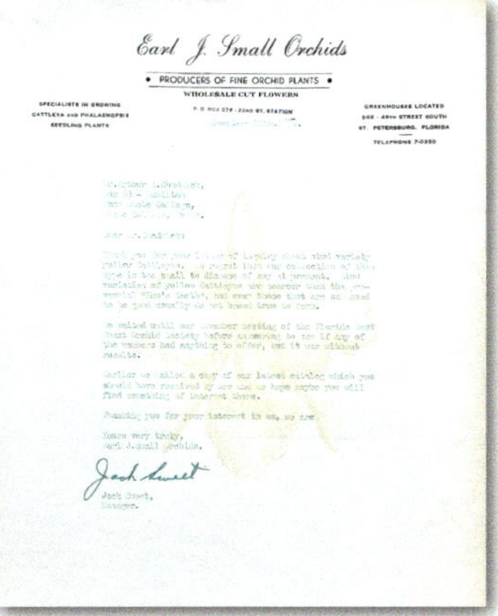

Earl J. Small Orchids
• PRODUCERS OF FINE ORCHID PLANTS •
WHOLESALE CUT FLOWERS
SPECIALISTS IN GROWING CATTLEYA AND PHALAENOPSIS SEEDLING PLANTS
GREENHOUSES LOCATED ST. PETERSBURG, FLORIDA